The Development of the Theatre

THE ORCHESTRA OF THE THEATRE OF DIONYSOS AT ATHENS

THE DEVELOPMENT OF THE THEATRE

A Study of Theatrical Art
from the Beginnings to the Present Day

by
ALLARDYCE NICOLL

FIFTH EDITION REVISED

HARCOURT, BRACE & WORLD, INC.
NEW YORK

Preface

The world of the theatre obviously has tremendous range and embraces within itself many diverse areas. In the present volume an attempt is made to provide a general account of the various developments in playhouse planning and in scenic design. This is a subject to which a great deal of attention has been devoted during the past twenty-five or thirty years—a period within which theatre history, as an independent subject of investigation, has fully come into its own: even a rapid glance at a comprehensive bibliography serves to demonstrate how much fresh ground has lately been explored both in fields which previously had attracted investigation and in fields hitherto almost unknown. A prime symbol of recent endeavour may be found in the increasing number of periodicals specifically designed to survey this subject in wide terms and to add to our existing store of information concerning particular movements in time or place.

Because of such expansion of interest in the history of the theatre the original text of this volume has been entirely revised and in part rewritten, with the object of presenting a kind of general map for those who wish to have an idea of the theme as a whole and also for those who may essay to engage in new investigations.

My thanks are due to Mr Sean Kenny and *The Observer*, and Mr Peter Moro and *World Premières Mondiales*, for permission to quote from articles; Dr Zdenek Stříbrný for securing on my behalf a complete set of photographs of the theatre and hall at Krumlov Castle; Signora M. Muraro for much help given to me at the Cini Foundation Instituto di Storia dell'Arte in Venice; and Mr Sullivan Kaufman for friendly advice and assistance. My thanks are also due to numerous officials at the various libraries and museums at which I have worked in gathering pictorial and other material for this volume.

A. N.

Contents

Illustrations

CHAPTER I

Introductory:
Theatres of the Orient

THE term "modern theatre" is one exceedingly difficult to define. During the earlier half of this century it would immediately have been interpreted as indicating those many playhouses which, in New York and London, even in Delhi, Peking, and Tokyo, had been built in the familiar proscenium-frame manner, with the audience accommodated in stalls, pit, and balconies. By the time we reach the sixties, however, this hitherto fairly standard pattern, while still remaining dominant, can no longer be styled "modern"; rather, that adjective must be applied to the dozens of experimental theatrical shapes and forms which, particularly in the United States of America and in numerous European countries, run the gamut from "theatre-in-the-round" to buildings designed in various ways to banish the proscenium-arch relationship between the public and the players.

If we proceed to search for the origins of these two types of twentieth-century playhouse, a peculiar paradox emerges. Although the latest of the "modern" stage-plans have been worked out in direct opposition to the earlier "modern" plans, both descend in clearly perceptible but different ways from one single source—the ancient theatre of Dionysos in classical Athens. It is to that theatre, accordingly, that we must turn at the very start, regarding it not only as the dim ancestor of the earlier "modern" but also as the creative impetus inspiring most of the more recent "experimental" designs, no matter how bizarre these may be, no matter how different they may seem at an initial glance from their far-off forerunner.

While this direct connexion between the original Greek and the latest of modern theatres is certain and easily demonstrable, it is, however, to be borne in mind that several oriental lands developed at various periods their own indigenous stages, and that some of these, besides displaying interesting features of their own, have exerted at least a tangential influence in recent times upon Western playhouse-planning and convention. Since these oriental theatres lie outside the main line of development from Athens to Broadway and Shaftesbury Avenue, and to Stratford, Ontario, it may accordingly be convenient to look at least briefly at what Japan, China, and India had to offer in the field of theatrical activity.

The stages originated in these three countries are quite distinct from each other, yet interestingly we find that they are all dominated by certain qualities shared in common; simplicity and formalism dictated the shape of each stage structure, and each in its own particular way aimed at encouraging conventional movements on the part of the performers.

The early Chinese theatre may be taken first. This consisted of no more than a rectangular wooden hall, with a balcony running round three of its sides, and with an acting-platform jutting forward into the space reserved for the audience. At the back of the stage there was only a curtain, from the sides of which the players could make their entrances and their exits

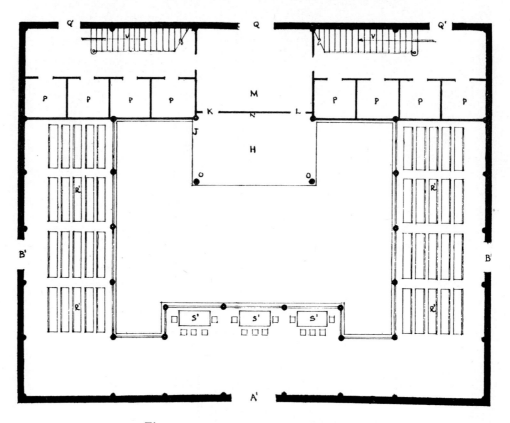

Fig. 1. A CHINESE PALACE THEATRE

(Fig. 1). During the present century, through the influence of Western models, scenic decoration, sometimes very elaborate, has been introduced in China, but originally no attempt was made to put before the spectators anything in the way of what may be called static visual display, whether employed realistically to present a fictional locality or symbolically to suggest it. On the other hand, the public was allowed to feast its eyes on what might be styled "dynamic scenery"—the rich and colourful array of costumes worn by the actors. These actors, moreover, were expected to deal with their parts by means of a complex system of traditional gestures and movements; through these, both the situations in which the performers were supposed to be involved and their emotional states were expressed in formal terms. Thus the joy of theatre-going was intimately based upon the spectators' expert knowledge of the significance of the gestures, something perhaps akin to the nineteenth-century English spectators' appreciation of the "points" made by the performers in Shakespearian rôles. No doubt it was this emphasis on traditional movements which explains a peculiar feature of Chinese play performances. Normally, in East as in West, audiences come, and came, to the theatre prepared to remain there for the complete duration of a play: in China, apparently from earliest times, it was the custom for those attending the shows to enter and to leave when they pleased. The stories told in the dramas were traditional and familiar, and thus their beginnings and their ends were known, so that a man might, if he so chose, watch without loss, and with full appreciation, even a few selected scenes. As the Chinese dramas are lyric plays, to be likened rather to operas than to the straight drama of the West, another parallel may be permitted: just as a keen Italian opera-goer can derive pleasure from listening to no more than a single act of *Aïda* or *Madama Butterfly*, so the Chinese spectator could delight in witnessing and in listening to selected excerpts from the music-dramas whose content he knew so well.

In China, the theatre was largely a popular entertainment; the ancient Indian Hindu stage was predominatingly associated with the courtly aristocrats: yet strangely the theatres erected in the latter country bore a peculiar likeness to those of the former. Despite the fact that an attempt was made in India to achieve greater intimacy between players and privileged spectators, the royal playhouses were established on a basis not essentially different from that of the Chinese popular houses. Indeed, the one really distinctive feature of theatre-building in ancient India is the series of precise measurements which the architects had to observe: there might be three playhouse sizes, but each had to have its own established proportions; thus, for example, the most usual type of theatre had its dimensions fixed at exactly 96 feet by 48 feet. This rectangle, in turn, was neatly divided into two, one part serving to accommodate the audience and the other being apportioned to the actors. A long narrow space at the rear of the performers' area was utilized as a dressing-room, and this left a large rectangular platform, extending the full width of the house, with two "wings" at the sides; between these side-wings was a curtain which could be drawn or left open as desired. The stage itself was further extended by what in the English theatre would be called an "apron," a curving platform jutting out into the midst of the spectators. Here, once more, realistic settings were completely absent; here the miming of the actors, although rather less symbolic than that displayed by the Chinese performers, was eagerly awaited by the prince and his company of courtiers at special festival productions. For this theatre Kālidāsa and his companions penned their Sanskrit plays, capturing, by a strange chance, a romantic tragi-comic spirit not unlike that which animated so many English and Spanish plays in the late-sixteenth and seventeenth centuries.

Neither the Chinese nor the Hindu stage has made so great an impression on the modern Western theatre as the third of these oriental forms, that of Japan. There, if we leave out the highly developed and skilfully manipulated puppet theatres, we find ourselves confronted by two distinct stage structures and methods of performance—the aristocratic Nō and the more popular Kabuki.

The first of these, the Nō, demanded a "theatre" no less exactly shaped than the ancient Indian. The stage itself was 19 feet 5 inches square, no more and no less; its height above the auditorium-level was 2 feet 7 inches; reverberating jars, to help the acoustics, were placed underneath at predetermined places (Figs. 2 and 3). Four pilasters supported a roof protecting the actors and their rich costumes from inclement weather. Three sides of this square platform were surrounded by the spectators; the other side opened up into a further platform appropriated to the orchestra and stage-attendants. Here, however, we encounter something highly characteristic and indeed unique—a long "bridge" leading off from the rear platform towards the dressing-room area. Nothing was provided scenically for the eyes of the audience, but traditional formalism called for the exact placing of certain objects on or about the stage. All round the forward three sides of the acting-platform was a barrier of white sand, and to this some steps descended. Two of the pilasters as well as two positions near by were strictly assigned to the two main character-types introduced into the Nō plays, the *shite* and the *waki*: at the rear of the back platform was a panel on which an old twisted pine was painted: on ground-level, against the forward side of the bridge, were set three small pines.

Obviously we are here confronted by a theatre in which formalism is dominant, a theatre minutely designed for the effective presentation of the delicately patterned plays belonging to this tradition. Despite the fact that much of the formalism can be appreciated only by those

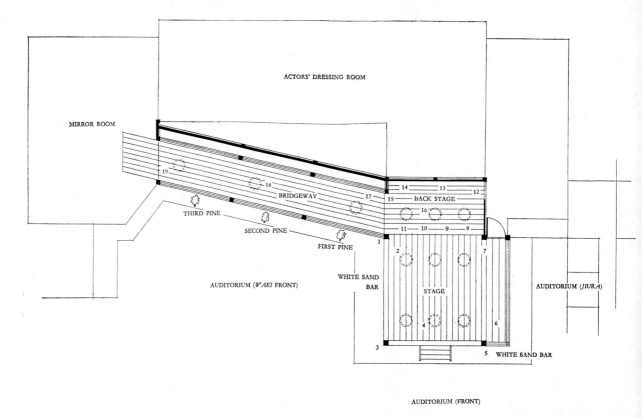

Fig. 2. PLAN OF A JAPANESE NŌ THEATRE

intimately and expertly acquainted with its significances, the perfection achieved in this style of aristocratic Japanese production has been seized upon excitedly by numerous Western enthusiasts, so that for a time, in certain literary-dramatic circles, the Japanese influence came to rival, and indeed at times almost to supplant, the influence of the Athenian dramatists. And for some directors that bridge leading, as it were, through the audience became a perplexing challenge.

The bridge, called the *hana-michi*, or "flower-way," was a feature too of the Kabuki stage, although here, instead of leading back to the dressing-room area, it jutted forth more boldly into the midst of the spectators. By no means so strictly controlled by tradition, the Kabuki theatre differed from the Nō by admitting the presentation of scenic effects, and one means of shifting the scenes through the operation of a revolving platform provided the inspiration for all those revolving stages which, in Western playhouses, have at once aided the producers to achieve flexibility and encouraged them to indulge in needless whirlings and gyrations.

It would appear that in recent times the force of all these traditional oriental forms is declining in face of the constant pressure exerted by Western-style realism, and presumably it is possible that in the not-too-distant future they will disappear entirely, or else remain only as museum oddities: yet, whether they continue to exist or not, clearly it is important that we should bear them in mind as we proceed back to ancient Greece, striving to trace the history of Western theatrical forms from their earliest origins on to the present.

Fig. 3. A JAPANESE NŌ THEATRE

CHAPTER II

The Greek Heritage

1. Introductory

THE Greek theatre has for us a kind of threefold interest. The citizens of the Greek states were the first European communities to raise dramatic performances to the level of an art, and the dramatists who established the forms of tragedy and comedy— Aeschylus, Sophocles, Euripides, and Aristophanes—have maintained their eminence all through the long centuries from their own times down to the present. Thus an attempt to grasp at least the essentials of theatrical form and convention during the classical period has an importance in and for itself. Nor does this primal interest exist only within the area of historical investigation. The Greek playwrights still exercise a potent creative force, and scores of modern dramatists have found strength in the process of adapting their legendary themes to modern conditions. In the same way, the shape of the classical theatres and the styles of production employed in them do not remain now only as objects confined within the limits of the study. Festival performances at Epidauros and elsewhere are clearly not museum exhibits, and much modern theatre design has either borrowed from the Greeks or else evolved new forms based on a study of the old. And, thirdly, there is the fact that, from the Renaissance onward, the forms and conventions of the classic playhouses set an indelible seal on the playhouses of modern times: an eighteenth-century French opera-house, a nineteenth-century English Theatre Royal, or an American theatre built in the twentieth century may seem far enough removed from classical models, yet when we look more closely we realize that all of these stem from the one, single tradition.

It is, however, necessary to remember that when we speak of the "Greek theatre" we refer not to one thing, but to several things. Usually, in employing the term, we have in mind the great theatre at Athens, but besides this famous structure there were many other play-houses at diverse localities erected over a lengthy span of years; and it will be readily realized that since different places and different generations witnessed the building of these monumental edifices, no two theatres are identically alike. There can thus be no absolute "ideal" of a Greek theatre, although for convenience we may divide the existing build-ings or those for which there is at least some sure archaeological evidence into four main kinds.

(1) The first type has only historical significance—the pre-Aeschylean wooden theatres which recent investigations suggest were constructed in a trapezoidal and not in a circular plan. Here tiers of benches set at angles were arranged so that they almost surrounded a dancing-place, maybe also trapezoidal in form, known as the orchestra. (2) Precisely when these pre-Aeschylean wooden playhouses first came into being remains uncertain, but certainly they were adumbrated long before the second type, the classical Athenian, took shape in the fifth century B.C. (3) That in turn gave place to the Hellenistic, so called because it is the

Fig. 3a. ANCIENT MINOAN "COURT THEATRE" AT PHAESTOS, CRETE

It is not certain for what kinds of performances this "theatre" and that at Knossos were built, but they probably played some part in the development of the later classical Athenian theatre of the fifth century B.C.

form of theatre erected from the fourth century onward, mostly in territories outside Greece proper but under the impress of Greek or Hellenic culture. It corresponds, in theatrical art, to that movement which, in history, is symbolized in the conquests of Alexander the Great. (4) Finally, when the Greek civilization was coming to an end, it met with the rapidly spreading Roman culture, and in the society thus established sprang up a fourth type of theatre, for convenience called the Graeco-Roman. Pre-Aeschylean, classical Athenian, Hellenistic, and Graeco-Roman playhouses require to be kept distinct from each other, yet clearly one shades into another, and there are certain buildings which lie, as it were, on the borderland between type and type. Unquestionably the second, if only because of its association with the masters of old Greek tragedy and comedy, has the greatest intrinsic interest, but from the point of view of the student of the theatre the later forms have equal, if not greater, value, since through them the Hellenic model was carried forward into a later age.

Before proceeding to an account of these forms, it is essential to remember that, despite all the work devoted to the study of their principles and practice, despite all the painstaking archaeological investigations, some questions still remain baffling, and the answers propounded are subject to debate. That this should be so need occasion no surprise. The greater Greek dramatists reached their culmination by the middle of the fifth century B.C., yet only a few stones dating from that period exist among the ruins of the famous Dionysian theatre at Athens, while outside Athens nearly all the partially extant playhouses are of later construction.

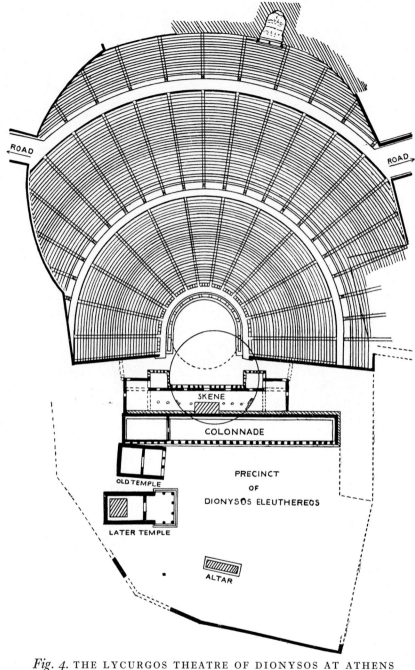

Fig. 4. THE LYCURGOS THEATRE OF DIONYSOS AT ATHENS

The inner circle shows the position of the earliest orchestra.

Purely archaeological study, therefore, must leave many features, even important ones, uncertain, and recourse must be had to other, literary, bodies of information or suggestion. Of these two are chief, and both require to be handled circumspectly. First come the comments upon theatrical building and procedure made by Vitruvius and Pollux, authors who gave to Renaissance architects almost all that then was known about the classical stage and whose writings still have prime value. At the same time, in reading their books we need to be constantly on guard. Vitruvius penned his comprehensive work on architecture about the year 15 B.C., four centuries at least after the time of Sophocles— just about the same gap which separates us to-day from the year when Shakespeare was born. Pollux, whose *Onomastikon* is a kind of encyclopaedic fount of information, lived almost two centuries later still, and here the modern parallel would be a gap between our own age and that of Chaucer. It stands to reason that neither of these writers could speak with firsthand authority about that which interests us most—the antique theatre of Athens; and any doubts which arise from this consideration must inevitably be increased when we find that even their comments on the theatres of their own time, Graeco-Roman and Roman, partake of a decidedly idealizing and generalizing tendency. Thus, for example, Vitruvius' description of a typical Roman playhouse corresponds with no exactitude to the shape of any extant or partially extant structure belonging to that period. While the works of Vitruvius and Pollux remain invaluable, therefore, they can in no wise be trusted when their views run counter to evidence gathered from other sources. The second treasury of information comes from the plays themselves. It need hardly be said that these plays were written by practising dramatists, and that, accordingly, all their scenes must have been planned in such a way as to permit of their being easily represented on the stage. Nevertheless, no one familiar with stage production requires to be told that particular effects desired by playwrights can be secured very often in a variety of different ways and that dramas originally designed for one form of theatre may effectively be presented in theatres entirely different. *A Doll's House*, penned for Ibsen's naturalistic, peep-show stage, can yield its quality in an arena production, and at Chichester Sir Laurence Olivier can win success for his production of an *Uncle Vanya* intended for the only type of theatre that Chekhov knew. In looking at these Greek plays, accordingly, even while we recognize that they have to be interpreted in practical theatre terms and that they provide evidence of prime import for an understanding of the theatres for which they were originally written, we must remember that it is essential to avoid concluding that any particular scene must have been presented in any one particular way. Our minds have to remain open for the consideration of possibilities other than those which, perhaps, first occur to us.

2. *The Ancient Athenian Theatre*

Although we are concerned here with the playhouse and not with the play, an appreciation of the origins and development of tragedy and comedy in Greece is essential before we proceed to look at the main features of the classical stage. Concerning the origins much again is unsure, but in general it may be said that the source of tragedy is to be found in choric dithyrambs sung in honour of the god Dionysos; that these dithyrambs were originally improvised and rhapsodical in essence; and that, as time passed by, they were "poetized," or rendered literary, possibly by Arion of Methymna. The dithyramb was not confined to any one region in Greece; the movement towards literary composition was one which probably saw developments in widely different regions, the whole taking shape as a kind of formal chant, sung by the devotees of the god, and no doubt directed by one man as leader or guide. Then came Thespis, who, whether on his own initiative or elaborating on the practice of others, definitely made this leader into an actor whose words were answered by the chanting chorus, and who turned to deal with subjects not specifically connected with the stories of Dionysos. This was in the sixth century B.C.; the drama had been born, and, with the introduction of a second actor and later a third, it grew to maturity in the hands of Aeschylus (525–456 B.C.), Sophocles (495–406 B.C.), and Euripides (480–406 B.C.), the masters of Greek tragedy.

Comedy had a somewhat similar history. It arose out of the less decorous mummery associated with the κῶμος (*komos*; the Latin *comus*), a voluntary procession organized by the townsfolk in honour of Dionysos and ending with a phallic song. Our word "comedy" is derived directly from this word κῶμος added to ᾠδή (*ode*, song). Apparently the *komos* revels consisted at first of just the procession, a sacrifice, and a chant; but, owing to the fact that the words of the chant were often satiric, what had been originally the back-chat of the crowd of onlookers became a part of the whole ritual, so that comedy, when at last it emerged as a literary form, was distinguished from tragedy by the presence in it of two choruses instead of only one—a standard structural element in the plays of Aristophanes (*c.* 448–380 B.C.).

Even from this brief sketch of the rise of the two chief dramatic forms in the sixth and fifth centuries B.C. it becomes obvious that theatrical representations, coloured by religious sentiment, directed their appeal towards the whole of the community, and that, when theatres came to be built, the primal need was for ample space to accommodate the audience. It is also obvious that, both in tragedy and in comedy, the chorus was a basic feature of the plays; thus the acting-area had to be sufficiently large to permit them to make those elaborate dancing movements which had always been associated with the chanting of the lyric verses. To meet these two requirements the earliest "theatres" probably consisted of no more than a round level space for the performers, set at the foot of a sloping hillside for the convenience of the spectators. The level space, with an altar at its centre, was known as the ὀρχήστρα (orchestra): as yet the word "theatre" (θέατρον, theatron), derived from the verb θεᾶσθαι (theasthai, to see), applied, not to a locality, but simply to the assembled group of onlookers. There existed no word to describe the combined orchestra and auditorium.

Starting from this simple arrangement, where a round dancing-place was all that converted natural ground into a playing-place, the Greek theatre easily and logically developed. First came a few wooden seats towards the inner edge of the orchestra, designed for the principal men of the district or for honoured guests: later, other wooden benches, or ἴκρια (ikria), arranged up the hillside, provided a formal auditorium. Quite understandably, as we have seen, these wooden benches appear to have been constructed angularly, but when, at the very beginning of the fifth century, stone came to supplant wood, both the orchestra and the seats for the audience were shaped in circular form. Owing to the facts that the hillside sloped only one way and that even in the most primitive type of dramatic performance there was only one side to the action, the seats did not completely encircle the orchestra, but it was found that spectators could still have an excellent view of the performers even if the seats were carried on somewhat beyond an exact semicircle, with the terminating sides running obliquely to the diameter of the orchestra.

Excavations undertaken at Athens show that in the original Dionysian theatre there the orchestra had a diameter of 78 feet. Since it was placed on the slope of the Acropolis itself, the ground-level could not be obtained without some banking-up at the rear, so there was a drop of some $6\frac{1}{2}$ feet between its farther edge and the ancient temple of Dionysos (Fig. 5). It is the fact that up to 465 B.C. this simple arrangement endured, which explains the settings and some of the conventions in the earliest plays of Aeschylus. Thus the *Suppliants* (c. 490 B.C.), the *Persians* (472 B.C.), and *Prometheus Bound* (c. 470 B.C.) are all laid in open, desert country-side unflanked by any building. Use, even, was made of the drop at the rear edge of the orchestral circle. In *Prometheus Bound* a dummy figure was evidently employed for the captive fire-bringer, and this figure at the close of the drama sank into the abyss, thus allowing

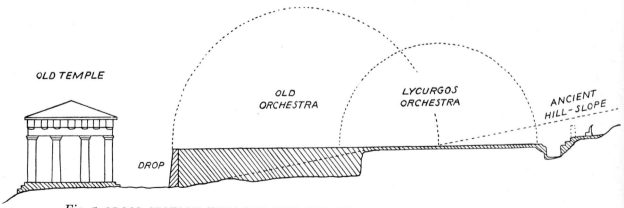

Fig. 5. CROSS-SECTION THROUGH THE OLD AND NEW ORCHESTRAS AT ATHENS
The drop at the rear of the former should be noted.

a live actor to take its place and to ascend at the beginning of the lost *Prometheus Unbound*. The drop, inconvenient as it might seem to be, had provided an opportunity for Aeschylus, who, like all dramatic masters, was alert to utilize all the physical conditions of his stage for the purpose of enriching his actions. Other examples are numerous. For instance, the fact that the performance of the dramas usually started at sunrise led to time references in the dialogue which made fictional and actual conditions harmonize. In Euripides' *Iphigenia at Aulis* the situation begins with the last darkness before dawn. "What star is that there sailing?" asks Agamemnon, to which his attendant replies, "Sirius, in his middle height near the seven Pleiads riding." Some time later, the sun's light colours the east, and a character declares:

> That silver light
> Shows the approach of morn, the harbinger
> Of the sun's fiery steeds.

The rest of the action takes place in the broad light of day. What effect this synchronization of dramatic setting and actual physical phenomena must have had may readily be imagined even by those who have not had the opportunity of being thrilled by kindred unrehearsed effects—the sudden swirling of pigeons in the Salzburg Domplatz towards the close of *Jedermann*, or the mysterious hooting of owls as the *Bacchae* at Epidauros draws to its sad end.

3. The Scene-buildings and the Stage

With the introduction of two and later of three actors, whom the necessities of the performance constrained to appear in a diversity of parts, it became imperative that a hut should

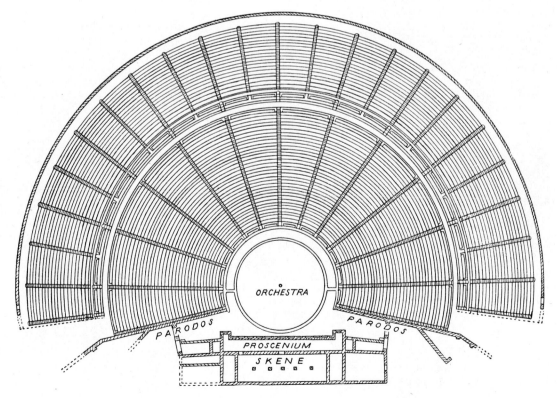

Fig. 6. PLAN OF THE THEATRE AT EPIDAUROS

be erected for the convenience of those concerned in the production. In Athens the close proximity of the old temple of Dionysos would have rendered the building of such a hut or dressing-room almost impossible, and it is likely that the moving of the ancient orchestra some 50 feet northward was dictated by this consideration: the result of the change in position was that a free space was left at the rear of what had been the acting-area, and here a small wooden σκηνή (*skene*, scene-building) was set up. Its original function was unquestionably a purely practical one, the provision of a concealed location in which the actors, out of sight of the audience, could make themselves ready, and to which they might retire when their particular actions were done; but soon it was found to offer many opportunities when considered as a scenic background. It is from this time that plays, instead of being set in open country, are presumed to take place before a temple or a palace. What this early scene-building looked like we cannot tell; unpretentious undoubtedly it was, presenting in all probability a plain front unadorned save for possible paintings erected to symbolize the scenic action. Within a few years, however, something more ornate had been planned and executed. About 425 B.C. a firm stone basis was laid for an elaborate scene-building consisting of a long front wall interrupted at the sides by projecting wings or παρασκήνια (*paraskenia*). Between these projecting wings we may suppose that there existed a very low stage, possibly raised but a foot from the orchestra-level, yet providing that elevation which actors of all ages and of all climes have

Fig. 7. THE THEATRE AT EPIDAUROS

sought and used. Immediately behind this stage may have come a
columned προσχήνιον (*proskenion*,
proscenium), built of wood like
the rest of the scene-building.
The front wall of the scene-building itself was probably pierced by
three doors for the exits and the
entrances of the actors.

It is obvious that this scene-
building, often extending to beyond the diameter of the orchestral circle, nearly met the oblique
lines formed by the seats in the
auditorium. In other words, a
passageway was made at each side
by the edge of the auditorium and
the ends of the scene-building.
These passageways, used by both
chorus and spectators, gained the
name of πάροδος (*parodos*), and
were in later times adorned with
richly sculptured gates.

In all probability the wooden
scene-building thus erected on a
stone foundation at the end of
the fifth century B.C. was of two
stories, the upper of which was
the ἐπισχήνιον (*episkenion*) and

Fig. 8. THE STAGE BUILDINGS OF THE THEATRE
AT TAORMINA, SICILY

was utilized for the "machines," of which an account will be given below. It is likely that
the slightly raised stage was called the λογεῖον (*logeion*, speaking-place), although that word
and the term θεολογεῖον (*theologeion*, speaking-place of divinities) have both been applied to
the top of the proscenium or first story of the scene-building itself. By the time that the scene-
building was elaborated and sometimes constructed of stone, the regular palace convention
for tragedy had become fully established, to pass on in imitative forms to the dramatists of
the Renaissance.

4. The Hellenistic Theatre

During the course of the fourth century B.C. social conditions began to change, and with
them came alterations in the theatrical form. Already in the plays of Euripides there is evident
a declining of the ritualistic element in tragedy, the introduction of a new almost "realistic"
note in the handling of situations and dialogue, and an emphasis on complications in the
handling of plots. Obviously, for a dramatist who might be regarded as the angry young man
of his day, the chorus, with its formal movements which often seemed to hold up the development of the action, was troublesome, and it is not surprising that in his works it comes to be
treated in a cavalier manner, sometimes serving to do no more than present lyric songs only

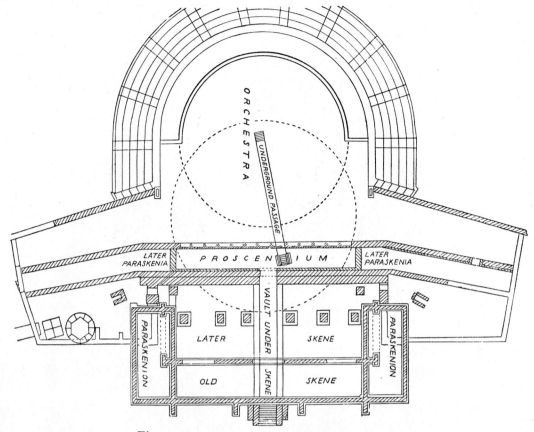

Fig. 9. PLAN OF THE THEATRE AT ERETRIA

Note should be taken of the old passageway leading to "Charon's steps" in the centre of the orchestra.

tenuously connected with the subject-matter of the plays themselves. Still further, the tragic grandeur so apparent in the works of Aeschylus and the equally tragic tension in those of Sophocles tended to be reduced, so that "tragedy" began to shade itself into "drama," or what later ages would have called "tragicomedy." At the same time, the effervescent Old Comedy, the style in which Aristophanes' greatest plays were conceived, began to alter shape

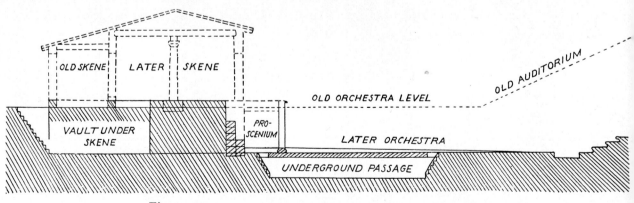

Fig. 10. CROSS-SECTION OF THE THEATRE AT ERETRIA

Comparison with Fig. 9 shows clearly the arrangement of the underground passage.

Fig. 11. THE SKENE OF THE THEATRE AT OROPOS
The proscenium pillars and the front wall of the scene-building are here shown.

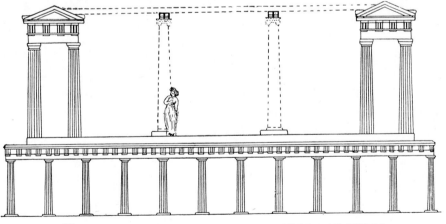

Fig. 12. RECONSTRUCTION OF THE STAGE AT DELOS

until it reached the form known as the New Comedy—presenting more realistically drawn, commonplace characters, and, inspired by the writings of Euripides, placing much emphasis on story and plot. Here, too, the chorus was an encumbrance, and in the plays written by Menander (*c.* 343–292 B.C.) it remained only as a sad relic of its former self, serving merely to provide what may be styled *entr'acte* entertainment.

Fig. 13. THE THEATRE AT PRIENE

Fig. 15. SCENE FROM A PHLYAX COMEDY

Fig. 17. SCENE FROM A PHLYAX COMEDY

Note should be taken of the platform stage and of the decorated doorway.

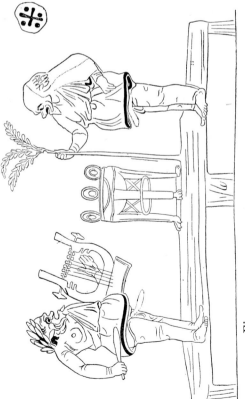

Fig. 14. SCENE FROM A PHLYAX COMEDY

Note should be taken of the plain wooden stage.

Fig. 16. SCENE FROM A PHLYAX COMEDY

Naturally, with the growth and establishment of this fresh style of playwriting, the original "classical" theatre no longer met the needs of the time; and consequently, as the Hellenistic culture spread outward over the whole of Magna Graecia, modifications were introduced which did not completely alter the form of the stage but which brought in a kind of different orientation.

By good fortune, sufficient structures of this kind, at Epidauros, Eretria, Oropos, Delos, Priene, and elsewhere, have been preserved to give us a fairly clear idea of their general shape. Essentially, this general shape was determined by the fact that, whereas the older playhouses focused all attention upon the orchestra, the new playhouses sought to direct the spectators' attention to the stage on which the actors moved. Two or three alterations in plan are worthy of particular attention. In general the auditorium remained either as a semicircle extended at its diameter, or else was modified so that the semicircle was slightly enlarged by the carrying on of the benches for some yards at right angles to the diameter; but there were considerable changes in the performers' part of the playhouse. Instead of a low stage, the actors were set upon a long elevated platform, 10 to 13 feet in height, supported by rows of columns, between which painted wooden panels were commonly inserted. With the introduction of this raised stage came a corresponding new development of the scene-building. Between the columns at the stage-front (called the *proskenion*, literally "the part in front of the *skene*") the painted wooden panels (*pinakes*) were given merely a wash of colour or were simply decorated with formal designs; but above, as a background to the actors, provision was made for something far more elaborate. In this Hellenistic theatre the rear of the stage had a wide, ample façade, with three huge openings (called *thyromata*) into which large painted *pinakes* could be set, and we may believe that, in accordance with the subject-matter and tone of the New Comedy, these pieces of scenery tended at least towards the realistic.

The general effect provided by this fresh treatment of stage and background is excellently suggested, although in a primitive way, by a series of vase-paintings which come from Sicily and the lower eastern coast of Italy. In these localities Greek settlements had been set up at an early date, and among them flourished a vigorous kind of burlesque performances named the *phlyakes*. Their stages were wooden, and probably restricted in area, but, if we allow for this fact, the designs serve to indicate the basic appearance of the Hellenistic playhouse. Figure 14 shows one of these paintings, depicting the actors' platform in its simplest form—no more than a series of wooden planks, set upon rough-hewn beams. Very similar supports and planks appear in Fig. 15. When we turn to Fig. 16, however, we encounter something different: the wooden stage and the props are more or less the same, but the space below has been filled in with panels on which are painted purely formal designs, and steps lead down to the ground-level. The wooden platform is again to be seen in Fig. 17, but here the stage front has been filled in with draped curtains: furthermore, at the rear of the performers there

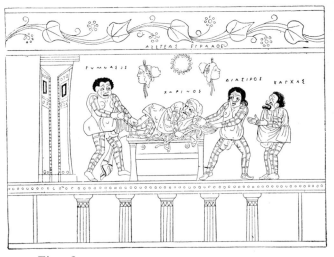

Fig. 18. SCENE FROM A PHLYAX COMEDY

Note should be taken of the formal stage supports and the suggestion of scenery.

is a partial indication of a decorated background. Finally, in Fig. 18 we reach the conclusion. Here the stage is not so clearly made of wood, formal columns have taken the place of rough-hewn or square-planed props, and the scenically depicted doorway at the back has been more firmly suggested.

It was not, of course, only the front of the *skene* which became more prominent at this period. The whole building became larger and was generally divided into several rooms, while at the same time architectural elaboration, as in the majestic gateways between the edges of the auditorium and those of the scene-building, was frequent. It need hardly be stressed that, although these theatres were still vastly unlike the playhouses which have sprung into being in the modern period, insensibly we are moving in the direction of the later styles, with the shift of interest from orchestra to stage, with the banishing of the chorus and the concentration upon the actors, with the emphasis upon plot in plays, with the trend towards realism, and with the accompanying trend towards scenic elaboration.

5. Graeco-Roman Theatres

Towards the end of the second century B.C. still further modifications in theatre form became apparent which were to lead directly towards the quite distinct playhouse-planning of Roman times. Theatres such as those at Termessos, Sagalassos, Patara, Myra, Tralles, Magnesia, and Ephesus exhibit, with minor variations, a common form with characteristic features. (1) In the first place, the auditorium for the most part retained its old shape, stretching beyond the regular semicircle (Fig. 19). (2) The orchestra, however, which had hitherto been

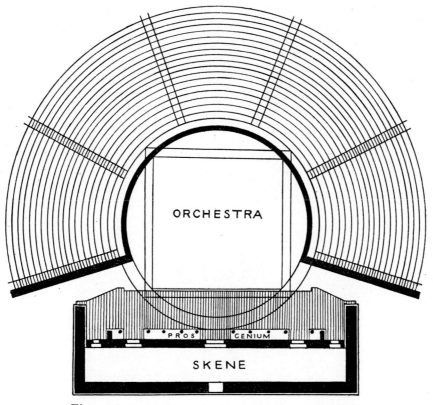

Fig. 19. PLAN OF THE THEATRE AT TERMESSOS

completely circular, was encroached upon by the moving forward of the scene-building, although always it remained more than a semicircle. In many of these theatres the orchestra if carried round in a complete circle would touch at its circumference the forward edge of the scene-building, the stage jutting out for about half its radius. (3) The lowest row of seats usually abutted directly onto the orchestra. (4) The stage-front was enlarged and made more rich, although the front of this stage was usually plain or else set with unadorned panels. (5) The long narrow stage of the Hellenistic playhouses gave way to a much lower and deeper platform, sometimes as much as 20 feet from front to back.

The plan of the theatre at Termessos (Fig. 19) clearly shows the main features of this new model, and the view of its remains (Fig. 20) equally clearly demonstrates the way in which the scenic background was being made more sumptuous and impressive. By this time the stage and the "setting" have come to possess a dominating importance, and the path leading from the purely Greek style to the Roman is amply apparent.

6. Machines

Although all these playhouses were open-air structures it must not be thought that, even in early times, they were lacking in means for securing scenic and similar effects, and the devices employed for securing such effects must be associated with a number of conventions connected with the doorways and other means of ingress.

Pollux thus starts, in his account of some nineteen theatrical devices, with discussion of the traditional associations of the three main doors in the background. The middle door, usually larger than the others, was the "royal" entrance. It was regarded as the doorway of a palace or was presumed to belong to the protagonist in the drama. That on the right was the door by which the second actor entered, or was supposed to lead to guest-chambers, while that on the left belonged to a minor person, or formed a fictitious ruined temple, desert, or prison. These were the doors which led directly into supposedly actual buildings; for persons who were presumed to come from a place outside the two entrances onto the orchestra, the *parodoi*, had to suffice, one leading towards the forum, the other to the outskirts of the city.

These doors were, of course, permanent scenic features, and provided what may be styled symbolic or conventional settings, but besides that something must have been attempted in the way of representational effects. Vitruvius declares that Aeschylus invented scene-painting, while Aristotle ascribes the credit of this to Sophocles. Painted scenes of some kind, therefore, must have been in use, and we may assume that these came into existence at a time when the activities of these two dramatists coalesced, or,

Fig. 20. THE THEATRE AT TERMESSOS

in other words, at some period immediately previous to 456 B.C. We have evidence that *pinakes* were used not merely to fill in the spaces between the proscenium pillars, but for the purpose of providing a scenic background. Some of these may have been fixed to the wall behind the actors, but normally they seem to have been attached to the περίακτοι (*periaktoi*), which are described for us by both Pollux and Vitruvius.[1] These seem to have been triangular prisms, on each side of which was painted a certain scene. Placed on a central pivot, they could thus be revolved in order to display a change of setting. Probably they were fitted with a small ledge which could, if need be, accommodate the god who, in Vitruvius' words, is to appear with sound of "sudden thunder." The exact position of the *periaktoi* has not yet been definitely determined, but it would seem probable that they stood in or by the two side-doorways—a suggestion which corresponds with the conventional significance of these doors, for the *periaktos*

Fig. 21. TERRA-COTTA RELIEF OF A STAGE WALL

on the left displayed distant country scenes, while that on the right showed parts of the city.

More important still is a consideration of the machines regularly employed at least in the Hellenistic period, and here Pollux becomes our principal guide. (1) First comes the ἐκκύκλημα (*ekkuklema*). Described as a platform upon which a throne is set and obviously derived from the verb ἐκκυκλεῖν (*ekkuklein*, to roll out), it was clearly some device whereby the result of interior action, such as dead bodies after a murder, could be shown. Many references to it are made both in the plays themselves and by later commentators, and considerable discussion has been devoted to it by modern scholars. A view which is commonly held gives to it a semicircular shape, so that the low platform could be swung out at any of the three main stage-doors. (2) Evidently associated with this machine is the ἐξώστρα (*exostra*), which Pollux identifies with the *ekkuklema*. It is possible that the machine indicated here was a low platform, not revolved as the *ekkuklema*, but pushed out on wheels or rollers. (3) Still more common was the machine proper, or μηχανή (*mechane*), mentioned by several classical writers. This appears to have consisted of a hook and pulley set at the very top of the *skene* to the left-hand side of the stage. By its means divinities could be raised or lowered. Examples of its use are numerous after about 430 B.C., when, no doubt, it was introduced in a perfected form. Aristophanes hangs Socrates in a basket by its help in *The Clouds*, while a similar device is to be noted in

[1] καταβλήματα δὲ, ὑφάσματα, ἢ πίνακες ἦσαν, ἔχοντες γραφὰς τῇ χρείᾳ τῶν δραμάτων προσφόρους· κατεβάλλετο δὲ ἐπὶ τὰς περιάκτους (Pollux, iv, 311).

Secundum autem spatia ad ornatus comparata, quae loca Graeci περιάκτους dicunt ab eo, quod machinae sunt in his locis versatiles trigonoe habentes singulares species ornationis, quae, cum aut fabularum mutationes sunt futurae, seu deorum adventus cum tonitribus repentinis, versentur mutentque speciem ornationis in fronte (Vitruvius, v, 6).

The Birds. In tragedy an early form seems implied in at least two plays of Aeschylus, and it occurs frequently in Euripides. It is from this use of the *mechane* that there arose the phrase θεὸς ἀπὸ μηχανῆς, repeated in Latin as *deus ex machina*, which, originally applied solely to the physical appearance of the divinity, came to signify a dramatic device introduced for the purpose of bringing a problem or an action to a swift, and often to an unsatisfactorily artificial, conclusion.

The *mechane* possibly appeared under a variety of different names. Thus Pollux enumerates also (4) the *theologeion*, (5) the crane, and (6) the suspension machine, while Suidas suggests ἐώρημα (*eorema*) as a synonym for the *mechane*. Concerning the *theologeion* opinions differ; by some it is thought to have been merely an upper platform, by others it is assumed to have been a regular piece of theatrical machinery. Pollux says little to guide us save that here gods made their appearance. The crane (γέρανος) seems to have been a machine used for swifter effect, particularly employed when a body had to be snatched from the stage. The suspension machine (αἰῶραι, *aiorai*) may simply be a name for the ropes by which divinities were suspended in the air, but was probably distinguished from the *mechane* by the fact that the ropes were invisible and that there was no platform. Finally (7) Pollux mentions as the equivalent of the *mechane* in comedy the *krade* (κράδη), or "fig-branch"; this is referred to also by Plutarch.

A peculiar device is suggested by Pollux when he deals (8) with the *skope* (σκοπή), which he tells us is made for those who view the action. It seems probable here that he is referring to a particular vantage-point from which the "director" could supervise the play being performed below. (9) Little information is given us of the "wall" (τεῖχος, *teichos*) save that it and (10) the tower (πύργος, *purgos*) were raised parts from which persons might look down upon the stage. It may have been that these were lofty practicable platforms. (11) The beacon-tower (φρυκτώριον, *phruktorion*), declares Pollux tantalizingly, requires no explanation. (12) The *distegia* (διστεγία), literally "the second floor," provided the means whereby actors could mount to the roof of a house and thence survey the characters below. (13) The κεραυνοσκοπεῖον (*keraunoskopeion*), or "lightning-machine," is described by Pollux as a kind of *periaktos*. It may have been a prism with the three sides coloured black, across each of which was painted a lightning-flash. (14) With it naturally goes the βροντεῖον (*bronteion*), or "thunder-machine"; this machine consisted of jars filled with stones, the latter being poured noisily into a vessel of brass. (15) The "semicircle," says Pollux, is sufficiently indicated by its name. It stood by the orchestra and gave a view of a far-distant landscape—a portion of a city or sailors upon the sea. The description seems to suggest some kind of a cyclorama. (16) The στροφεῖον (*stropheion*), which from its name seems to have been a revolving machine, showed heroes who had been taken into the company of the gods, or those who had met their deaths by sea or in battle. (17) "Charon's steps" must simply have been trap-doors, possibly in the orchestra, through which ghosts and spirits made their appearance, a simple device (see Figs. 9 and 10), elaborated perhaps in the (18) ἀναπιέσματα (*anapiesmata*), which apparently raised the spirits mechanically from the deeps.

Perhaps scholars have not made quite as much of these machines as they deserve. It is true that we are unaware when the majority of them came into being, but we have the testimony of Pollux, supported by many other scattered authorities, that they existed at one period or another during the career of the Greek or Graeco-Roman theatre. Their importance lies in the facts that they show the stage-managers of those times to have been almost as eager as managers of to-day to secure spectacular effects, and that these passages of Pollux were eagerly conned by the theatre innovators of the Renaissance. Perhaps a performance in an ancient theatre was not so statuesque, so innocent of purely "theatrical" devices as sometimes we think; by these machines it was put in touch with the theatres of the modern world.

It will be readily understood what a service the elaborated scene-building and its accompanying contrivances did to the dramatists of the time. We have only to analyse the difficulties which must have faced any contemporary playwright to realize the fresh realms which were opened before him by successive improvements in the theatrical craft. Thus as a typical example one might take the prohibition imposed on the dramatist in regard to the presentation of murder on the stage. Originally due, apparently, to the religious associations of dramatic performances, this prohibition was almost absolute. In the earliest period the only method of informing the audience of some scene of violence was by introducing a messenger—a device rendered necessary by the physical conditions surrounding the dramatist, but essentially dull and uninspiring. With the appearance of the scene-building, however, a further means of overcoming the prohibition was presented. Behind the closed doors the cry of a Clytemnestra could be heard; or, still more effective, an actor could stand at the door and in broken words tell the audience of what he sees within. The last stage is reached when the ἐκκύκλημα is invented. Now the dramatist can present not merely the cries of the victim, but the dead body of the victim itself. All that he has to do is to arrange a tableau of murderer and murdered on the semicircular platform, wheel that round, and display it to the wondering and terrified gaze of the spectators. It is obvious that this effect could not have been secured by the mere opening of the central doors. Only those directly in front could have seen the tableau; it would have remained out of the line of sight of those who sat towards the sides of the auditorium.

7. *Acting and Production*

It is, of course, very important to remember that in the classical period performances were not given regularly throughout the year and that they formed part of civic festivals, religious in scope, which were sponsored by those in authority. Still further, the works of several dramatists were entered in competition, a highly esteemed prize being offered to the dramatist considered worthiest.

The two chief festivals were the City Dionysia, held in March each year, and the Lenaea, held in January; but conditions in these two were by no means the same. Since navigation was often unsafe in the latter month, the audiences at the Lenaea consisted mainly of Athenian citizens, whereas in March there were likely to be numerous representatives of allied states crowding into the town: a homely atmosphere characterized the one festival, and a cosmopolitan spirit the other. How this might affect the writings of the comic poets, at least, is well shown by the fate of Aristophanes' *The Babylonians*. That satirical piece, which represented the allies as ground down by the tyranny of Cleon, was performed at the City Dionysia, and the author was impeached by the enraged demagogue—not because he had dared to make fun of the government, but because he had done so παρόντων τῶν ξένων—in the presence of strangers. Such slips as this of Aristophanes, however, were not frequent, and in general a restraint and marked care are to be seen in the comic dramas written for the more mixed festival.

The fact that plays in Greece aimed at securing a prize, awarded by judges appointed by the people, influenced both the comic and the tragic poets. The judges were not always uninfluenced by popular displays of approval or disapproval, and as a result playwrights frequently made direct bids to capture the plaudits of the mass. Openly the comic poets sought to please the crowd, sometimes going so far as to scatter tit-bits among the audience—a practice ridiculed by Aristophanes when, in the *Peace* (421 B.C.), he caused one grain of corn to be given to each of the spectators. More decorously, but not less eagerly, the tragic authors vied with one another, penning, often with tongue in cheek, passages which were calculated to gain the applause of patriotic Athenians.

For the over-all conduct of each festival an archon was responsible: they made the preliminary selection of the plays to be presented, and, when they had made their choice, they assigned to each dramatist a choregus to act as "producer." Nothing more clearly shows the popular and civic nature of these performances than the fact that the choregus was always a rich citizen who, on being assigned the duty, was compelled by law to accept it—which meant that he had to provide the money necessary for all the expenses of production, nearly always an onerous burden.

At the very start, as we have seen, the chorus, with its dithyrambic chanting and with its dance movements, alone occupied the orchestral circle, but things changed when first an actor (ὑποκριτής, *hypokrites*, literally, one who answers) appeared as a separate figure. This actor originally was the dramatist; we know, for example, that Aeschylus himself interpreted the heroic rôles in his earliest plays. Such a fusion of actor and dramatist could, however, not endure when two main characters, and later three, made their bow in tragedy. Even although attempts were made to adjust the ancient practices to changed conditions—the playwright acting the chief rôles and giving instruction to his subordinates—it was inevitable that gradually the actors should assume independent status. By the year 449 the performers were selected by the archons and prizes for histrionic skill were established alongside the prizes for poetic excellence. Once this stage had been reached, it was again almost inevitable that the players began to take precedence over the authors. An actors' guild came into being at Athens in the third century B.C., and soon similar guilds sprang into existence throughout the realms dominated by Greek culture, and these guilds are a symbol of the pre-eminence attained by the player.

At the same time, certain changes in histrionic style are to be observed. In the early days, when the chorus was still the conventional core of the drama and when the number of actors was strictly limited, a definitely formal grandeur pervaded the productions. The masks had a statuesque grandeur; the manners depicted in the plays were mostly those of an heroic age, not of contemporary times; memories of Homer were all-pervasive. As, however, during the passing of the years tragedy declined and the New Comedy took the place of the Old, in the interpretation of both a kind of realism supplanted the traditional formalism. The tragic masks assumed more lifelike features, and the manners depicted in the comic plays became theatrical reflections of the manners of the spectators; what had been the core of the earlier drama, the chorus, vanished. The Hellenistic stage did not differ from the classical only in structural form: all the productional elements in it breathed the spirit of a new age.

8. *The Unities and the Acts*

Perhaps in mentioning the chorus a word or two may be said concerning the famous unities and concerning the division of dramas into acts, even although these affect only indirectly theatrical representation. It has been often asserted by historians that the unities, as elaborated and expressed by Renaissance critics, were almost wholly unknown in Greece. On the other hand, Greek drama does present the basis on which the later theories were based. The unity of time was referred to vaguely by Aristotle when he declared that tragedy, in contradistinction to the epic, was generally limited in duration, often being confined to twenty-four hours. It is obvious, first of all, that this general statement is strictly true, and, secondly, that it was more imperative to confine the duration of the action in Greek than in modern drama. The chorus, we must remember, stood continuously in the orchestra. Because of its presence the dramatic action had to be rushed forward to its conclusion. Yet we must observe that the Greek dramatists evidently felt the restriction, for they have employed in the words of the chorus itself a certain species of idealized time. Indeed, we meet in Greek drama that peculiar phenomenon which, by critics of Shakespeare, is called a "double clock," where two separate impressions, or sets of facts, are presented before an audience. It is observable also that the tradition of the trilogy, by which three plays on the same general theme were produced together, provided the Greeks with a method of escape. Where the Orestes story would hardly be fully intelligible by itself, the conjunction of an *Orestes* with a preceding *Agamemnon* and a succeeding *Furies* supplied the spectators with what a modern dramatist might well have included in a single play. The unity of action, in the broadest significance of the term, has naturally to be preserved in all drama; but even in the narrower sense as implying an insistence upon one theme and upon one theme alone, it was never strictly adhered to in the realms of the Greek drama. Even in what seems at first sight to be the purest tragedy, comic elements were occasionally introduced. Old nurses and messengers were depicted with frequent touches of humour, so that the impression could not have been so simple and mono-emotional as Renaissance critics declared it ought to be. Finally, there is the unity of place, not mentioned at all in Aristotle's *Poetics*. At first glance it might seem as if this unity of place would have been indelibly impressed upon Greek drama because of the physical conditions of the playhouse; but even in this respect the stricter assumptions of the pseudo-classic critics are not justified. Both in Aeschylus' *Eumenides* and in Sophocles' *Ajax* the rules are broken, even if there is nothing of that violent and frequent alteration of locality which is such a marked feature of modern theatres. Undoubtedly there were limits beyond which the Greek dramatists could not go; undoubtedly, as compared with playhouses of today, their theatres imposed upon them restrictions which proved ultimately the basis for the theories of Renaissance philosophers. At the same time we must note that the restrictions were not final and critically imposed; that there was always a margin of licence; and that the dramatists, not being critic-bound as were those of later days, succeeded in securing an even greater concentration of effect and sometimes an even more delicate subtlety in the seizing of situation, through the conventions within which they, as artists, had to work.

This question of the unities, itself dependent on the structure of the Greek playhouse, is intimately connected with the division of dramas into portions or acts. The Old Comedy of Aristophanes knew naught of formal dividing, and, although we can trace in general various portions fairly clearly marked, there is no norm which we can establish as the ideal to which the dramatists looked for their model. We may on the other hand state in bold terms that the comedies of Aristophanes do as a rule fall into seven separate parts or scenes. There is, first of all, the πρόλογος (*prologos*, prologue), in which the general outline of the plot is presented, followed by the πάροδος (*parodos*, entrance), the entrance-song of the chorus. These two parts are preparatory for the ἀγών (*agon*), or dramatized debate between the principal characters of the comedy. The ἀγών over, the chorus comes forward to address the audience in the παράβασις (*parabasis*, from παραβαίνειν, *parabainein*, to come forward), a part which is itself apportionable into many subdivisions. This choral ode is followed by a number of ἐπεισόδια (*epeisodia*), or episodes, in which action enters more into play, the episodes for the most part illustrating the theme which in the *agon* had been treated in an abstract and theoretical manner. When the histrionic action has ceased the chorus sings its στάσιμα (*stasima*) or χορικά (*chorika*), in which, addressing the audience once more, it draws conclusions from the ἐπεισόδια and sometimes from the ἀγών. Finally, leaving the theatre, the chorus sings its last song, the ἔξοδος (*exodos*, exit-song), often addressing the audience directly and pointing out salient features of the play. In tragedy a simpler division is apparent. Here, in spite of a certain amount of variation, we can trace a general tendency towards the presenting of five main portions of histrionic action (ἐπεισόδια) separated by four or more choral chants. It seems probable that, when the chorus disappeared as an integral part of the drama, these five portions, indicated even in Greek days as τὰ πέντε μέρη (the five parts), were standardized and that this example was that which Horace followed when he advised the would-be writer to make his tragedy of neither more nor less than five acts.

9. *Masks and Costumes*

The performance of a Greek play, whether comedy or tragedy, differed from a modern production not only in the facts that the theatre was an open-air structure and that a chorus played so large a part in the dialogue. The costumes, and above all the masks, gave to it a special character of its own. In any consideration of the costumes of the tragic actors it must be remembered that the manners and themes presented in most of the tragic dramas reached back to the cycle of Homeric legend. For the Greeks, however, no thoughts of historical accuracy prescribed a dress which copied exactly that worn in previous centuries, and a solution seems to have been found in a conventionalized stage-costume which was similar to, yet differed widely from, the dresses of ordinary life. That this typical tragic costume was fully established, if it was not actually invented by him, in the time of Aeschylus is amply proved from references in later writings, and it endured down to Roman days, traditional conservatism having for-

Fig. 22. ANDROMEDA IN STAGE DRESS

bidden experimental alteration. In simple terms we may say that the fundamental article of dress was the χιτών (*chiton*), a loose-flowing garment which extended from the neck to the ankles. Such a robe, of course, was worn in daily life as well, but the stage χιτών was distinguished from the ordinary χιτών by several peculiarities. (1) Because they were thought to be degenerate and effeminate, sleeves were eschewed by the Athenians. The stage-garment, however, was provided with such sleeves extending to the wrists. (2) Whereas the ordinary χιτών was usually belted at the waist, on the stage the girdle was worn just below the breast. This, as will be seen, was due to the exaggerated height of the tragic actor. (3) Instead of being always composed of white or of self-coloured materials, this χιτών was often adorned with many bright hues and was ornamented, now with formal designs, now with painted animals, figures, or symbolical forms (Fig. 22). This richness of colouring must ever be borne in mind when we speak of the "statuesque" quality of classical Athenian performances.

Above the χιτών was thrown a cloak, which might either be the ἱμάτιον (*himation*) or the χλαμύς (*chlamus*). The former was a long covering thrown over the right shoulder, the latter a short mantle cast over the left shoulder. These, like the χιτών, were gorgeously coloured, and, judging from the account of Pollux, we may hazard the conjecture that the colours were employed for symbolic effect. Thus it would seem that dark or dim colours signified grief or mourning (symbolism of emotion), and that queens wore garments in which purple played a predominant part (symbolism of station). In all probability the Greek dramatists were aided in their delineation of character and of soul-state by these means. It is undeniable, also, that while normally the principal figures in a Greek tragedy all wore this conventional costuming, special garments were occasionally employed to signify either the profession of the wearer or his immediate condition. Thus Pollux informs us that Telephus and Philoctetes, being in a state of abject misery, were clad in rags, and we may presume that the lower-class characters, such as servants or messengers, wore garments nearer to those in ordinary use. Small details of apparel too helped to make distinctions. Kings wore their crowns as they did in the Elizabethan theatre. A Persian sported his turban over the ordinary stage-dress. Hercules carried his club and lion's skin. Old men rested wearily on a stick or crutch. Granted that there was an understanding on the part of the audience, this conventional symbolism of attire must have gone far towards making the natures and the status of the various characters perfectly plain.

In connexion with the garments mention may be made of two peculiar features which the Athenian stage shared with the stage of China today. Probably because of the vastness of the Grecian playhouse the actor was usually raised to an abnormal height by the use of the κόθορνος (*kothornos*, cothurnus), variously known as the ἐμβάτης (*embates*) and the ὀκρίβας (*okribas*). These were boots with a heavy wooden sole, generally painted, no doubt with symbolic colouring. If the origin of the cothurnus, however, was due to the desire to make the actor seem taller than he was in reality, the prevalent wish for symbolism certainly entered in to give it a subordinate importance. Thus the height of the cothurnus varied in accordance with the importance of the character. A monarch was entitled to a loftier boot than was one of his attendant lords. Along with this cothurnus must be taken the ὄγκος (*onkos*), a lofty head-dress which towered over the mask, reminding us at times of the feathered head-gear of Restoration heroes and of the weirdly dressed performers in Chinese drama. This *onkos* and cothurnus, as is obvious, must have raised an actor of 6 feet to well over 7 feet 6 inches, and, to prevent his appearance from seeming unduly slim, padding was freely used to increase the bulk as well as the height. Perhaps this bulk corresponded also with the dignity of the characters. We know that kings wore a special short garment, heavily padded, to which was given the name of κόλπωμα (*kolpoma*).

The great characteristic of the Greek tragic actor was, however, not a portion of his dress, but the mask which rendered in conventional forms an indication of his age, station, and prevalent mood. While the mask owes its being without question to the religious ceremonies from which tragedy was born, it was, partly at least, dependent upon the theatre in which the performances were given. Facial expression would have been lost in the vastness of the Athenian playhouse; the mask gave typical expression in more easily visible form. The small number of actors allowed could not, without its help, have sustained their many parts. The aid given through the resonance of the widely opened mouth must have proved a welcome assistance even in theatres where, as we know, the acoustic properties were well-nigh perfect. For many reasons, then, traditionally religious as well as theatrical, the mask was retained as a prime feature of the actor's attire. Made of linen, cork, or wood, these masks provided much

Fig. 23. COTHURNUS, MASKS, AND ONKOS ON THE MODERN CHINESE STAGE

Fig. 24. TERRA-COTTA FIGURE OF AN ACTOR

information to the audience. For our knowledge of the typical varieties the account given by Pollux, if meagre, is invaluable. In his work are enumerated nearly thirty masks for tragedy, and we gather that the mask-maker endeavoured, above all other things, to indicate the age of the person represented. Six old men are described in the *Onomastikon*. (1) First comes the shaven type, the oldest of all, with a few white locks attached to the *onkos*. His mask depicts extreme age. This is the type of Priam. (2) Then there comes the man who is not quite so old—the "white" man, as he is styled by Pollux—with grey locks, a thick white beard, hanging eyebrows, and, above, a small *onkos*. Thus, no doubt, was Cadmus played. (3) Coming downward, we meet with the grey-haired man, of a dark or sallow complexion, the Oedipus of these type-characters, on the verge of old age. (4) Middle-aged men come next. The tyrant with thick black locks and beard, sharp face, and lofty *onkos* is nearest the age of Oedipus. Aegisthus must have been of this nature. (5) Blond hair seems to have indicated earlier manhood, for there next comes the "fair" man, of a pleasant complexion and sporting a lower *onkos*, the "hero" proper, companioned (6) by the "fairer" man, rather paler and displaying a countenance which betokens distress or sickness.

This list of the older men in Pollux is followed by a list of eight young men, again distinguished by the colour of their hair, complexions, and *onkos*. (1) The eldest of these is the "good-for-all-work," a character who has no beard, but is granted thick black hair and locks. He is somewhat tanned in face, but has a good complexion, and is typified in the person of

Fig. 25.

A TRAGEDY KING

The actor is shown with
hair disarranged, as if he
had but newly taken off
the mask which is placed
on the table to his left.

the youthful hero. (2) The character with crisp flaxen hair, fierce countenance, and bushy eyebrows comes next, accompanied by (3) another, just a little younger. The description seems to be that of the youthful hero, corresponding in temperament with the last two types of middle-aged men, who obviously belong to the hero class. (4) Contrasted with these comes the "soft" type, pale of face, jocund of appearance, shining, as Pollux says, with a godlike beauty. A youthful divinity, such as Dionysos or Apollo, may well have appeared in such a mask. Perhaps Castor and Pollux belong to the same group. (5) There come next the "squalid" characters with livid cheeks, light hair, and eyes downcast through misery. These are the youths whom misfortune has driven into despair. (6) Finally we reach the "pale" type and his companion (7) the quasi-pale type, the first very fair-haired, with lean, emaciated cheeks, the second more like the "good-for-all-work" but wasted by suffering. The former appears as Polydore's ghost in *Hecuba*, the latter as the fainting Orestes and as the lovelorn Haimon in *Antigone*.

The servants of tragic drama appear next in Pollux' account, three varieties being noted. (1) The old man clad in leather, with a leather cap in place of an *onkos*, white locks, sallow face, sharp nose, and raised eyebrows, is the more intelligent servitor or the old tutor. (2) The servant with the peaked beard is middle-aged. He bears a high and wide *onkos* hollowed round

Fig. 26. MASK OF A TRAGIC HERO

Fig. 27. STATUETTE OF A TRAGIC HERO

Note will be taken of the *onkos*, the *cothurnus*, and the ornamented robes.

the circumference. His hair is light in colour and his countenance ruddy. He is the typical messenger. (3) With him appears another snub-nosed messenger, fair also, with a ruddy complexion and hair parted at the middle of the head.

The three servants complete the list of male parts, so that we may now turn to the women characters. These, like the men, are arranged by Pollux in order of age. (1) There is first the grey-haired old woman, above the rest in years and position. She wears a medium-sized *onkos* and is pale of face. (2) The free old woman has grey hair, pale features, a smaller *onkos*, and locks streaming down to the neck. (3) Next comes the old woman slave with ruddy cheeks and a sheepskin bonnet instead of an *onkos*. This is a typical old nurse. (4) The middle-aged servant has a small *onkos*, is pale of face, and has hair streaked with grey. (5) The *diphtheritis*, or leather-clad woman, is younger than this type. She has no *onkos*. (6) "The woman with flowing hair" is dark, with pale, sad complexion, companioned by (7) another with long hair at the sides and short hair on the forehead. (8) The newly violated woman has a special tonsure. (9 and 10) The young girl with shorn locks has a pale complexion; of this type there seem to be two varieties. (11) Finally we find the very young child.

Both in tragedy and in comedy, of course, these type-masks were supplemented by the use of special masks which indicated either the mental or physical state of the wearer, or the legendary attributes of some fictitious person. The horned Actaeon, the blind Phineus or Thamyris, the many-eyed Argus, Achilles in despair over the death of Patroclus, Rivers, Hours, Muses, Furies—these are among the many similar characters which, as Pollux notes, were provided with special masks of their own.

While comedy in many ways reproduced for another purpose forms found in tragedy, naturally the comic actor wore a dress fundamentally different from that of his tragic colleague. Padding (which was named σωμάτιον, *somation*), as in tragedy, was regular, but it was designed to create a ridiculous, not a dignified, appearance. Puffed out in front and behind, and without the long χιτών, the comic actor bustled his way, Falstaff-like, on the stage. Over his padded stomach he sometimes wore an abnormally short χιτών, with occasionally an equally short χλαμύς. Sometimes, however, he was completely clad in a tight-fitting, skin-like garment which clung closely to his limbs and was coloured to represent flesh or was striped with some dyes. Characteristic of his appearance was the phallus, which symbolized the prevailing licence of the Athenian comedy. Apparently these typical garments were carried over to the New Comedy, in which, however, a greater realism prevailed, some of the persons at least wearing the dress of ordinary life.

Fig. 28. MASK OF THE LONG-HAIRED HEROINE

Like the tragic actors the performers in comedy wore masks, although without the *onkos* so typical of tragic grandeur. Pollux again provides us with a long list of these—although here perhaps should be introduced a note of caution. No doubt his catalogue of tragic types was over-formalized and included mask features which belonged to the later development of the stage; at the same time, we may believe that, in general, he has described what spectators of the earlier classical period must have seen on the stage. When he turns to comedy, however, it is evident that Pollux was thinking largely in terms of the New Comedy. He has little or nothing to say about the fantastic figures whom Aristophanes delighted to introduce into his ebullient plays, and his catalogue evidently has been based chiefly upon the New Comedy and its Roman imitations. As in his treatment of the tragic masks, he starts with the more elderly persons. (1 and 2) First come two characters called *pappos*. The first of these, an ancient grandfather, is almost bald but long-bearded. His face is pale and lean, his eyes dim; but his whole countenance betokens cheeriness. He is thus contrasted with his companion, who is still thinner, but is given a severe look with a ruddy, cantankerous appearance. Callipho and Simo in *Pseudolus* are later representatives of these types. (3 and 4) Alongside of these are two "old men" or stock comedy fathers, of whom Menedemus and Chremes in *Heautontimoroumenos* are typical. The former is called by Pollux the "chief." He has a hooked nose with a broad mask. The eyebrows have a certain peculiarity in that the right side is raised, the left horizontal, so that one profile indicates anger, the other calm, the actor being forced to turn his face one way or the other to reveal the fictitious emotions of the character he is representing. The second old man has a long, trembling beard, thick hair, and a certain phlegmatic appearance. (5 and 6) The Hermonios and Second Hermonios gain their names apparently from that of an actual actor-contemporary of Aristophanes. The chief of these two has a bald head, raised eyebrows, and a severe countenance. The second is barely described for us, but the short, pointed beard seems to have been a characteristic feature. (7) A pointed beard is worn also by another character, called by Pollux simply "the man with the pointed beard." He is marked by an air of intractability, which is

Fig. 29. TERRA-COTTA STATUETTE OF A COMIC ACTOR DECLAIMING

Fig. 30. MENANDER RELIEF, SHOWING MASKS OF YOUTH, COURTESAN, AND OLD MAN

Fig. 31. COMEDY SCENE, SHOWING CHEERY AND TESTY OLD MEN, FLUTE-PLAYER, YOUTH, AND SERVANT

indicated in his raised eyebrows. Lyco in the *Curculio* is of this type. (8) The brothel-keeper, the *leno* of the Roman stage, resembles the next-described character, Lycomedeios, save that he is bald and has contracted brows and distended lips. (9) Lycomedeios sports crisp hair and a double expression, one eyebrow being raised, the other horizontal. He is the sycophant and busybody of the comic dramas.

The youths come next in order. Of these there are eleven, to correspond with the nine old and elderly men. (1) First comes the young man, "good-for-all-work." He is ruddy in colour, has raised eyebrows and a crown of hair on his head, with the general appearance of a robust, athletic youth—the lover, the "juvenile lead" of to-day, the Clitipho of the classical *Heautontimoroumenos*. (2) The "dark young man" is a trifle his junior. His eyebrows are not raised, and he looks like a student or a follower of the gymnasium. He is obviously not so riotous as his elder brother. He is opposed to the (3) "young man with curled hair," who is more beautiful of feature and ruddy of complexion, with one wrinkle on his brow. His well-tended hair and general appearance betoken the man of luxurious life. (4) Still more effeminate is the "delicate young man" with a pale complexion, obviously reared in ease and unathletic habits. He too has a crown of hair on his head. He is the youngest of all and is typified in the Dinarchus of *Truculentus*. (5) In addition to these typical young men, lovers and their kin, appear seven other class types, of whom the "rustic" first claims our attention. His hair is black and bound in a crown on his head. His cheeks are tanned, his lips wide, and his nose flat. Next (6

Fig. 32. SET OF MASKS: OLD MAN, FAIR YOUTH, YOUTH WITH CURLY HAIR, AND SERVANT

and 7) comes the "boasting soldier," of which type there are two varieties, one having black hair and dark complexion, the other blond hair and fair complexion. Both are distinguished by an enormous headdress of threatening proportions. Obviously Pyrgopolinices in the *Miles Gloriosus* of Plautus is the type representative of this class. (8 and 9) The flatterer and the parasite naturally go together, the former distinguished by evil eyebrows, the latter by a cheerier and more obsequious countenance. Both have dark hair, hooked noses, and broken ears. (10) With these goes the "Sicilian," a kind of third parasite, who is not described for us. (11) Finally there is a character called by Pollux merely a "portrait mask," a stranger, well dressed, with a clean-shaven chin. He is probably the gull of the rascal crew described above.

The servants of comedy in some respects follow closely on the lines of the other characters. (1) Thus the first servant mentioned by Pollux is the *pappos*, a grey-haired old man who has been liberated for his long service, as is shown by the arrangement of his hair, which is as worn by freemen. (2) Next to him is the "chief slave," distinguished by a coil of red hair, raised eyebrows, and contracted brows. (3) There is a servant who is lean and ruddy, with raised eyebrows and a head partly bald. (4) The "crisp slave" also has red hair. His eyes are peculiarly screwed up and his lips distended. (5) With these goes Maison, the Greek cook, who is bald and has hair of a yellowish red. (6) Tettix, the foreign cook, boasts a bald head streaked with two or three black locks, a dark complexion, and a deceitful face. (7) Finally, there is a type of boasting servant with an enormous headdress, a kind of double of type 2, represented in the Sceledrus of *Miles Gloriosus*.

The women's masks, some seventeen in all, now must occupy our attention. First there comes a group of three "old hags." (1) The lean or "wolfish" old woman, with thin net of wrinkles, white-haired and pallid, has crooked eyes, which correspond with the general rapacious nature of the type. (2) The "fat old woman" has deep wrinkles on her face, while her hair is caught in a band. (3) Thirdly, there is the old domestic servant, flat-nosed, with two molar teeth only in each jaw.

The "young women" correspond to the "young men," ranging in age from about forty-five down to extremest youth. (1) First comes the "talkative woman," a perennial type. She has long hair, straight eyebrows, and a fair complexion. (2) The "crisp woman" is distinguished by the appearance of her hair, and it has been thought that this is the type of the silent, modest spouse. No doubt the two are represented in the Philumena and Pamphila of Plautus' *Stichus*.

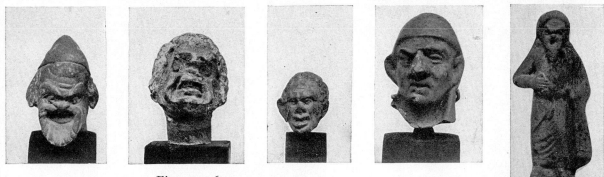

Figs. 33–36. TERRA-COTTA MASKS

Fig. 37 (far right). TERRA-COTTA STATUETTE OF AN OLD MAN

Fig. 38. MASK OF A TRAGIC HERO

Fig. 39. MASK OF A MESSENGER

Fig. 40. MASK OF A TRAGIC
HEROINE

Fig. 41. MASK OF THE GOLDEN COURTESAN

(3) The "virgin" is the young heroine, with straight dark eyebrows and a pale countenance. (4 and 5) Next come two "false virgins," girls of good family who have fallen into distress and have been the victims of violation. Whereas the virgin wears the usual maiden's headdress, the plaited locks separated by a parting, the first false virgin has her hair in a knot after the custom of young brides, and the second wears the maiden's locks without the parting. Both are pallid in complexion. With these we leave the world of upper-class life and pass to the *demi-mondaine.* (6) The "talkative mistress" is an elderly courtesan who has become a bawd. (7) The "mistress" has her hair done in the style of married women, which indicates the fact that she has been accepted by some wealthy man as his concubine. (8) The "accomplished courtesan" is somewhat like the false virgin, but is ruddier and has locks of hair about her ears. (9) The "young courtesan" is largely unadorned and only has a fillet binding her head. (10 and 11) The courtesan proper has, however, two companions, the "golden courtesan" and the "courtesan with the bandeau." The former, as her name shows, wears a profusion of golden ornaments in her hair; the latter binds her head with a gaily coloured ribbon. Both are older and more experienced than the young courtesan. (12) Among the courtesans we find, last of all, the *lampadion,* so called because of the fact that the hair is caught in a pointed tress on the

head. Perhaps, as has been thought, this is the mask of the young noble-born girl who, seized away from her parents in youth, is thought to be a courtesan until discovery is made of her birth—the Marina of the classical stage. (18) The "dainty servant," clad in a white under-girdled tunic, is the true lady's maid, while (14) the "servant with smooth hair," dressed in scarlet and snub-nosed, is clearly the confidante of the courtesan, typified in the Milphidippa of *Miles Gloriosus*.

So ends the list of the masks in Pollux, and we can see from the indications given by him how age, class, birth, and nature were symbolized by special features. Colour of hair indicates the first; while snub-noses are apportioned to those of low birth. Colour and ornaments characterize the courtesans, and hair-dress the married and unmarried women. Eyebrows, lips, and complexion are freely used to indicate temperament and mental condition, the object of the whole being to allow the spectators at a glance to grasp the main features of the persons represented.

CHAPTER III

The Roman Theatre

1. *The Playhouses*

PERHAPS the essential distinction between the Roman stage performances and those of ancient Greece is that the former had virtually no real religious associations. Such a statement, it is true, requires both qualification and explanatory comment. In Rome the many days in the year during which plays and other spectacles could be presented were technically connected with festivals in honour of the gods; shrines were frequently included in the theatrical buildings; and play performances were fairly frequent parts of funeral games. Nevertheless, as we look at the theatres of Rome, we realize that these connexions have no basic significance: when the Romans went to the playhouse they sought for entertainment merely, and as the centuries moved on the appeal tended to become more and more directed towards the illiterate mass: farcical business and sensational incident were all the rage. We must, of course, admit that the Hellenistic playhouses also had lost the intimate connexion with divine service which had characterized the theatre of Dionysos at Athens, yet these playhouses could not quite forget that out of which they had grown.

At a very early date the Greek colonies established in Sicily had brought from their homeland the passion for the erection of theatre buildings, and there many famous Athenian tragedies and comedies were presented. For the most part, however, the first stages erected for displays of acting, those connected with the *phlyakes* and the Roman farcical Atellanae, were simple wooden structures. Gradually, and again largely under the inspiration of the Hellenistic colonists, various townships began to substitute stone theatrical buildings, most of them exhibiting a fresh architectural approach, so that by the time, 55 B.C., that Pompey's great playhouse was set up in Rome itself, a new model had been established.

This new model had many interesting features. The Roman *proskenion*, now, in the Latinized form of *proscaenium*, often applied to the whole acting-area and its background, was usually ornamented in front with columns and niches. The stage itself was made lower and considerably deeper. Behind the actors rose a sumptuous *scaenae frons*, majestic in its proportions. Still more important were some other novelties. Throughout the whole of its history, the Greeks had shown a predilection for the larger-than-semicircle type of auditorium, but in these Italian playhouses the auditorium (called the *cavea*) was reduced to a strictly semicircular shape. In harmony with this, the orchestral circle was halved, and an indication of the way in which its theatrical significance had now declined is shown by the fact that in some of these playhouses seats for distinguished spectators were actually placed within its confines.

Since the front of the stage now coincided with the diameter of the attenuated orchestra, it is

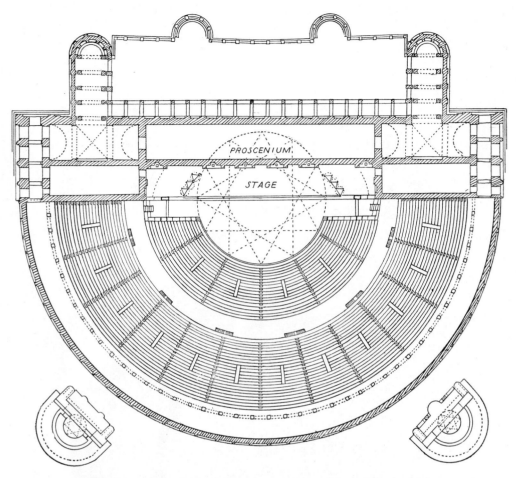

PROSCENIUM

STAGE

Fig. 42. PLAN OF THE MARCELLUS THEATRE AT ROME

Fig. 43. STAGE FRONT AT DJEMILA

Note will be taken of the steps leading from stage to orchestra.

obvious that the portion of the theatre which was reserved for actors and that which was given over to spectators had no clearly marked lines of demarcation. Whereas the Greek theatres had always been composed of either two or three separate parts, here the entire trend was towards the creation of a single architectural whole.

The integration of auditorium, orchestra, and stage-buildings meant that the ancient open entrance passages at the sides of the stage could be filled in, thus formally and logically completing the process of integration, and on the tops of the walled-in structures, the so-called *tribunalia*, special seats could be provided for those concerned with the production or for favoured guests. Furthermore, the fusion of the original separate parts meant that no longer was there the need of building the auditorium on sloping ground. In some outlying parts of the Roman dominions the old Greek choice of location persisted, but generally it was found that this Roman theatre could more effectively be constructed when the whole was planned to occupy a level space. This meant, in turn, that the entire building had to be enclosed with

Fig. 44. THE THEATRE AT ASPENDOS

high walls—and the Roman architects eagerly seized the opportunity of adorning these with majestic stone columns and arches.

From the time when the Pompey theatre thus offered a fresh model, dozens of similar buildings arose all over the Roman Empire, becoming ever more and more stupendous, more and more elaborate. The *cavea*, vast in extent, was divided by corridors and ramps (the *vomitoria*) and often took shape as a series of "floors," each with its own order of architectural ornament (Fig. 44). Frequently the orchestra was enclosed by a wall, since this space was used on occasion for gladiatorial displays or, when flooded with water, for mimic sea-fights or water ballets (Fig. 45). It seems to have been usual, also, for steps to lead down from the stage-level to the enclosed orchestral area; such steps are still to be seen in the theatre of Djemila in North Africa (Fig. 43). Sometimes, as in the Phaedrus alterations in the theatre at Athens (third or fourth century A.D.), the desire for decoration led to sculptured shapes being set along the front of the long stage: there an elaborate frieze of kneeling figures was put into the place of what had once been a comparatively blank wall (Fig. 52). To balance the height of the *cavea*, the *scaenae frons* soared upward in a serried forest of architectural decoration (Fig. 46), and often, as in the theatre at Aspendos (Fig. 44), a roof was erected over the stage to protect the architect's embellishments and the actors below.

The presence of this roof in some theatres leads, finally, to a consideration of two particular innovations in these Roman theatres. Owing to the facts that the theatre was now treated as a single unity and that the top of the *scaenae frons* was level with the top of the *cavea* (shown clearly in Fig. 44) there was now the possibility of covering the entire structure with an awning, to which was given the name *velum* or *velarium*. Thus, in effect, the Roman playhouse, although its stonework still presented the features of an open-air edifice, was being brought reasonably close to the indoor theatres of the modern period. And a second innova-

Fig. 45. A WATER BALLET

Fig. 46. SCAENAE FRONS OF THE THEATRE AT LEPTIS MAGNA

tion brought them even closer: the Romans invented a front curtain, called *aulaeum*, which, presumably fixed on a frame, could be dropped into the orchestra and raised again; and still another type of curtain, known as the *siparium*, could be used to cover parts of the façade behind the actors.

Fig. 47. RECONSTRUCTION OF THE SCAENAE FRONS AT ASPENDOS

Fig. 48. RECONSTRUCTION
OF THE SCAENAE FRONS AT
ASPENDOS

Fig. 49. THE OUTSIDE WALL
OF THE THEATRE AT ORANGE

Figs. 50 and 51. THE THEATRE AT ORANGE

Fig. 52. RELIEFS ON THE HYPOSCENIUM OF THE THEATRE AT ATHENS

Fig. 53. A ROMAN STAGE

Majestic and imposing as the remains of these Roman theatres may be, we must believe that in general they were less intimately adapted than the Greek stages for the performance of plays. No doubt at Orange and elsewhere comedies and tragedies are still presented effectively in festival productions, but, when we consider the decay of drama during the centuries of the Roman Empire, we are bound to acknowledge that these impressive buildings were originally designed rather as monuments of civic pride than as places wherein the drama might be most satisfactorily presented.

2. *Actors, Costumes, and Masks*

Nothing more clearly indicates the decline of Roman drama than does the inferior social position occupied by the actors. At the very start some comic or tragic poet might engage his own company and perhaps take a leading part himself, but soon conditions changed. Permanent dramatic troupes came into being, each under the control of a "commercial" manager, each consisting of slaves who might be flogged or even put to death at that manager's will. Naturally, therefore, the profession of acting became despised, and even after Roscius had won fame and esteem for himself, there never was in Rome that dignity surrounding a performer which is evident in the records of the Greek stage. As generation succeeded generation conditions worsened. Gradually the written drama disappeared from the theatres, preserving only a precarious and unsatisfactory half-existence in the shape of dramatic "poems" designed for no more than private recitation. When mimic sea-fights and gladiatorial shows did not occupy the theatres, only the *mimus*, the work of improvising mimes, took the place of what, in Athens, had been the solemn production of the plays of Sophocles.

During the two centuries preceding our era, it had seemed for a time that the spirit of Menander's New Comedy was to find a fresh home in the Roman culture, and it is true that the works of Plautus (*c.* 254–184 B.C.) and especially of Terence (*c.* 195–159

Fig. 54. MASKS FOR THE "ANDRIA" OF TERENCE

B.C.) were responsible for conveying to the modern stage
something at least of the atmosphere of the later Greek
comedy. There was even at this period a method of production not dissimilar from that pertaining in Hellenistic times.
For tragedy actors wore long sweeping robes (*syrmata*), and
in comedy the garments frequently recall those familiar in
earlier days. Wigs (*galeri* or *galearia*) were usually worn,
and the tragic performer sported buskins, or *cothurni*, as
in Greek days. Still colour symbolism seems to have been
employed: old men were usually dressed in white, young
men in purple, parasites in grey, courtesans in yellow. As
in Greece, masks were familiar parts of the attire sported
by the comic players. An interesting relic of their use is
to be found in one of the manuscripts of Terence's *Andria*
where the several masks apportioned to the characters in
the play are set up in rows, just as possibly they may have
been in some storage cabinet placed in the actors' dressing-
rooms (Fig. 54, and see Fig. 55).

Fig. 55. SYRUS IN THE "HEAUTON-
TIMOROUMENOS" OF TERENCE

But all of this was forgotten after the passage of a few centuries, so that, when the Roman
Empire collapsed, the only theatrical or dramatic elements remaining were the dubious
performances of the mimes, the still more dubious exhibitions of pantomimic dancers, and the
stilted works of poets who were writing works calculated, not for performance, but for reading.

CHAPTER IV

Performances in the Middle Ages

1. Relics of the Classical Tradition

APPROXIMATELY a thousand years separated the first primitive emergence of drama in Athens from the final collapse of the Roman civilization. For almost exactly a thousand years after that the Greek and Roman theatres were forgotten, until once again the classical tradition, rescued from obscurity, demonstrated its enduring creative strength.

For a short time after the fall of Rome, it is true, some kind of debased spectacles still were displayed before the populace: *scaenici* continued to give their performances during the sixth century when the Ostrogoths wielded power in Italy. In Byzantium, the seat of the Eastern Empire, they endured still longer: professional actors remained active there as late as the close of the seventh century. Soon, however, all this was to disappear: after the coming of the Lombards in 568 we hear no more of *spectacula* or of theatres at Rome, while in the East problems more serious soon set people thinking of things sterner than merry supper-parties with groups of dancing girls.

It is, of course, possible that, although the use of theatres disappeared from men's minds, some slight, tattered remnants of at least the mime tradition were carried on throughout the Dark Ages. Not infrequently the writings of pious Christians allude to *histriones* and *mimi* in terms which suggest that these performers were familiar figures. "Melio est Deo placere quam histrionibus"—"It is better to please God than the actors"—Alcuin warns a young friend, and the warning would have been pointless if there had not then been actors to please. "Melius est, pauperes edere de mensa tua, quam istriones"—"It is better to feed paupers at your table than actors"—declares the same author to the Bishop of Lindisfarne, and once again there is the implication that the entertaining of performers, even by prominent ecclesiastics, was at that time by no means unknown. Still further, when the term *jongleur* came into being in the sense of "entertainer," many men associated it with a far-reaching tradition. Derived from the classical Latin *iocularis*, "merry," the medieval Latin *ioculator* found its place in almost every European language—the Old French *iogleor*, the Spanish *juglar*, the Italian *giocolatore*, the Old High German *gaugalâri*, the Middle German *goukelaere*; and perhaps, as the English "juggler" suggests, these entertainers for the most part delighted their audiences, not by the exhibition of any dramatic scenes, but simply by conjuring and acrobatics. Nevertheless, we read in an early glossary that *istriones sunt ioculatores* (actors are jongleurs), while *mimi seu ioculatores* (mimes or jongleurs) is a common phrase. Thus medieval writers clearly regarded them as the direct descendants of the more ancient mimes. And throughout these centuries there are not a few scattered references which appear to show that at least some of the performers did, in fact, indulge in something which approached the dramatic.

Apart from this tradition existed another. Throughout the Middle Ages one Latin play-wright maintained his position. In spite of the distrust of all that pertained to the theatre, Terence's works continued to be read because of their delicate and incisive literary style; there were not lacking attempts to imitate his writings; and maybe this imitation went some-what further than is commonly admitted. At any rate, from a period between the seventh and the tenth century comes a little dialogue in Latin in which two characters are made to converse: one is Terence himself, the other is called *Persona Delusoris*. It has all the appearance of having been a prologue either for a performance of one of Terence's plays or for that of some farce-comedy based on his works. Such extant vernacular pieces as the English *Inter-ludium de Clerico et Puella* (An Interlude of a Clerk and a Girl) and the French *Le Garçon et l'Aveugle* also suggest that the imitation went at times considerably beyond the sphere of the literary exercise.

2. *The Growth of Medieval Drama*

Whatever evidence of this kind we may bring forward, however, it need hardly be said that the characteristic drama of the Middle Ages was an independent development, owing absolutely nothing to the earlier tradition. As is well known, its source is to be sought for in a far different place, in the very heart of the Catholic Church. Finding its basis in the symbolic nature of the service of the Mass, this new drama developed out of a desire on the part of the clergy to place the salient facts of Christ's life more realistically before their congregations. At the two great festivals of the Church, Easter and Christmas, arose little dramas, or dramatic scenes, which displayed the birth and the death of Jesus. The story of these two dramatic scenes (generally called liturgical dramas because still associated with the service or liturgy) has often been told and need not be repeated in any detail here. Only such few facts as may serve to make plain the setting are required.

The earliest form of the Easter play is a piece of four-lined dialogue in which a couple of priests, arraying themselves in white as angels, are confronted by two other priests whose robes show that they are women.

Quem quaeritis in sepulchro, o Christicolae?

"Whom do you seek in the sepulchre, O Christian women?" asks one of the angels.

Iesum Nazarenum crucifixum, o coelicolae,

"Jesus of Nazareth Who was crucified, O heavenly ones," the women reply, and are immediately answered:

Non est hic: surrexit sicut praedixerat.
Ite, nuntiate quia surrexit de sepulchro.

"He is not here: He has arisen even as He foretold. Go, announce that He is arisen from the sepulchre."

It is here evident that we have the foundations of what is true drama, and, the scene pleasing the audience, additions soon crept in. Mary Magdalen lingers behind and meets Christ clad as a gardener; Peter and John run frantically towards the sepulchre, one outstripping the other; the Marys buy perfumes from a little stall set outside the fictitious tomb. At Christmas there is the same development. The shepherds see the star which heralds the birth of Christ,

4

and come to lay their rustic gifts on His cradle. Later three Kings arrive with their more precious presents; and, still later, Herod rants and raves when he hears that a King of Kings has been born into the world.

All of this, of course, is in Latin, but soon vernacular comes to take its place, and portions of the liturgical drama, as in the English Shrewsbury fragments, are spoken in medieval French or German or English, for, it must be remembered, this was no national development, but a movement which is to be traced in almost every European country. The next stage is the separation of the primitive play from the regular Church services. Partly because these dramas were growing so rapidly in extent, partly because the largest churches were not sufficiently great to accommodate all the vast concourse of people who flocked to see the plays, the drama was moved outside onto the steps of the great west door, the spectators standing in the church-yard without. Then came doubt in the minds of the ecclesiastical authorities. This thing which they had called into being was becoming too great a force in the lives of the people; and accordingly came edict after edict, criticism after criticism, until the clergy were prohibited from taking part in performances—at least in such performances as were conducted outside the walls of the church itself. The drama, however, had been born and had grown into a lusty and lovable child; it could not die now, and the rôle of guardian was assumed by the laity. In England the powerful town-guilds took over the production of plays; in France and in Italy special societies or associations, such as the famous Confrérie de la Passion, were formed as vast amateur acting bodies. The subject-matter of their performances still remained Biblical, but its range was mightily extended, and the dialogue now was in the common vernacular tongues. Thus grew into being the sprawling collections of plays known in their own time collectively as "miracles" or *mystères* or *sacre rappresentazioni*, and commonly described to-day as "mystery cycles."

3. Medieval Theatres and Mise-en-Scène

As might naturally be supposed, we cannot describe the appearance of any one "theatre" used in medieval times. The question is rather one of the "theatres" (in the broadest sense) employed during those years between the appearance of the first liturgical drama and the comic interludes of the sixteenth century. In general, we may divide these into several main groups, each to be considered separately: (1) the church as a theatre; (2) the church-like arrangement

Fig. 56. THE SEPULCHRE

Note will be taken of the angels who raise the lid of the (practicable) sarcophagus. The original is in the Church of St Paul at Dax.

Fig. 57. CHRIST RISING FROM THE TOMB

Note will be taken of the realistic treatment both of the sarcophagus lid and of the figures depicted.

Fig. 58. CHRIST RISING FROM
THE TOMB

Note will be taken of the figure of Christ half
seated in the sarcophagus. The original is in
the Museum of Toulouse.

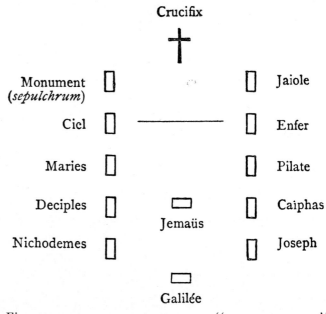

Fig. 59. THE MANSIONS IN THE "RESURRECTION"

of the acting-place when first the drama was brought to the open air; (3) the stationary setting; (4) the round; (5) the pageant; and (6) the curtained platform.

(1) We start first, then, with the arrangements made within the church for the performance of the liturgical plays. The sepulchre used at the Easter play could be of various kinds. At first no doubt it was merely an *assimilatio quaedam sepulchri*, a kind of symbol of a sepulchre arranged at the high altar to the east of the church, but this soon gave way to a regularly built tomb, whether of wood or stone, set usually in the north aisle. Some indication of what this sepulchre looked like is provided for us in details of twelfth-century church architecture. Up to the twelfth century Christ's tomb is nearly always shown, in conventional Byzantine manner, as an architectural building with two arches. With the development of the liturgical play, however, new designs enter in. The tomb is now clearly a sarcophagus, sometimes with the lid half-open or wholly open (Fig. 56) and frequently accompanied by an angel who points within as if saying *Non est hic* (Fig. 57). Still further, Christ Himself, Who is never depicted by Byzantine artists as coming from the sepulchre, is now shown rising out of it (Fig. 58). The location of this "theatrical" tomb was always either in the eastern or, more commonly, in the northern end of the church. With the slow elaboration of the *Quem quaeritis* playlet, however, the need of having more than a single fictional "set" immediately arose. Thus, for example, when the Marys, walking up the nave towards the tomb, stopped to purchase their spices, they did so at an unguent-seller's stall. At first this stall was represented merely by a chair, but soon some simple structure was specially fashioned for the occasion. Thus even at its most primitive stage the liturgical drama showed a tendency towards what might be described as extension of acting-space: the whole nave of the church could be used by the ecclesiastical actors, and within this space different particular fictional localities could be indicated.

(2) Passing from this, we reach the period when more fully developed and diversified plays were being put before the public and when as yet the minds of those responsible for the productions were still dominated by thoughts of the church-as-theatre, even although these

plays had moved outside its precincts. Here several texts and plans come to our aid, most notably a French twelfth- or thirteenth-century *Resurrection*, an Anglo-Norman twelfth-century *Adam*, a plan (dating from the sixteenth century, but probably reproducing a much earlier setting) of a production formerly called the Donaueschingen mystery play, but now definitely proved to have emanated from Villingen, and a second plan, of the same date, from Lucerne. In the first of these there is a kind of preface or prologue which indicates the positions to be occupied by the emblems of the various fictional localities. From this we learn that the crucifix is at one end, no doubt where it would have appeared above the high altar in a church (Fig. 59). On one side are a tomb, a heaven, and places for the Marys, the Disciples, and Nicodemus. Opposite these are five places—a jail, hell, and locations for Pilate, Caiaphas, and Joseph. Opposite the crucifix we find Emmaus and Galilee.[1]

At this point, it is necessary to pause for a moment to consider how these various fictional localities were shown to the public. Originally, as we have seen, chairs must have served for this purpose in the presentation of the earliest liturgical playlets, and even when we have moved on into the sphere of the mystery cycles we encounter descriptive terms such as *sedes*, *estals*, and *sièges*. Alongside of these we also have *lius* (*lieux*) and *loca*. But in later days the commonest technical words are *domus*, *mansions*, or *houses*, and we know that in the productions the *seats*, *houses*, or *places*, whether belonging to named characters or else indicating such areas as Heaven or Hell, were, in fact, small stages, usually with posts at their corners supporting curtained frameworks. Their actual appearance may, however, be left aside for the moment: what is important to observe is that in the *Resurrection* these mansions are all placed alongside each other, their positions being determined by memories of performances within the churches.

[1] The prologue runs as follows:

"En ceste manere recitom	"In this respect let us recite
La seinte resurreccion.	The Resurrection play to-night.
Primerement apareillons	First of all we detail here
Tus les lius et les mansions:	All the houses that appear:
Le crucifix primerement	First a crucifix we fit;
E puis apres le monument.	The sepulchre comes after it.
Une jaiole i deit aver	There too must be a prison cell
Pur les prisons emprisoner.	To keep the prisoners in well.
Enfer seit mis de cele part,	On that side Hell must be,
E mansions de l'altre part,	Mansions on the other see.
E puis le ciel; et as estals	And Heaven is there, and then
Primes Pilate od ces vassals.	A place for Pilate and his men.
Sis u set chivaliers aura.	Six or seven courtiers there,
Caiphas en l'altre serra;	And Caiaphas on another chair.
Od lui seit la jeuerie,	The Jewish folk are near by
Puis Joseph, cil d'Arimachie.	With Joseph of Arimachie.
Et quart liu seit danz Nichodemes.	Don Nichodeme comes fourth of all.
Chescons i ad od sei les soens.	Each has his servants within call.
El quint les deciples Crist.	Next the disciples' company we see,
Les treis Maries saient el sist.	And sixth there are the Maries three.
Si seit pourvéu que l'om face	Galilee is placed fair
Galilée en mi la place;	In the middle of the square;
Jemaüs uncore i seit fait,	Emmaus also must be reared
U Jhesu fut al hostel trait."	Where Jesus to his friends appeared."

With this prologue may be compared another cited from manuscript in Gustave Cohen's *Histoire de la Mise en Scène*, pp. 76–77. There too Paradise and Hell are on opposite sides.

Still more information is provided by the play of *Adam*. Here again the church arrangement is followed: to the east stands the crucifix, with Paradise to the left of the spectator and Hell to the right. Particularly valuable is the description of these two mansions. Paradise, we learn,

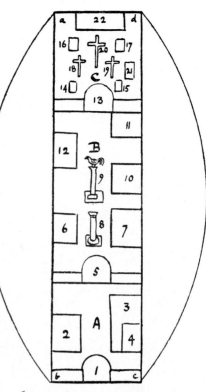

Fig. 60. THE MANSIONS IN THE VILLINGEN MYSTERY PLAY

> constituatur ... loco eminenciori; circumponantur cortine et panni serici, ea altitudine, ut persone, que in paradiso erunt, possint videri sursum ad humeros; serantur odoriferi flores et frondes; sint in eo diverse arbores et fructus in eis dependentes, ut amenissimus locus videatur.... Quicunque nominaverit paradisum, respiciat eum et manu demonstret.[1]

Of Hell we learn that

> singuli alii diaboli illos venientes monstrabunt, et eos suscipient et in infernum mittent; et in eo facient fumum magnum exsurgere, et vociferabuntur inter se in inferno gaudentes, et collident caldaria et lebetes suos, ut exterius audiantur.[2]

Evidently verisimilitude of a kind was sought after even in the twelfth century.

Next we may take the plan of the Villingen mystery play (Fig. 60), which presents a more complicated arrangement. Here clearly the three cross divisions indicate sanctuary, choir, and nave. Heaven in this case is in the east (*i.e.*, at the altar), and Hell is placed on the left instead of on the right—*i.e.*, in the north-west, but its position is determined by the fact that it is the place farthest from Heaven.

1. First door   2. Hell   3. Garden of Gethsemane   4. Mount Olivet   5. Second door   6. Herod   7. Pilate   8. Pillar of scourging   9. Pillar for cock   10. Caiaphas   11. Annas   12. Last Supper   13. Third door   14–17. Graves   18–19. Thieves' crosses   20. Cross   21. Holy Sepulchre   22. Heaven.

The plans of the Easter play presented on two successive days at Lucerne provide a fitting parallel. Here the market-square was used as the "theatre" with Heaven, the seat of the Pater Eternus and His seven angels, at the end onto which abutted the Cornmarket Street and the New Place. The plan showing the arrangement for the second day (Fig. 61) gives a view of the square, while the turreted Heaven mansion is clearly delineated in the first plan (Fig. 62). At the opposite end of the square, and to the left-hand side, a rough sketch of a many-toothed monster marked "Die Höll" indicates the seat of "Lucifer & 6 Tüffel." The other mansions, as is evident, are set along the four sides of the square. From the sketches some of these seem to have been ordinary timbered houses, others decorated in a manner peculiar

---

1 "Is to be placed on a raised spot; curtains and silk cloths are to be hung about it at such a height that persons in Paradise are visible from the shoulders. Fragrant flowers and leaves are scattered there; in it are divers trees with hanging fruit so as to give the impression of a most lovely place. . . . Whoever names Paradise must look toward it and indicate it with his hand." The terrestrial Paradise in the famous *Mystère du Viel Testament* is similarly adorned; it is "bien garny de toutes fleurs, arbres, fruictz et autres plaisances, et au meilleu l'arbre de vie plus excellent que tous les autres." A technical word for the *loggie* of French theatres—"*Paradise*"—is a relic of the raised Paradise described here. Its elevated position may be due to the use of choir galleries in the medieval church.

2 "Certain other devils point at them as they come, and seize them and bear them to Hell; and in Hell they shall make a great smoke arise, and they shall shout out to each other in Hell in jubilation, and clash their pots and kettles, so as to be heard without."

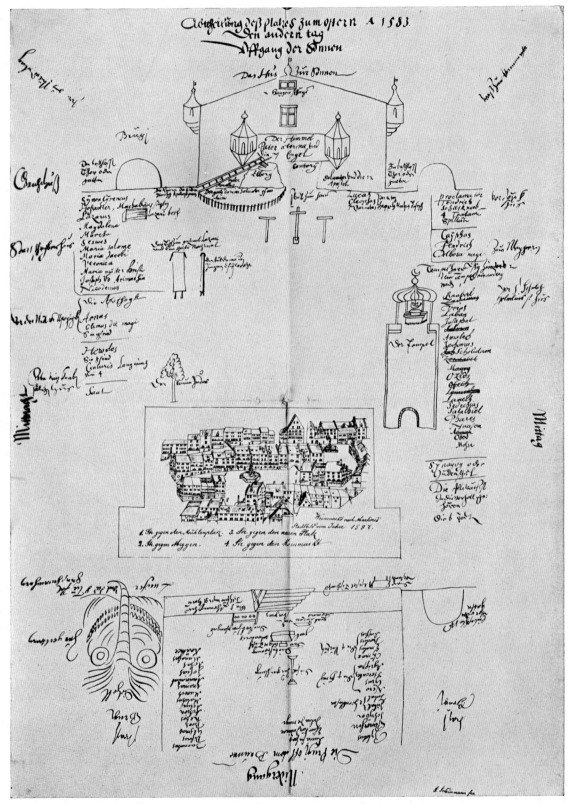

Fig. 61. THE LUCERNE EASTER PLAY, 1583: SECOND DAY

to their purposes. "Der Tempel" on the right-hand side has thus a kind of Eastern cupola, apparently surmounted by a crescent.

Such "market square" productions were frequent in widely scattered towns. The elaborate mystery-play at Mons in 1501 was so presented, as was that at Angers in 1486.

(3) Obviously, the arrangement of the mansions in a way which recalls the arrangement of the seats in church performances is of less importance than the principles underlying this medieval method of staging. That principle basically depends upon the acceptance by the audience of three conventions—(*a*) the symbolic representation of fictional localities by means of mansions, (*b*) the placing of these mansions in close proximity to each other, and (*c*) the using for acting purposes of such actual ground space as surrounded, was enclosed by, or lay in front of, the mansions. During a performance the spectators were expected to forget all other mansions save that particular one involved in the scene being presented at the moment, and if this mansion was too small effectively to provide room for all the participating actors, so that some of them had to take their positions in front of the mansion at ground-level, then this space of ground had to be taken by the public as belonging to the sphere of the mansion concerned. The ground-level area thus made available for the actors was technically named the *platea* or, in English, "playne" (plain), or "place." It is perhaps best to think of it as an unlocalized area to which a fictional locality could be assigned by the performers themselves: commonly, if a performer stepped down from his mansion, or house, and continued his action on the ground-level, then the spot where he stood was taken as part of his mansion; on the other hand, if an actor had to make a fictional journey from one mansion to another, then the ground on which he trod was conceived of as representing, in attenuated form, the tract between two far-distant fictional locations. Thus, for example, the demons in *Adam*, issuing from Hell, run about *per plateas* (that is, over the ground-level) before they approach Paradise for the purpose of tempting Eve. The *platea* was, in other words, "anywhere."

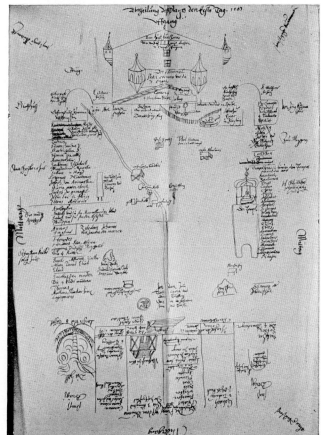

If this was the principle, then it did not matter precisely how the separate mansions stood in relation to each other; and, as the mystery-play productions became ever more elaborate, those concerned with them found that one very convenient arrangement was to have the various houses placed before the audience either in a straight line or in a slightly curved disposition. The Valenciennes miniature (Fig. 63) well illustrates the first of these. The mansions here are set directly facing the spectators in a row. To the extreme left is Paradise, followed by a small temple before which is a gate. Jerusalem succeeds, and then a castle. The

Fig. 62. THE LUCERNE EASTER PLAY, 1583: FIRST DAY

Fig. 63. THE VALENCIENNES MYSTERY PLAY, 1547

Fig. 64. MEDIEVAL DEVIL COSTUMES AT ZURICH

House of Bishops and the Golden Gate lead towards the extreme right, where appear a prison and Hell. This Hell is composed of two parts: behind is a house of torture, peopled by demons, while in front is a terrible monster's head from which some devils are issuing. The drawing excellently shows how some of the houses were coming to assume shapes more elaborate than that of the simple curtained booth—and all the evidence we have indicates that it was to Hell first and foremost that the medieval machinists and "managers" devoted their attention. The Lucerne drawing sketches in the monster, and a variant of the gaping and closing Hell's Mouth appears in Fig. 64. The monstrous head, "faicte en manière d'une grande gueule se cloant et ouvrant quant besoign en est,"[1] is probably a reminiscence of Leviathan, and it is coloured in the miniatures in striking hues. Here the medieval artist comes closest to the modern elaboration of scenic background.

For the curving line of mansions we may turn to a famous drawing by Jehan Fouquet, showing the martyrdom of Saint Apollonia (Fig. 65). Here in the foreground we see the torturing of the saint, and it is important to observe that this is being carried out on the

[1] "Made like a great gargoyle which closes and opens when need be." It was so described at Rouen in 1474.

platea and that it is being pursued with grim realism under the watchful eye of a prompter, or master of ceremonies. Behind is a series of booths with steps leading down to the ground-level. To the left there is a house crammed with angels who surround a throne evidently representing Heaven. Next comes a house of trumpeters providing celestial music, followed by a large box with an empty throne, probably that left vacant by the Emperor, the figure standing immediately behind Saint Apollonia. Then, most interestingly, we reach two booths occupied by women, and we can be almost certain that one of these elevated platforms is designed for spectators: in the medieval productions a sharp demarcation between those enacting the plays and those looking on was frequently absent and, indeed, was often impossible to secure. At the extreme right is Hell, framed of two parts: above is a platform on which two devils are standing, and below is a great gaping monster's head, from which a masked demon is issuing.

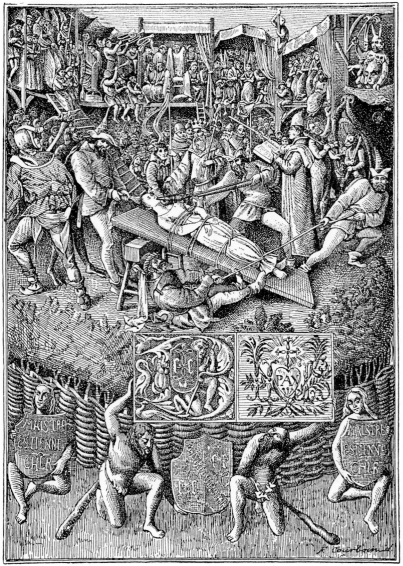

Fig. 65. "THE MARTYRDOM OF ST APOLLONIA"

(4) It is just possible that the performance drawn by Fouquet was in fact presented in a "round" of which the artist felt himself incapable of delineating more than half. In France we know that use was occasionally made of the still-standing Roman playhouses, such as those of Nîmes, Arles, and Orange, although it is not quite certain how, in such circumstances, the mansions were arranged in the ruins of such buildings. What appears eminently possible, however, is that the ancient Roman tradition of the amphitheatre lies behind those "rounds" in which the Cornish mysteries were performed and of which at least faint traces are to be found elsewhere in England. Of these the most important are the two circles which can yet be seen in St Just and Perranzabuloe. The former, of stone, has a diameter of 126 feet; the latter, of earth, is 4 feet larger. The manuscripts of the Cornish mystery plays happily furnish a plan which shows the arrangement of the mansions during the performances. For the *Origo Mundi*, for example, we have booths representing *Celum* (Heaven), followed by one marked

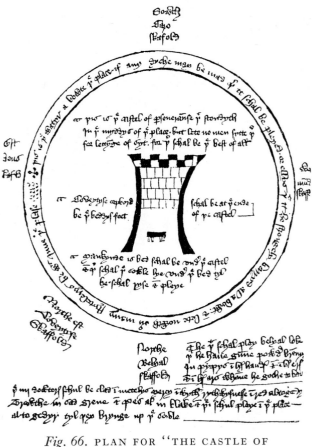

Fig. 66. PLAN FOR "THE CASTLE OF
PERSEVERANCE," *c.* 1425

The circle represents a ditch; the castle is in the centre with
"Mankynde [h]is bed" below it.

Tortores (Torturers), no doubt equivalent to the Hell prison of the French dramas, since *Infernum* (Hell) has been set next to it, and these are accompanied by houses for Pharaoh, David, Solomon, and Abraham. This plan may be compared with another interesting early diagram, that for a "morality" play which dates from the reign of King Henry VI, *The Castle of Perseverance*. Not only does the play itself provide proof of the utilization outside Cornwall of the round setting; it also offers valuable interpretative comments. Here (Fig. 66) again is a large circle, enclosed by "watyr a bowte the place if any dyche may be mad ther it schal be pleyed; or ellys that it be stronglye barryd al a bowte: & lete nowth ower many styte-lerys be withinne the place." Obviously, then, the whole of the histrionic action, as well as the opportunity given to the public of seeing that action, was planned within the circle's circumference: a water ditch or a strong fence surrounded the "theatre," and "stytelerys," or marshals, were provided, no doubt to see that order was maintained and space left for the moving about of the players. In the very centre was erected a building representing the Castle, and the several mansions were arranged round it according to the points of the compass. God's scaffold comes in the east, that of Belial in the north, with Caro in the south, and the World in the west; Covetousness occupies a position in the north-east. Quite clearly

Fig. 67. TWO MEDIEVAL PAGEANTS

audience and actors here were in closest proximity, and we must suppose both that the former would have moved from time to time towards the particular mansions which were being currently used, and that the latter carried their movement, processionally or otherwise, among the massed spectators.

(5) In England it would appear that the stationary setting, except in the form of rounds, was not common. There the guilds preferred to stage their plays on what came to be known as "pageants," which may be regarded as separate mansions placed upon wheels so that they might be shifted from place to place: they were thus similar to the *wagenspel* which was employed for similar purposes in the Netherlands. In describing the Chester plays as presented in the sixteenth century, a contemporary gives us a brief account of their use and construction. The actors, we are told,

> first beganne at ye Abbaye gates; & when the firste pagiente was played at ye Abbaye gates, then it was wheeled from thence to the pentice at ye highe crosse before ye Mayor; and before that was donne, the seconde came, and ye firste wente in-to water-gate streete, and from thence vnto ye Bridge-streete, and so all, one after an other, tell all ye pagiantes weare played.

The audiences gathered at these diverse locations saw before them

> a highe place made like a howse with ij rowmes, being open on ye tope: the lower rowme they apparrelled and dressed them selves; and in the higher rowme they played; and they stood vpon 6 wheeles.[1]

"Theatres for the severall Scenes, very large and high, placed upon wheels" is Dugdale's later account, while at Norwich in 1565 we are told that the Grocers' pageant was "a Howse of Waynskott paynted and buylded on a Carte with fowre whelys." In all probability they can be seen in two interesting contemporary miniatures (Fig. 67): in one of these a group of men, in the other a group of women, are shown watching performances being presented on the upper floor of tall booths, and the curtained spaces below these could clearly have served as convenient (or perhaps not so convenient) dressing-rooms.

Like the mansions used in the stationary settings, these movable pageants were sometimes made in symbolic representation of the locality or scene they were intended to indicate. Thus at Coventry the Cappers' pageant possessed a "hell-mouth," as did that of the Drapers. The latter was fitted with a windlass, means of belching fire from the mouth, a barrel for simulating an earthquake, and some apparatus for setting three worlds on fire; so that it was equipped with quite a nice collection of "machines." Usually, we may suppose, the Noah play-pageant was formed to represent a ship: at Hull a shipwright was paid in 1483 "for clinking Noah's ship"; in 1494 further money was expended on "making Noah's ship" and "rigging Noah's ship." In the Valenciennes miniature a practicable little vessel floats on a man-made pond, but here at Hull the ark moved on dry land—a farthing was paid in 1483 "to straw and grease for wheels."

The method of using these pageants is quite plain. The upper level was the main acting-area, and it seems as though the pageants themselves were often supplemented by movable open platforms set alongside them; but the street below could also be used as a *platea* when occasion demanded: at Coventry, a stage-direction indicates that Herod "ragis in the pagond & in the street also," while later "the iij Kyngis speykyth in the strete." Thus, except that the mansions have been separated from each other and made movable, they are the same as those set close together in the stationary settings.

[1] This description exists in two early manuscript versions: in one six wheels are referred to, in the other the number is given as four.

Fig. 68.

Fig. 70.

SIXTEENTH-CENTURY PLATFORM
STAGES

Fig. 69.

(6) Finally, we must bear in mind that the medieval world had, in addition to the elaborately decorated mystery plays, others of a humbler, but no less interesting, sort. Many secular playlets, sometimes with "moral" themes but often dealing with purely farcical episodes, have been preserved in France, and from other countries scattered remnants show that there was similar activity elsewhere. Some of it may have been amateur in scope, but for the most part its practitioners were professional entertainers, usually acting in small groups and usually, too, forced to offer their little plays in the simplest possible manner; as itinerants they were forced to perform, at times, without any kind of stage, and they could not have been expected to carry with them anything beyond such costumes as were required and perhaps a few hand properties. Thus, during a fairly long stretch of years in the late-fifteenth and early-sixteenth centuries, the extensive productions of the mystery plays and the kindred productions of lengthy "moralities" co-existed alongside a type of production of a completely different kind.

In England, for example, in addition to such a work as *The Castle of Perseverance*, we may take, as a specimen of a "morality" based on the mystery-play tradition, a drama called *Mary Magdalen*, where six main localities, each subdivided, were placed at the one time before the audience: here was a set of mansions representing Magdalen's castle and the houses of the Emperor, Herod, and Pilate; a pair of mansions for Hell; Jerusalem with a tavern, the house of Simon the Leper, and an arbour; Marseilles with a castle, a temple, and a sea-coast; Heaven with a wilderness near by; and the Holy Land with a mountain. It need hardly be said that such a piece could have been produced only by amateurs possessed of adequate resources. At this same time, however, we turn to the "interludes" given by professional actors, and in these we realize that the action of the play was intended to be offered to the public in the simplest possible manner. If need be, the players could act it on bare ground or on a hall floor; if the performance was in a hall, then the doors served them for entrances and exits; if they played outside, then even the doors were not essential. If they did on occasion have anything in the nature of a bare platform, they asked for nothing more than a curtain behind them; probably most of their performances were carried out standing, and, should a particular play demand a throne or some such object, an ordinary chair would be sufficient to serve their purposes.

No contemporary English print or picture is extant to give us an idea of what these performances looked like; but numerous early European engravings and paintings amply illustrate what must have been familiar to audiences wherever the itinerant actors wandered (Figs. 68–70). Whether the players were little professional troupes giving their interludes, or French comedians offering their farces, or Italians improvising on the basis of a scenario, they all must often have walked the rough planks of narrow trestle-stages, making their entrances from behind a curtained backing, or pushing their way through the spectators and mounting the platform, or, with the aid of a short ladder, peering from over the curtain as though they were looking down from the window of a house. Their means were of the simplest, and yet the meagre inheritance they left to their successors was destined to become the foundation of a rich patrimony.

4. Machinery, Effects, and Costumes

That the medieval mystery-cycle stage did not lack machinery entirely, in France, in Italy, and England, is amply proved by stage-directions and by eyewitnesses' accounts. In France a head of Saint Peter, severed, jumped thrice upon the stage, and "à chacun yst une fontaine."[1] There too the Holy Ghost descended like a "grand brandon de feu artificiellement fait par eaue-de-vie,"[2] while a statue of the Virgin moved her head and arms, and raised her eyes to heaven. Italy, naturally, because of her artists and painters, was not slow to make full use of these machines—*ingegni*, devices, they were called to correspond with the French *secrets* or *feyntes*. Vasari notes that one of the early masters of Italian perspective, Filippo Brunelleschi, invented or superintended the mechanical arrangements for a Paradise, which may have come near to those described by the same author elsewhere. Here there was

> un altro cielo sopra la tribuna maggiore, nel quale alcune ruote grandi fatte a guisa d'arcolai, che dal centro alla superficie movevano con belissimo ordine dieci giri per i dieci cieli, erano tutti pieni di lumicini, rappresentanti le stelle. . . .[3]

Mechanical effects find frequent mention. In a *Passione* "apronsi li monumenti, e vengono li tremuoti, e tenebre appariscono,"[4] while in a *San Lorenzo* play "viene una saetta dal cielo, e fallo rovinar tutto in pezzi."[5]

Effects of a similar kind, although not quite so ornate, were known in England. "Fyftie fadam of lyne for the cloudes" figured in the accounts of Chelmsford in 1562–63; while *Mary Magdalene* had a "hevyne" (Heaven) which could open. The Cornish plays presented "the

---

[1] "At each jump flowed a fountain."   [2] "A firebrand artificially made by spirits."

[3] "Another sky above the great rostrum, in which were some huge wheels constructed as if in the air, moving from the centre to the edges in most beautiful order, ten orbits for the ten heavens, all full of little lamps, representing the stars. . . ."

[4] "The monuments are opened, earthquakes come, and darkness descends."

[5] "A bolt comes from on high and casts it all in ruins."

father . . . in a clowde," and when he spoke "yᵉ levys" (leaves) opened. There Paradise, like
the Paradise of the French *Adam*, had "ii fayre trees," a "fowntaine," and "fyne flowers."
At Dublin we find a camel which is "peynted" and evidently carried by several "Portors."[1]
In many of the English mysteries ascents and descents of angels are frequent, while in *The
Salutation and Conception* of the Coventry series

> þe[2] holy gost discendit with iij bemys[3] to our lady, the sone of þe godhed nest[4] with iij bemys to the
> holy gost the fadyr godly with iij bemys to þe sone. And so entre all thre to here bosom.

There are flaming swords and burning altars in the Ludus Coventriae plays of *The Fall of Man*
and *Cain and Abel*. The play of *Mary Magdalene* is likewise rich in visual effects. A "bad
angyl" there enters "into hell with thondyr"; some devils set a "house one a fyere"; a
"moment"[5] is made to "tremyll and quake"; while later "a clowd" comes "frome hevene,
and" sets "þe tempyl one a fyer."

Most realistic, however, as has been seen, must have been the effects connected with Hell.
"A skin of parchment and gunpowder" was bought at Kingston-on-Thames in 1520, and
from other records we know well what it was used for. In the Cornish plays Lucifer "goeth
downe to hell apareled fowle wᵗʰ fyre about hem"; "he that schal pley belyal" (Belial) in
The Castle of Perseverance is bidden to "loke that he have gunne powder brennyng in pypys in
his hands and in his ers." That this was not merely a national custom is proved by a description of similar demons in France:

> Adonc fit la monstre de la Diablerie parmy la ville et le marché. Les diables estoient tous capparras-
> sonnés de peaux de loups, de veaulx, et de beliers, passementées de testes de moutons, de cornes de
> bœufz, et de grands havetz de cuisine: ceinctz de grosses courroies, esquelles pendoient grosses cymbales
> de vaches, et sonnettes de muletz à bruit horrifique. Tenoient en main aucuns bastons noirs pleins de
> fusées: autres portoient longs tizons allumés, sur lesquelz à chascun carrefour jettoient pleines poignées
> de parasine en pouldre, dont sortoit feu et fumée terrible.[6]

This description of the costumes of the medieval devils is exceeedingly interesting, and
may be compared with the pictures of such characters in Figs. 63 and 64. The animal heads
and grotesque dresses seem to have been a traditional stage convention. Of the other costumes
of actors in England we have nothing but vague references, but such as they are they have
their interest. Masks, or "visors," seem to have been fairly common. In 1391 a list of properties
at Beverley in Yorkshire included

> j karre,[7] viij hespis, xviij stapels, ij visers, ij wenges angeli . . . j worme . . . ij paria camisarum[8] and j
> gladius.[9]

Visors formed an entry in the accounts of Bungay, Suffolk, in 1566, and an item in the Canter-
bury records is the "payntyng of the hede and the Aungell of the pagent." Lucifer in the
Cornish mysteries had a serpent form "wᵗʰ a virgyn face & yolowe heare vpon her head." Wigs,

---

[1] This, it is true, is in a processional show rather than in a play. [2] the.
[3] trumpet-calls.   [4] next.   [5] idol.
[6] "Then the show of the Devils was made in the town and square. These devils were all clad in skins of wolves,
calves, and rams, surmounted with sheep-heads, bull-horns, and cockscombs: girdles of thick skins, from which hung
cows' or mules' bells with horrible noise. Some carried in their hands black rods full of squibs: others long flaming
spars, on which at each turn they threw handfuls of powdered resinous pitch from which issued terrible flame and
smoke."
[7] car or pageant.   [8] pairs of shirts   [9] sword.

with or without masks, were also freely utilized, as is indicated by a record of 1504 at Leicester:

> Paid for a pound of hemp to mend the angels heads, iij^d.

In 1585 at Tewkesbury there were "eight heads of hair for the Apostles, and ten beards, and a face or vizier for the Devil."

As for the costumes themselves there are many entries, but few descriptions. At Chelmsford in the sixteenth century we learn of a coat "of lether for Christ" and are treated besides to a pretty little list of properties:

> ij vyces coates, and ij scalpes, ij daggers (j dagger wanted)
> v prophets cappes (one wantinge).
> iiij flappes for devils.
> iij shepehoks, iiij whyppes (but one gone).

Fig. 71. HELL-MOUTH FROM THE CAEDMON MANUSCRIPT (ELEVENTH CENTURY)

"A new coat & a peir of hoes [hose] for Gabriell" appears at Coventry in 1544, while three skins were used for Noah's coat at Hull in 1494. Three yards of "dorneck" were needed for a player's coat at Kingston in 1513–14, where likewise was demanded a pennyworth of thread "for the resurrection." "Jesus hoose" are mentioned at Leicester in 1504; while Norwich provides an interesting record of

> A cote & hosen w^{t1} a bagg & capp for dolo^r,[2] steyned.
> 2 cotes & a payre hosen for Eve, stayned.
> A cote & hosen for Adam, Steyned.
> A cote w^t hosen & tayle for ye serpente, steyned, w^t a w^t heare. . . .[3]
> An Angell's Cote & over hoses of Apis Skynns. . . .
> A face & heare for ye Father.
> 2 hearys[4] for Adam & Eve.[5]

The costumes of Adam and Eve are more fully described for the Cornish dramas. There "Adam and Eva" are "aparlet [apparelled] in whytt lether," no doubt representing skin, and a stage direction bids "ffig leaves redy to cover ther members," the pair being provided later with "garmentis of skynnes."[6] The costumes, except for a few thus distinctly outlined, were no doubt the ordinary dresses of the day. At Worcester in 1576 an inventory hardly distinguishes any save a king's and a Devil's:

> A gowne of freres gyrdles. A woman's gowne. A K^s cloke of Tysshew. A Jerkyn and a payer of breeches. A lytill cloke of tysshew. A gowne of silk. A Jerkyn of greene, 2 cappes, and the devils apparell.

It is possible, however, that colour played a fair part in the general symbolism of the drama.

---

[1] with. [2] dolor, grief. [3] white hair, or wig. [4] hairs, or wigs.

[5] A very similar list of costumes for an Italian play in 1339 is given in A. D'Ancona, *Origini del Teatro Italiano* (1891), i, 164.

[6] It would seem that in France, if not in England, complete nudity on the stage was known. In the fourteenth-century *Miracles de Notre Dame* (Anciens textes francais, iii, 124–125) a woman disguised as a monk is, on death, revealed on the stage "toute nue."

The stage-directions in *The Castle of Perseverance* thus bid that

> the iiij dowters schul be clad in mentelys, Mercy in wyth,[1] rythwysnesse in red al togedyr, Trewthe in sad grene, & Pes al in blake,

while in the French *Adam* "Chaym sit indutus rubeis vestibus, Abel vero albis."[2] No doubt this general scheme was followed out in other plays. Rarely, however, do we have such detailed descriptions as that written by Jacques Thiboust of a costume worn by Nesron (Nero) in an *Actes des Apôtres* of 1536:

> Nesron . . . estoit vestu d'une saye de veloux bleu toute pourfilée d'or à grands rinceaux d'antique, et découpée a taille ouverte, par ou apparoissoit et flocquetoit a gros bouillons la doublure, qui estoit d'ung satin cramoisy, pourfilée semblablement d'ung autre ouvrage de fleurons et entrelacs de fil d'or; elle estoit doublée de veloux cramoisy a collet de mesme, faict a pointes renversées, entremesleés l'une dans l'autre, et semées par grands prodigalité de grosses perles, aux quelles pointes pendoient grosses houppes d'autres perles . . . Sa couronne d'or a trois branches estoit remplie de tant de sortes de pierreries . . . Il portait l'un de ses pieds sur une escrin couvert de drap d'argent et semé de quelque nombre de pierreries . . . Portoit en sa main une hache d'armes bien dorée; son port estoit hautain et son maintien magnifique; son dit tribunal et lui dessus estoit porté par huict roys captifs qui estoient dedans, desquels on ne voyoit seulement que les testes couronnés de couronnes d'or.[3]

With this account may be compared the notes regarding the costumes to be used for the sixteenth-century Lucerne play mentioned above. There, for example,

> Pater aeternus soll haben das gewöhnliche Diadem, schön altväterisch, graues langes Haar und Bart. Einen Reichsapfel in der Hand . . . . Eine weisse Rippe im Aermel.[4]

5. Actors and Performance

Concerning the actors in the English mystery plays little more may be said than has been given above. The guilds, having taken over the management of the cycles, provided the actors from among their own members. Generally these actors were paid a small fee. At Coventry one man received three shillings and fourpence "for pleayng God," another fourpence "for hangyng Judas," another fourpence "for Coc croyng [cock-crowing]." Five shillings was apportioned "to iij whyte [saved] sollys [souls]," five shillings "to iij blake sollys," and one shilling and fourpence "to ij wormes of conscyence." Similar records occur in the accounts of other towns. At Hull one Thomas Sawyr received tenpence for "playing God," a Jenkin Smith received one shilling for taking Noah, whose wife was awarde eightpence. This was in 1494; eleven years previously Noah and his wife got only one shilling and sixpence between them, and God only sixpence. The salaries of actors were evidently rising.

---

[1] white. [2] "Cain is to be clad in red garments, Abel in white."

[3] "Nero was clad in a lined cloak, all blue striped with golden bars after the antique style, and slit with open seams so that the lining of crimson satin appeared, adorned also with another design of ornaments and knots of gold thread; it was lined at the collar with crimson velvet, made with inverted points, intermingled one with another, and prodigally scattered with large pearls. At these points hung large strings of other pearls. . . . His golden crown of three tiers was decorated with all sorts of precious stones. . . . He supported one of his feet on a stool covered with silver cloth and ornamented with a large number of precious stones. . . . In his hand he carried a beautifully gilded battleaxe; his carriage was haughty and his demeanour grand; his tribunal and he were carried by eight captive kings who were within and of whom nothing was seen save their golden-crowned heads."

[4] "The Pater aeternus must have the customary diadem. He is an old man with long grey hair and beard. An imperial orb is in his hand. . . . A white rib in his sleeve."

In France conditions were similar and dissimilar. The *corps municipaux*, the town guilds, there as in England, took a large part in the organization of the mysteries, but they shared their activities with several others apparently unknown in England. The *confréries pieuses* played a prominent rôle in the management of the cycles, most famous of all being the Confrérie de la Passion established at Paris by letters patent of Charles VI, on December 4, 1402. It is with the establishment of this company at the Hôpital de la Trinité that we first meet in Europe with a permanent dramatic troupe settled at a definite theatre. The Confrérie de la Passion will also occupy our attention later. Alongside of these *confréries pieuses* there existed a number of peculiar groups of actors, professional and amateur. The Goliardi often busied themselves in the organization of performances. Les Basochiens, famous for their *triomphes* and *tableaux* "sans parler ne sans signer," laid their impress on the interlude stage. Les Sots, clad in hoods of yellow and green, assears, and costumes of similar colours, the green signifying hope of renewal and the yellow gaiety, passed over great tracts of France, at their

Fig. 72. THE FOOL AND THE DEVIL

head the well-known Enfants Sans-Souci. Finally there were the many *confréries des fous*. Deriving, apparently, from the notorious medieval Feast of Fools, these men, called Cornards or Connards at Rouen and Evreux because of their horned caps, Suppôts du Seigneur de la Coquille at Lyon, Sots at Amiens, Foux at Auxerre, L'Abbaye joyeuse de Lescache Profit at Cambrai, Gaillardons at Chalon-sur-Saône, Diables at Chaumont, Trompettes-Jongleurs at Chauny, and Mauvaises Braies at Laon, played interlude and scandalous farce to the shame of many serious men and the delight of many merry ones.

In presenting their performances these medieval entertainers, having no newspaper press in which to advertise themselves, made free use of the *cri*, or cry. This *cri* was usually accompanied, as in a present-day circus, by a lengthy procession. A full account of *le cry et Proclamation public* made for the exhibition at Paris of *Le Mystère des Actes des Apostres* in 1540 has been preserved, and a similar proclamation for the Chester plays, dated 1544, provides an interesting parallel. The object of both is the same—to announce the plays, present authority, and demand that no disturbance be made.

Normally in medieval drama all parts were taken by men. This is almost certainly true of England; although in France there are at least three records previous to 1550 which inform us of women players. One young amateur actress at Metz in 1468 spoke no fewer than 2300 lines as Saint Catherine—winning as her reward the hand of a gentleman in marriage. The general level of performance, no doubt, was crude, but a devout air of seriousness pervaded the whole. This acting business was so obviously not merely a game, but something of real importance for the world. Anachronistic as the drama regularly was in main outline, little details had to

5

be scrupulously exact. There must be the bladders of blood and the sheephooks and the instruments of torture. The effect of Christ's crucifixion could not be complete unless the actor himself suffered. M. le curé, one Nicolle, of Metz took the part of Jesus in 1437, and he "cuyda mourir en l'arbre de la croix, car le cœur lui faillit, tellement qu'il fût été mort, s'il ne fût été secouru."[1] From the same locality we learn that a priest named Jehan de Missey "portoit le personnage de Juda," but "pendit trop longtemps" and "fut pareillement transi et quasi mort; car le cueur lui faillit, par quoi il fut bien hâtivement dépendu et fut emporté en aucun lieu prochain pour le frotter de vinaigre et autre chose pour le réconforter."[2] If the Fouquet miniature is at all a representation of the reality we may truly pity the young performer of Saint Apollonia. The tooth-drawer is most businesslike and the rope-pullers most energetic.

As is evident, in this medieval drama and its theatre we have a set of conditions surprisingly like those provided in Greece. A drama, lyrical in origin, which springs from religion; actors devoted to the presentation of the plays; the whole performance a thing not of a class, but of the community—these are features which the Middle Ages possess in common with Athens of the age of Aeschylus. Beyond these similarities, however, there are many differences. The medieval people lacked that classical feeling for simplicity and unity of effect which characterizes Greek sculpture and Greek thought. The gargoyles will always be peering out from behind the soaring windows and the intricate traceries of stonework. The devils with their squibs will ever be pressing among the actors of more serious rôles. The medieval theatre is obviously a thing of the "Gothic imagination." Where the Greeks forbade violent action on the stage the audience of the Middle Ages demanded blood and rant. Herod has to rage on the pageant and on the street also. Where the Greeks endeavoured to secure an harmonious unity of effect, the medieval playwrights huddled serious and comic together. The shepherds crack their rustic jokes ere viewing Christ's manger; Noah and his wife have their comic tussle as the Deluge sweeps over the world.

6. *Tournaments, Entries, and Disguisings*

Obviously, since these medieval theatrical activities endured in various forms for so many centuries, the traditions thus set were destined to remain potent even when men, inspired by new concepts, moved out of the Middle Ages into the atmosphere of the modern world. It is true that the drama of Shakespeare and his companions was utterly unlike both the sprawling diffusiveness of the mystery cycles and the brief interludes presented in private halls or on market-square booths; and yet, when we examine these later plays carefully, we can easily trace, sometimes to our surprise, clear signs of the medieval inheritance. And this inheritance came not only from productions specifically theatrical; it was increased and enriched by diverse other semi-theatrical activities with which the people of earlier centuries had sought to enliven and cheer their spirits.

Among the courtly, tournaments provided rich and exciting spectacles. Lists were prepared, and special structures designed to accommodate the more distinguished spectators: elaborate costumes, tricked out in symbolic colourings, delighted the eyes. On darker winter days, the dullness of candle-lit courts was brightened by numerous disguisings, when groups

[1] "Would have died on the rood-tree, for he fainted and was like to have died had he not been rescued."

[2] "He took the part of Judas, but hung too long and fainted and was like dead; for his heart failed him, wherefore he was hastily taken down and carried to a place near by and sprinkled with vinegar and other things to bring him round."

of young men, clad extravagantly in outlandish costumes, entered gaily into the banqueting halls, often bringing in with them what can be described only by the word "scenery"—chariots with built-up fortresses or ships or rocky mountains. Such disguisings cannot properly be called plays; at the same time they did present something of dramatic action; the costumes worn by the performers were of a theatrical kind; and carpenters gained experience in the contriving of scenic structures composed of wood, canvas, and paint.

The carpenters, too, added materially to this kind of experience through their work on the adornment of open-air fabrics designed to celebrate royal "entries." A king or an emperor came on a visit to some city; sometimes, if the city lay outside his own dominions, a fellow-ruler strove to welcome him by commissioning his craftsmen to build triumphal arches or the like, generally with provision of space for symbolic *tableaux vivants* so fashioned as to give honour and pleasure to the visiting monarch; sometimes, if the city was part of his own territory, the citizens strove to display their loyalty and love by similar means. Here, again, we cannot call these entries theatrical; yet the influence of such street-theatres was long-enduring, and the triumphal arches definitely played a part in the early development of the post-medieval playhouses.

Apart from these more spectacular recreational activities, others less elaborate must not be left out of account. If the courtiers had their disguisings to amuse them, the humbler folk had their mummings and quasi-dramatic games, stray relics of which have come down even to our own times; and they too formed part of the heritage passed on from the medieval period.

Thus, as we leave the Middle Ages we must carry with us memories of various sorts of theatrical or semi-theatrical traditions. (1) First, and perhaps most important, is the productional method used in the presentation of the mystery plays—the setting-up of mansions

Fig. 73. A SETTING FOR "ST LAURENTIUS" AT KÖLN, 1581

representing separate localities, together with the use of an open *platea*, or place, shared by players and by spectators alike. These mansions might be set in a straight line facing the audience, or placed in semicircular form, or arranged as a complete circle, or scattered dispersedly in a market-square, or even erected upon carts and pulled from location to location. (2) Quite clearly, the vast, extensive display of mystery-cycle mansions can be simplified; and during the later years we can see how it is being brought indoors and adapted to the more restricted area of a platform-stage. One of the best illustrations of this is provided in a sketch made for a Saint Laurentius play at Cologne in 1581 (Fig. 73). There is no doubt about the platform: there it is, plainly supported on beams. On this stage, to the right appear a pagan altar and an obelisk, and to the left there is a tree. At the rear of the stage and to its sides a row of canvas frames and doorways, joined together, represent the houses of the High Priest of Jupiter, Augustus, Valerius, the Praetor, Hippolytus, Sixtus, and Faustina—together with two Thrones, a Prison, a Street, a Monument, and a Gate. As in the representations of the mystery plays, so here the audience was expected to ignore all the mansions except the particular locality called for in the scene being acted out on the stage. (3) The simplification, however, can be carried still further, and, instead of the row of painted frames, only a curtain can be used to back a plain platform-stage. This type of unadorned "theatre" probably was frequently employed by the small groups of English interlude players; it was certainly used by touring companies in France; and many of the Italian *commedia dell'arte* troupes were content to offer their comic scenes in such a style as they wandered from city to city, gradually extending their range from Italy so as to make most of Europe into a circuit. (4) And, finally, this simplication can be seen in its extremest form in the indoor presentation of some of the early interludes, when the players perform at one end of a hall, sometimes entering by whatever door or doors may be available, sometimes pressing their way through the little crowd of spectators watching their display.

All these various forms of theatrical presentation are bound together by two essential principles. The first is the close connexion between audience and actors. Even in the "St Apollonia" miniature we can see one built-up mansion clearly reserved for privileged spectators, set in between the other mansions belonging to the play itself; and in the production of the interludes those who watch are inextricably intermingled with those who perform. The second principle might be styled the "emblematic" or the "non-illusionistic." Nowhere, even in the most spectacular productions of mystery cycles, is there any attempt to depict realistically any particular scene. The built-up mansions were designed to suggest rather than to reproduce the reality, and when such built-up mansions were not available a plain curtain or the wall of a hall could serve as background for the players: their actions and words were sufficient to stimulate the spectators' imaginations into giving to airy nothing a local habitation and a name.

CHAPTER V

Renaissance Italy: Court Theatres and the Painted Scene

1. The Beginnings

IN 1500 tiny companies of English professional actors were displaying, on the bare hall floors of noblemen's mansions or on equally bare trestled booths in market-squares, their repertory of interludes, most of which now can be perused with interest only by specialized scholars: in 1599 the great company of the Lord Chamberlain's men was delighting audiences at the Globe with *King Henry IV* and *Julius Caesar*. During the years immediately before 1500 performances were being given, by Italian amateur actors, of classical comedies, presented on stages with little decoration save a row of curtained booths; by 1589 Florentine spectators were being enchanted by productions in which richly painted scenes continually changed, by seeming magic, before their wondering eyes. Thus within the course of a single century the theatre was brought from an ancient medieval world into a world perceptibly modern.

For convenience we may call this period the Renaissance, although in using that term we must remember that it can have a very wide application and that it is being employed here in a limited and special sense. Fundamentally, in so far as the theatre is concerned, four or five things have to be borne in mind. (1) This century of the Renaissance, in bringing men from the medieval realm onto the threshold of the modern, operated differently in different countries: consequently there is the necessity, as there was not in considering the medieval productions, of dealing with the various playhouses of these countries separately. (2) On the other hand, we must be careful not to fall into the error of assuming that, all at once, a complete change occurred. The Renaissance introduced entirely new concepts, yet much of its endeavour was, in fact, based on the medieval. Just as the structure of Shakespeare's *King Lear* may be explained only by reference to the medieval heritage, so the forms assumed by theatrical performances in sixteenth-century Italy will be found to incorporate many memories of earlier productions. (3) The force dominating the movement towards the modern theatrical world was inspired by two chief, and often conflicting, aims, one searching backward and the other questing towards the future. (*a*) On the one hand, there was the passionate desire to understand and to imitate the glories of Imperial Rome and the wonders of Greece. Eagerly the scholars ransacked the libraries for forgotten texts; into their ken swam numerous riches brought to the Italian courts by refugees from sacked Byzantium; the remains of classical theatres which, as it were, had simply been taken for granted in earlier years were now examined with care, measured, and in imagination reconstructed. (*b*) On the other hand, many of the painters and architects of the time were animated by a desire to achieve things fresh and new. They were discovering the joys of perspective, and in playhouse productions they realized that they had the opportunity of experimenting in ways beyond those permitted to them in their studios. Moreover, they came to appreciate, instinctively, that the theatre is basically a dynamic art and that the objectives of the stricter classicists were not only antiquarian but also directed towards the establishment of a static stage. Hence, as we watch the development of the theatre in Italy during the period from the end of the fifteenth century onto 1600 we can see a double force at work, the two impulses sometimes coalescing but eventually clashing and separating. (4) In addition to these things, we must also observe that practice and theory were continually interacting. Towards the middle of the fifteenth century, for example, some scholars had come upon Vitruvius' great work in manuscript, and one of them, Leon Battista Alberti, wrote a study called *De re aedificatoria*, which, although then known only to a limited group of scholars, began to stimulate the desire to build up something in the style of the classical stage. Experiments of this kind were being carried out when the first edition of Vitruvius, under the care of Sulpicio da Veroli, appeared from the press in 1486. This gave further stimulus and was followed by discussions of the true interpretation of the Latin text. Concurrently, however, the range of theatrical experiments was being extended, so that in 1545 Sebastiano Serlio could come forward with a work which did not aim merely at the reconstruction of the ancient but which concentrated upon the purely practical stage of the present. Although Serlio's study must be seen rather as describing what already had been attempted in the theatre than as putting forward novel concepts, the existence of this manual produced an impulse in the opposite direction and led the way to the appearance of a lengthy series of similar treatises, dealing with the construction of playhouses, perspective, methods of changing scenery, stage-lighting, and the like, which materially played their part in the elaboration of the new styles.

Obviously the story of this development of the theatre from the old to the new cannot be a complete one, since it may be fashioned only from such scattered records as chance has preserved for us: but sufficient remains to indicate with reasonable certainty at least the main steps in the growth of these playhouse experiments, and for some productions there exists a considerable amount of information both iconographical and descriptive. Clearly, of course, only the more outstanding contributions to the development itself can be outlined here. And first our attention has to be directed exclusively to performances in Italian courts and academies.

A start may be made by referring to two quite separate kinds of production. The first is that associated with the activities of Julius Pomponius Laetus (1425–98) in connexion with his Roman Academy. Inspired by a passionate love of all things classical, this man encouraged his group of like-minded friends and pupils to indulge in the presentation of some ancient tragedies and comedies, apparently aided by funds contributed by Cardinal Rafaelle Riario. One of these productions earned a complimentary notice in an epistle prefacing the edition of Vitruvius issued in 1486: there we are informed that a stage 5 feet high was erected in a courtyard and that this was "adorned" beautifully; it is also said that for another presentation of a Latin comedy a *picturatae scaenae facies* was built up. Precisely what is intended here we cannot tell, but some contemporary performances of a similar kind at Ferrara suggest that the staging may have been quite simple. In that of Plautus' *Menaechmi*, given in 1486, the production was also out-of-doors; a wooden stage was erected, and at its rear were five "battlemented houses" (*case merlade*), each with a door and a window. References to these houses, described variously as *castelli* and as *casamenti merlati*, occur in connexion with several slightly later Ferrarese performances. There seems to be a strong probability that nothing more was attempted here than the setting up of medieval-type booths, houses, or mansions placed so close together that they formed a single large unit. Whether these are vaguely represented in the illustrated edition of Terence published at Lyons in 1493 is not certain, but it seems probable that, even if the little scenes depicted in this volume belong to a woodcut tradition,

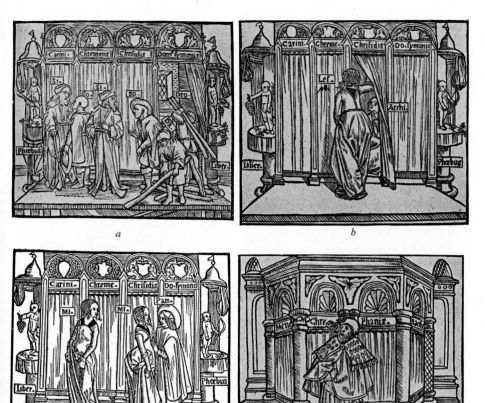

Fig. 74. a, b, and c. A SETTING FOR THE "ANDRIA" OF TERENCE, 1493

Fig. 75. A SETTING FOR THE "HEAUTON-TIMOROUMENOS" OF TERENCE, 1493

they offer us a fair idea at least of the principle involved (Figs. 74 and 75). From one point of view there is nothing new here: we are still confronted by curtained houses in medieval style. Nevertheless, two elements point to the future; and, since pictorial art and theatre were inter-related during those years, it hardly matters whether these features derive from the one or the other. The first is that in several of the woodcuts the houses are framed at the sides by decorated columns with statuettes in niches or by architectural motifs. This may not seem particularly significant, but, primitive as the device may be, it points to a desire on the part of those re-sponsible to treat the houses not as separate units but as a complete whole: indeed, it represents the first tentative movement towards the framework which later became the proscenium arch. Secondly, the binding together of the houses by means of other columns emphasizes a still more important break-away from the past. During the earlier period the mansions, or houses, were each treated separately, even when they were placed fairly close together, and more commonly they were spread out with spaces between them or set dispersedly within a larger area. Perhaps oftener than we realize, numerous Renaissance plays and entertainments were thus presented with mansions scattered over the hall of a palace. Although these mansions may have been constructed and decorated in a new style, their relationship to each other, together with the relationship of the performers to the spectators, was basically medieval. Thus, for example, when Angelo Poliziano's *Orfeo* was presented at Mantua in 1480, its settings appear to have been shown to the audience all at one time. As a variant of this procedure, there was the production of a play by Domenico Fosso at Bologna in 1487 wherein the houses, representing a hill with trees, a tower, a palace, and other localities, were actually wheeled from spot to

Fig. 76. THE SETTING FOR "LE BALET COMIQUE
DE LA ROYNE," 1581

spot. And if we seek for an illustration of what these performances looked like we have only to glance at the engraving which accompanies the original printed text of the *Balet Comique de la Royne*, as performed in France in 1581 (Fig. 76).

The essential novelty, therefore, in the row of houses used for the productions at Rome and Ferrara rests primarily in the fact that these houses no longer were separate but were regarded as component parts of a general city street, and secondarily in the associated fact that they were looked upon as a kind of single "picture" demanding some sort of frame. Although the Terence woodcuts and the descriptions of the performances at Rome and Ferrara may make us think that we are dealing here with something very primitive and perhaps somewhat ridiculous, we are in fact standing firmly on the threshold of a new theatrical age.

2. *The Painted Scene*

All that was now needed to set the new stage on its destined path was to substitute a perspectively painted background in place of the several houses; and such a background, forming the next chief step, certainly was displayed to the spectators at Ferrara when, in 1508, they attended the performance of Ariosto's *Cassaria*: this had "a painting and perspective of a scene with houses, churches, towers and gardens" (una contracta et prospettiva di una terra cum case, chiesie, campanili et zardini), and the artist responsible was Pellegrino da Udine. The audience present at this production, although they could not know it, were assisting at what was virtually a theatrical revolution soon fated to become the "establishment." Five years later, in 1513, at Urbino, the performance of *La Calandria*, a comedy by Bernardo Dovizi (who later became Cardinal Bibbiena), carried the revolution a little further. Here the setting was "a very lovely city with streets, palaces, churches, towers" all represented by "excellent painting and clever perspective" (una città bellissima con le strade, palazzi, chiese, torri . . . (executed with) bonissima pintura et prospettiva bene intesa), and further enriched with apparently three-dimensional structures. At each side, moreover, there were practicable towers, with battlements, within which the musicians were placed; an unhappily inconclusive reference to a cornice above may indicate the introduction of the very first proscenium arch known to us. In all probability, this important setting was the work of Gerolamo Genga (1476–1551). The same play, *La Calandria*, offers us still a third example of this rapid development in scenic design. One year after the Urbino production, it was revived in Rome with a setting by Baldassare Peruzzi (1481–1536), and there is good reason for believing that a drawing by this artist (Fig. 77) shows us what was then presented on the stage—and, looking at it, we

Fig. 77. A DESIGN BY BALDASSARE PERUZZI, PROBABLY FOR "LA CALANDRIA," ROME, 1514

immediately realize, almost with a shock, how far the stage had travelled within a space of less than twenty years.

Leaving the Middle Ages with its productions of new plays by means of dispersed houses, we have moved on to the Terence revivals with their rows of houses set together so that they become a unit and can be thought of as forming part of a street, then onward to the introduction of a flat "picture" extending in breadth rather than in depth, and on finally to a setting which obviously has depth and which equally obviously is of a different kind: there is a painted picture at the very rear, but the front buildings are composed in another way.

For an understanding of that other way, we may turn now to Serlio's treatise. In his practical account of how to construct a theatre four things are of special significance. (1) First, his plan for auditorium and stage (Fig. 78) assumes the use of a rectangular hall such as had familiarly been employed in courtly houses for dramatic representations. The stage is set at one end of the hall, and benches are shored up for the spectators. Significantly, his arrangement of these benches is borrowed from the *cavea* of the Roman playhouse, and indeed differs

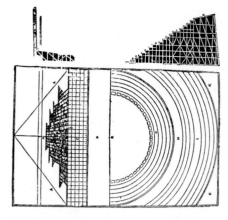

Fig. 78. PLAN OF A THEATRE BY
SEBASTIANO SERLIO, 1545

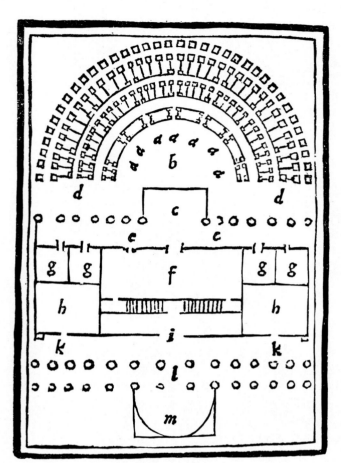

Fig. 79. PLAN OF A GREEK THEATRE IN THE
JOCUNDUS EDITION OF VITRUVIUS, 1513
This shows well the early humanist idea of the Greek stage; note
that the whole is enclosed within a rectangular wall.

Fig. 80. THE COMIC SCENE
ACCORDING TO SERLIO, 1545

Fig. 81. THE TRAGIC SCENE
ACCORDING TO SERLIO, 1545

Fig. 82. THE SATYRIC SCENE
ACCORDING TO SERLIO, 1545

from such a reconstructed "archaeological" plan as that given in the 1513 "Jocundus" edition of Vitruvius (Fig. 79) only in so far as the further portion of the sweeping semicircle is cut off by the side walls. Fundamentally, therefore, we have here the growth of a Renaissance auditorium out of the studies of the classical enthusiasts. (2) A kindred inspiration from the same source may be seen in the fact that the three designs (Figs. 80–82) which he presents are those of a comic scene, a tragic scene, and a satyric, which follows exactly the description contained in Vitruvius' work: "There are three types of scenes, one called Tragic, the second Comic and the third Satyric" (Genera autem sunt scaenarum tria: unum quod dicitur, tragicum, alterum comicum, tertium satyricum). These designs which he presents, therefore, are not intended for particular plays: they stand as stock settings to be used whenever any comedy, any tragedy, or any pastoral is being put before the public. In theory at least we are still here in the milieu of those who sought to revive the classical theatre. (3) Quite clearly both the comic and the tragic settings thus exhibited to us are closely associated with Peruzzi's design (Fig. 77), which seemingly was made for the production of *La Calandria* at Rome in 1514. We may, therefore, be reasonably sure that the method of scene-construction advised by Serlio in 1551 was that employed for the realization of this design some thirty-seven years before, and that the same method of construction was still in use at the middle of the century. (4) When we turn to the stage part of Serlio's plan and cross-section we see that he once more has started by following the form of the Roman acting-platform: the long, reasonably narrow acting-area immediately in front of the audience has been taken from that source. But as soon as we look beyond that, we find ourselves in another world. Instead of a columned *scaenae frons*, there is a sharply raked platform on which the perspective setting of a city street or square has been built up by a judicious admixture of built-up houses and painted canvas; these taper in until they are closed by a perspectively design-ed flat. The houses nearest to the front of the stage all have two sides, one parallel to the stage-front and one inclining inward. Since, in order to achieve the perspective effect, the various houses and painted canvas frames had to diminish rapidly in size, it is clear that the actors performed not *in* the scene but *against* it: perhaps the players might make use of the nearer houses, but if they stepped further back the whole perspective illusion would have been shattered.

3. The Teatro Olimpico at Vicenza

While obviously the kind of stage illustrated by Serlio was ultimately inspired by the classical, equally obviously this perspective set belonged wholly to the time of the Renaissance; and among those interested in the theatre at that period there were some at least who sternly

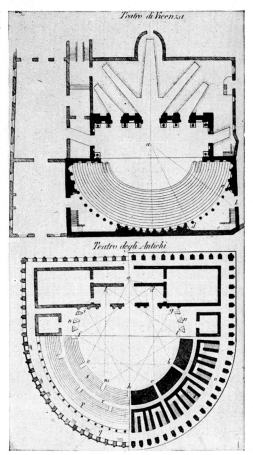

Fig. 83. PLAN OF THE TEATRO OLIMPICO, VICENZA, COMPARED WITH THAT OF A ROMAN THEATRE

Note the avenues for street scenes and the five entrances to the stage.

Fig. 84. THE TEATRO OLIMPICO, 1585

demanded something more rigorously Roman. We may be sure that there were various experiments made in this direction, but to understand them fully we have to turn to the final triumph of their endeavours, the theatre planned by Andrea Palladio (1518–80) for the Olympic Academy of Vicenza, a building which, although constructed of wood, happily still stands. On May 23, 1580, the work on it was started, but unfortunately Palladio died the following August, and the carrying-out of his project was entrusted to Vincenzo Scamozzi (1552–1616), who completed it, not without some variations from the original design, in 1585.

In general the building has been conceived according to the best classical ideas of the time, but it presents a number of very interesting deviations from what it aims to copy (Fig. 83). Instead of a completely semicircular auditorium, the seats are arranged in a semi-ellipse, thus providing better sight-lines for the spectators. Between the front rows of the auditorium and the stage itself is a shallow orchestra. The stage proper is rectangular, long, and narrow, as in Roman theatres, with a wooden floor painted to resemble marble. This is entirely enclosed by a *scaenae frons*, an ornamented architectural façade: below is a series of four pediments (Figs. 84–85) with statues, and above is a set of six statues surmounted by six decorative panels and a painted roof. On the wall facing the audience comes a large open arch, the *porta regia* of Vitruvius, flanked on the sides by two lesser doors (*portae minores*). Those portions of the façade which stand at right angles to the principal wall are also pierced by

Fig. 85. THE CENTRAL ARCHWAY IN THE
TEATRO OLIMPICO, 1585

Fig. 86. PLAN OF A ROMAN THEATRE
ACCORDING TO DANIELLO BARBARO,
1556

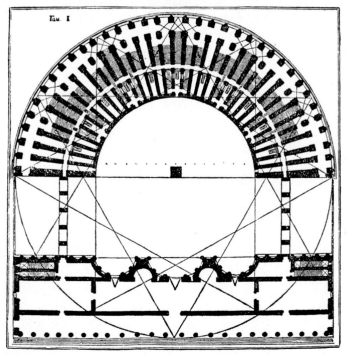

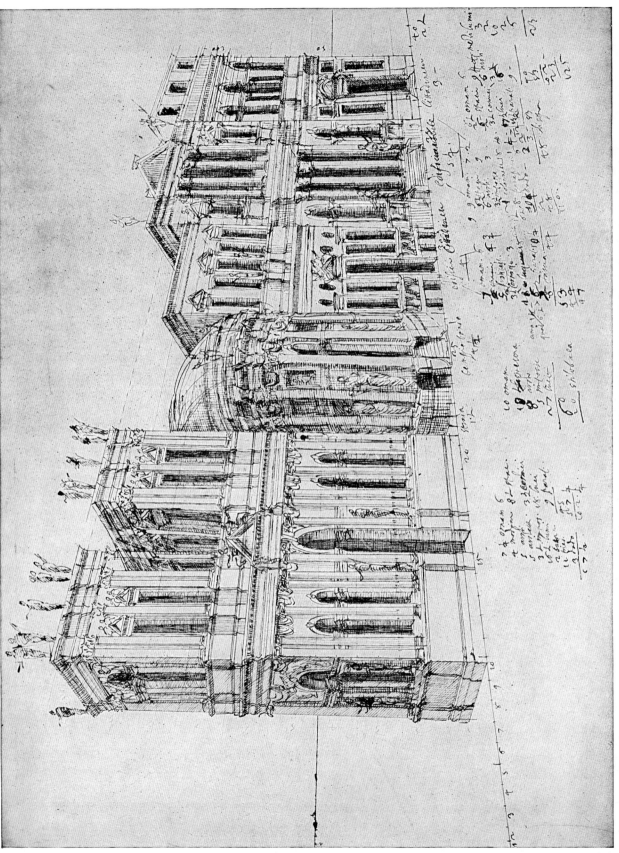

Fig 87 DESIGN BY VINCENZO SCAMOZZI FOR A STREET IN THE TEATRO OLIMPICO

doors which have above them boxes, apparently intended both for the action of the play and for spectators. Originally, it would seem, all these entrances were closed either by actual doors or by painted backcloths; but at an early date the Renaissance passion for perspective could not be denied entry even into this temple of classical inspiration.

The scholars, puzzling over their texts of Vitruvius, had been much intrigued by that author's reference to Greek *periaktoi* and, apparently quite correctly, they identified these as triangular painted prisms which could be placed at the openings in the *scaenae frons*. Daniello Barbaro shows them so set in his plan of a Roman theatre (Fig. 86), published in 1556. It was possibly with these *periaktoi* in mind that Scamozzi had the idea of constructing perspective alleys at each of the entrance-ways in the Teatro Olimpico, set at such angles that every person in the audience could see down one at least. The scenes here are permanent, and are supposed to represent streets running into a central courtyard (Fig. 87).

Thus the Teatro Olimpico came into being, one of the great landmarks in the history of the modern theatre, yet clearly backward-looking and largely out of touch with the movement which stemmed from Peruzzi's design of 1514.

4. Changeable Scenery

Throughout the greater part of the sixteenth century the city-square type of setting continued on its course, and gradually it came to be associated with a handsome proscenium arch (Figs. 89–90).

Exactly how this "frontispiece" developed has occasioned some debate; but it may perhaps be thought that attempts to attribute its origin to one thing or another are less likely to reach the truth than an endeavour to trace it back to several sources. Undoubtedly, during the earlier years, many productions must have offered to the spectators settings similar to that which is illustrated in Fig. 88, where apparently the Serlian-type stage is carried right up

Fig. 88. AN ITALIAN SETTING IN THE SIXTEENTH CENTURY
The 'Serlian' style is clear in this woodcut.

Fig. 89. AN ITALIAN-STYLE SETTING IN
THE SEVENTEENTH CENTURY

Fig. 90. DESIGN BY BARTOLOMMEO
NERONI (IL RICCIO) FOR "L'ORTENSIO,"
1561

This should be compared with Serlio's tragic scene.
Particular note should also be made of the formal
proscenium arch. The production took place at Siena.

to the walls on either side. When the frontispiece is used, then the setting, instead of being, as it were, a part of the hall, becomes a picture, framed by an arch or rectangular opening, separate from the auditorium. Now, it cannot be denied that in pictorial art a long-standing convention made use of archways through which scenes of all kinds might be seen; and it also cannot be denied that during the sixteenth century the employment of triumphal arches, set up in city streets and squares to celebrate special occasions, was common. We may also freely admit that there exists a close connexion between the theatrical frontispieces and both the pictorial convention and the three-dimensional triumphal arches. Yet we are left with a vague doubt as to whether, in fact, this tells the whole of the story. Quite obviously, the artists responsible for the city-square kind of setting must have realized how useful a masking frame might be, and we are not surprised to find some early designs wherein the two front houses have been dealt with in such a way as to give them the appearance of the sides to such a frame. No special ingenuity would be required to add a horizontal strip at the top, thus completing a rectangular proscenium. It has already been noted that even in the early Terence woodcuts the rows of houses have at least a suggestion of a framing design at their sides. It might further be observed that such a design as that given to us by Joseph Furttenbach in his *Architectura civilis* (Fig. 89) indicates another easy way in which the "framework" device could have come into being: here there is a picture, but it is seen edged at the sides and top by what is evidently intended to be a permanently opened pair of curtains.

The idea of having a frontispiece, therefore, need not in any respect have derived only from the pictorial arch convention or from the so-called street-theatres. Indeed, what must strike us as particularly suggestive is the fact that the majority of the early designs which do show a proscenium frame offer to our view, not an archway, but a rectangular masking device (see Fig. 90).

Proceeding in a different direction however, we might easily be inclined to view these proscenium arches as a kind of last relic of the Roman *scaenae frons*, and this apparent connexion becomes still more emphatic when we compare some later designs with the façade of the Teatro Olimpico. It might, indeed, be perfectly justifiable to say that several of the deepened and three-dimensional proscenium frames constructed during the seventeenth century look so much like the Teatro Olimpico façade with the central doorway opened out, that we cannot avoid assuming an influence exerted by the "classical" upon the "modern." Furthermore, and quite apart from the possibility of such later influence, it is of great interest to observe that one of the earliest theatrical sketches we possess from the Renaissance

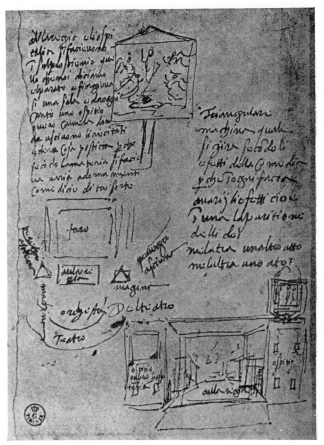

Fig. 91. A THEATRICAL SKETCH BY ANTONIO SAN GALLO THE YOUNGER

period hints strongly at a relationship between the Roman *porta regia* and the painters' frontispiece. This sketch (Fig. 91) was made by Antonio San Gallo the Younger (1485–1546), and, although parts of it are difficult to interpret, it seems without doubt to have been made with the idea of illustrating a classical playhouse in the light of contemporary theatrical activity. Particularly worthy of note, therefore, is the fact that the artist has clearly shown a city-square set in a rectangular central opening marked *aula regia*.

This sketch also offers us an introduction to the changing scenery which the later theatre-workers placed within their frames. Toying with the perplexing question of the *periaktoi*, San Gallo has set a *triangulare machina* of this sort on top of each of the *ospitij* indicated at the side of the stage—and these *ospitij* are obviously the *hospitalia* recorded by Vitruvius.

The *periaktoi* exerted peculiar fascination for the theatre-workers of this time precisely because they moved, and the Renaissance theatre was not content to stay still. The performances of revived classical plays and of plays imitated from those of classical authors were all very well, but neither the formally conceived acts nor the stabilized settings could hold audiences for long. No doubt, at the beginning, the perspective city-squares thrilled the spectators, yet familiarity always breeds contempt, and the spectators instinctively craved for movement and variety.

Because of that instinctive craving they welcomed and encouraged the free development of *intermezzi* or *intermedii*—colourful entertainments, having nothing to do with the play

Fig. 92. A SETTING BY BERNARDO BUONTALENTI FOR ONE OF THE INTERMEZZI GIVEN AT FLORENCE IN 1589

Fig. 93. DESIGN FOR CLOUDWORK AND DIVINITIES
This may be by Buontalenti. Cp. Figs. 94 to 97.

being enacted, which were inserted between the several acts of stiff tragedy and sometimes equally stiff comedy. For a considerable time, however, these *intermezzi* had to be content either with the long narrow stage, temporarily vacated by the play-actors, and with the orchestral space below, or else with scenic objects wheeled in after the medieval fashion. But clearly what many men were groping for, although some hardly realized what was the real object of their search, rested in the area of scenic change.

Fig. 94. DESIGN FOR CLOUDWORK

This groping spirit was aided by two things—the establishment of regular Court theatres and the growth of the *intermezzi* until they virtually absorbed all attention. Already in 1531 Ferrara appears to have had a hall or theatre specifically reserved for theatrical performances, and when, in 1585, the artist Bernardo Buontalenti (?1536–1608) was commissioned to construct a theatre in the Uffizi at Florence he was enabled to take the final step in the development of the Renaissance stage. Instead of a single unaltered setting, however beautiful, being placed immovable behind the actors, the spectators saw a continual series of ever-changing and ever-startling scenic displays set before their wondering eyes.

Fig. 95. DESIGN FOR A "DESERT" SCENE

The whole theatre here was 66 feet wide, 183 feet deep, and 46 feet high, with a raked auditorium. At the beginning appeared a perspective view of Florence. Then in the first of the *intermezzi* was seen a wondrous cloud-machine filled with allegorical characters; this was followed by its counterpart, "a horrible cavern full of the most terrible flames and dark vapours" (un' orrida caverna piena d'orribilissimi fuochi, con fiamme oscure e gosche); then came a scene of winter landscape magically transformed into spring; a seascape was next introduced; another cloud-effect was shown even more marvellous than that which had preceded; and finally came a spacious plain with trees and grottos, caverns and grottos. The

Fig. 96. THE COURT OF NEPTUNE

contemporary who describes these cannot conceal his admiration, excitement, and wonder at the effects produced.

Unquestionably such effects were created by Buontalenti through the use of many machines which became "the model from which the artificers of the whole of Europe took all their latest ideas and devices" (esemplare dal quale poi dagli ingegneri di tutta Europa furon presi i modi e gli artifizj più novi e più singolari). They must have involved the use of a number of large traps in the stage and also of complicated devices for the cloud-effects, anticipating the elaborate machines of similar kinds which were invented in the seventeenth

Fig. 97. MARINE MONSTERS

century. At the same time it is necessary to remember that these displays in the Medici Court have a sort of symbolic value quite apart from their tremendous practical achievements. They signalize the establishment of the stage in which the settings are made to alter so as to represent different localities within the scope of a single production, creating backgrounds for the performers in *entr'acte* entertainments.

Backed by the rich resources of the Medici Court, the genius of Buontalenti was thus enabled to present a truly lordly show in which a new concept was enshrined. About this time, however, other centres less lavishly endowed with wealth were becoming theatrically active:

some of the playhouses belonged to smaller Courts at which expenditures had to be more closely guarded than at Florence; still others came within the sphere of the "public" theatre. Before 1580, for example, there had thus been built two wooden playhouses at Venice, their cost defrayed by a couple of patrician families, those of Tron and Michiel, but both planned and directed as commercial ventures; elsewhere numbers of halls, or *stanze*, within which itinerant actors had been wont to perform, were gradually beginning to expand their activities and to take shape as regular theatres. All of these, animated by what had been achieved at the Uffizi, longed to have the opportunity of displaying something similar, even if their means were limited; and accordingly the need of the time was for some simple and relatively inexpensive method, less elaborate and costly than those in which Buontalenti had indulged, for offering to their humbler publics the delights of scenic transformation.

This need was met by the adaptation of the classical *periaktoi*, and consequently it is to these ancient machines that we must return. Vitruvius had suggested that such triangular devices had been placed in the doorways of the classical theatres; San Gallo, seeing them as machines for giving sudden appearances of celestial characters, proposed to place them, not on, but at the sides of, the stage. Soon, however, it must have occurred to some one that the two-sided frames which were described and illustrated by Serlio could, with very little difficulty, be modified so as to assume the shape of *periaktoi*: all that was required for this purpose was to add a third side, thus converting them into triangular boxes, insert a central pole passing below stage, and they could be made to turn in such a way as to reveal different scenes. Already in 1543 their use seems to have been familiar; at least so we must presume from an

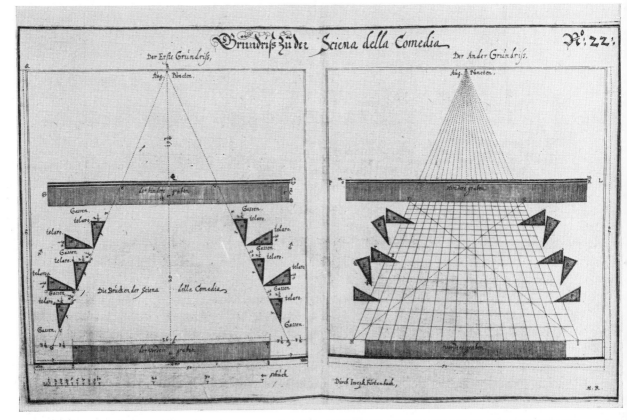

Fig. 98. PERIAKTOI ON THE SEVENTEETH-CENTURY STAGE FROM J. FURTTENBACH
"ARCHITECTURA RECREATIONIS," 1640

edition in 1583 of a posthumous work by Giacomo Barozzi da Vignola, *Le due regole della prospettiva pratica*, with comments by Egnatio Danti, where reference is made to their employment by Bastiano da San Gallo (usually called Aristotile: 1481–1551) at Castro; and two purely theatrical volumes, of some sixty years later, Nicola Sabbatini's *Pratica di fabricar scene e machine ne' teatri* (1638) and Joseph Furttenbach's *Architectura recreationis* (1640), give space to explaining how they might be put to service. Apart from the obvious fact that the employment of these *periaktoi* continued over a long period of years, the truly important observation to be made is that all these practical writers were engaged in expounding a theatrical procedure which not only succeeded that of Serlio but was essentially at variance with his: he had been concerned with the static set, whereas the minds of Danti, Sabbatini, and Furttenbach were steadily directed towards scenic change. There need be no wonder that they seized so eagerly upon the turning prisms which the classical scholars had dug up out of Vitruvius.

The engraving (Fig. 98) in which Furttenbach illustrates their use is virtually self-explanatory. All that happened was that the static Serlian wings took on the quality of movement, and every one, at least for a time, was made happy. Nevertheless, at their best these triangular wings must have been difficult to control, and their appearance from the auditorium must also have left much to be desired. Perhaps it was because of this that tentatively Sabbatini mentions two other methods of securing the desired result. One consists of making twin sets of two-sided Serlian frames, one fitting over the other: when an alteration in scene is required the one in front is slipped back, thus revealing the other behind. In the second alternative method, variously painted canvases are prepared, detachable from the lath frames which are eventually to hold them up: to effect an alteration, one of these is simply slipped onto the frame on top of the first canvas shown to the audience. Both of these devices, obviously, must have been even clumsier than the *periaktoi*, and it was the use of triangular frames, with the accompanying

provision of understage machinery, which was the true foundation of later theatrical development. The frames themselves may soon have vanished; but the essential principle involved in their employment remained.

The turning wings could be made to reveal different painted canvases in this way, but it need not be said that often they demanded some kind of masking at the top. Provision, therefore, had also to be made for the changing of the "heavens," and once more Sabbatini and Furttenbach outline the way of constructing cloud-borders (Fig. 99). If there was no necessity for altering the cloud-work, and if no celestial machines had to be flown upward or downward, the heavens (*cielo*) could be simply built entire (*intiero*): curved battens were attached for this purpose to the beams above the stage, with painted cloths nailed neatly to them. If, however, descents and ascents were necessary, then the sky had to be cut (*spezzato*), with several small battens placed one behind the other so as to leave gaps between them.

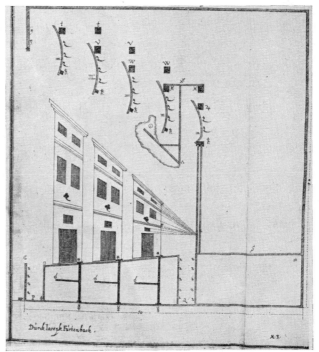

Fig. 99. CLOUD-BORDERS ON THE SEVENTEENTH-CENTURY STAGE FROM J. FURTTENBACH, "ARCHITECTURA RECREATIONIS," 1640

Fig. 100. THE SETTING FOR BONARELLI'S "IL SOLIMANO," 1620. DESIGN BY
ALFONSO PARIGI, ENGRAVED BY JACQUES CALLOT

In so far as the further perspective background was concerned, this could be painted on
two large frames or shutters drawn together centre-stage: if other similar frames were set
behind, then the drawing back of the front pair would immediately reveal a change of prospect.
Two things are worthy of note here. First, the word "immediately" is the operative term at
this point. Front curtains were known but were little used save at the opening of the performance, and during the earlier years they seem to have been so arranged that, like the Roman
auleum, they were dropped to the ground and not drawn upward: the rarity of their employment is well reflected in Sabbatini's half-hearted paragraphs devoted to their fashioning.
What appealed to audiences of this period was the suddenness of the scenic displays presented
to their eyes, and they were not content, like audiences at the end of the nineteenth century,
to wait interminably for the scene-shifters to complete a fresh setting behind a curtain's
concealment. Hence we find that all the theatrical theorists and all the practical men of the
theatre were mightily concerned with methods of altering scenes rapidly in full view of the
spectators. Remembering the use of that falling curtain, we may find that a metaphor introduced by Ariosto in the 1532 edition of his *Orlando Furioso* imaginatively captures the mood
of wonder and delight which accompanied these sudden appearances. The poet is intent on
describing a suddenly revealed and refulgent beauty, and he compares this with what he had
seen on the stage—

Quale al cader de le cortine suole
  Parer, fra mille lampade, la scena,
D'archi, et di più d'una superba mole
  D'oro, e di statue e di pitture piena—

As at the curtain-fall we see appear,
  'Mid candles multitudinous, the view,
The arches and the statues, paintings clear
  And massive buildings bright with golden hue.

So much was this suddenness an essential part of the effect that more than one contemporary treatise indulges in describing various methods of momentarily distracting the audience's attention while the change is being made—by having trumpets suddenly and unexpectedly sound from one side of the stage, or even by having accomplices raise an alarm at the rear of the audience—so that, when the spectators' eyes turn back once more to the prospect, they may be thrilled by the vision of an entirely fresh setting.

The second thing to observe is that it seems to have taken a considerable time for the theatre-workers of the period to grasp fully what could be accomplished by the use of straight flats instead of the two-sided Serlian frames or the *periaktoi*. Precisely when these came into

Fig. 101. THE SETTING FOR BONARELLI'S "IL SOLIMANO," 1620. DESIGN BY
ALFONSO PARIGI, ENGRAVED BY JACQUES CALLOT
This should be compared with Fig. 100. The setting in *Il Solimano* was constant throughout the five acts, but this shows the buildings in flames.

regular use we cannot tell for certain, but it was sufficiently late to make a discussion of their employment more proper in an account of the seventeenth-century stage than in an account of the stage during the earlier years.

Already, however, before 1600, and even as far back as the first decades of the sixteenth century, much had been learned. Ariosto speaks of the *mille lampade*, and we must remember that the impression created by these scenes was greatly enriched, indeed was largely dependent upon, the theatrical lighting of the period. In trying to convert the contemporary designs into a reconstructed reality, we must clothe them in the light which shone down softly from these hundreds and thousands of candles, easing the contours, mellowing the perspective painting, bathing everything in a gentle radiance. And we must, too, bear in mind that, although we are now well on the way towards the peep-show stage, yet the experience of looking, as we now look, from a darkened auditorium at a brightly illuminated stage was not that of these spectators. They themselves were in much the same light as the actors: there they sat, clad in their brocades and satins and silks, with scintillating jewels on the women's dresses and sometimes on the costumes of the men, harmonizing with and enriching the general theatrical impression. Nor, in spite of the difficulty in the control of the source of illumination, was the theatre without the imaginative use of light. For evidence on this we need go no further than the extremely interesting and significant "Dialogues," written probably about 1565 by Leone di Somi, which are presented as an appendix to the present volume. This practical man-of-the-theatre tells us that in his productions he always placed plenty of lights "in the streets, upon house roofs, and towers" when he was producing a comedy, in order to express the mood of gaiety with the very first view of the scene discovered to the audience; while in producing tragedy he contrived that, as soon as "the first unhappy situation occurred . . . at that moment the majority of the stage lamps which were not used to illuminate the perspective were shaded or extinguished." These candles and lamps were, it would seem, freely placed in the streets between the houses as well as behind the cloud-borders; footlights even were put to use; and from Serlio we learn of the colouring of the light by means of bottles filled, country-chemist-wise, with red or blue or other-hued liquids.

All sorts of machine-effects introduced variety, and Sabbatini gives full instructions for the making of many of these. The *periaktoi*, if soaked in spirits, lighted and rapidly turned, might give the appearance of a conflagration—although, as the writer warns, this device had to be employed with very great care. Houses could be made to fall in ruins by constructing frames on connecting iron bars which, when pulled away, would remove the necessary support. Seas could be made by painted cloths under which rollers turned, and perhaps crest-like strips of wood might be made to rise and fall between the billows. Transformation scenes, by the aid of trapdoors and understage machinery, could easily be arranged: caverns and trees and spirits could in a moment be made to materialize upon the stage.

It is, of course, very difficult for us to form an absolutely sure opinion concerning the effectiveness of these productions. Unquestionably we must give due weight to the facts that such scenic displays were then novelties and that, however skilful those responsible might be, they were compelled to work with materials less supple and adaptable than the corresponding materials so freely in use to-day. Nevertheless, against that must be placed another fact—that the majority of these theatre-men were distinguished artists in their own right, and that without doubt they must have brought much of beauty from their studios to the stage. It was not only the experience of something new which so excited contemporaries; their accounts show amply that they felt themselves in the presence of a loveliness which they could hardly find adequate words to describe.

CHAPTER VI

Renaissance France, England and Spain

1. *France: Relics of the Medieval Stage*

IT might have been thought that, since Italy was the source of so much of Renaissance inspiration, the proscenium arch and decorated stage developed in that country would have immediately spread its influence throughout Europe; but in fact many years had to pass by before this occurred. During the sixteenth century the Germanic lands, and the other lands to the east and north, were not yet ready for any widespread theatrical activities, while France, England, and Spain, for various reasons, pursued their own national paths. In Italy the existence of small cultured courts had offered an atmosphere peculiarly propitious for the invention and growth of the new theatre: these courts vied with one another in the encouragement of arts and learning; they supported numerous academies; the theatrical entertainments which they sponsored had to be rich since, partly at least, they were presented as visible demonstrations of the wealth, taste, and power of prince or duke; and all over Italy in these years the spirit of the Renaissance found its most characteristic expression through architecture, painting, and sculpture. In England this spirit discovered its characteristic medium in poetry rather than in the pictorial arts; politically the sixteenth century was for France a sad period of disruption; and Spain conservatively maintained a cultural attitude of its own. In these circumstances, therefore, there need be no particular surprise in finding that the spread of the new Italian theatrical concepts had to wait for many decades before they became the foundation for playhouse practice elsewhere.

In France, if we leave aside the trestle-stages used by itinerant performers, the most interesting theatrical activity during the century was that associated with the great Confrérie de la Passion, the organization which had been established in Paris for the performance of mystery cycles. In 1402 this company of men had been granted special leave "to make and play whatever Mystery they care" (de faire et jouer quelque Misterre que ce soit), while in 1548, when the mystery plays were rapidly fading in importance and by some were being looked upon askance, although the company was now forbidden to act "sacred mysteries" (*mystères sacrez*), it was offered an almost exclusive licence to act "other secular plays" (*autres mystères profanes*). Given this permission to present such dramas, the Confrérie promptly converted into a theatre a long rectangular hall in the Hôtel de Bourgogne; up to 1598 they played there regularly, and, while they had to abandon this stage for a short period, they took it over again in 1608 on being elevated in position by becoming the Comédiens du Roi.

Concerning their practice during the sixteenth century, evidence is not so plentiful, but fortunately there has been preserved an exceedingly significant record of their work in the middle of the century following. This consists of a *Mémoire pour la décoration des pièces qui se représentent par les Comédiens du Roy*, a detailed collection of notes and sketches for productions between 1633 and 1678. These sketches and notes are so clearly based on earlier methods that, despite their late date, we can be sure that they show the continuation of staging-procedure which had been carried on by the Confrérie since the days when they offered to the public only the medieval sacred mysteries. The chief artist concerned here was Laurent Mahelot, and the essential value of the volume rests in the fact that both comments and designs fully indicate that the material preserved in these pages was of a basically practical kind.

The designs themselves are all made up from sets of simulated houses painted on frames. It seems clear that in the construction of those houses Italian influence, and particularly the influence of Serlio, has been operative. Moreover, in a very few of the designs there is evident an attempt to build the houses into a single unity: occasionally a set for comedy or tragedy reminds us in general outline of the comic or tragic scene as illustrated in Serlio's treatise. On the other hand, such sketches are comparatively rare, and we are bound to realize that behind the Italian-type frames, behind even these apparently unified settings, another principle is at work.

This principle is wholly medieval, and it may be described as the attempt to place upon a restricted stage area, at one and the same time, as many houses representing different localities as a particular play might demand. The staging-principle itself, we further realize, was bound up with current dramatic practice. In Italy the classically inclined theorists had laid heavy and severe hands upon play-writing, and, although many writers struggled, the idea of unity of place within a given drama was firmly imposed. It was this method of constructing a comedy or a tragedy with a single place of action which made possible all the city-square designs which were so typical of Italian sixteenth-century playhouse endeavour. In France, however, despite the presence of numbers of similarly inclined critics seeking to hold to the supposed classical "unities," the French secular dramas which formed the repertoire of the Confrérie were mostly inspired by romantic sentiment, so that the fictional localities of the various scenes were many and varied. It is obvious that such a play can be presented in the theatre in three ways and in three ways only: (1) by the use of curtains, the imagination of the audience creating the surroundings; (2) by the use of changing scenery; and (3) by the use of the *décor simultané*. It was the last which Mahelot adopted. A typical example may serve to make the principle clearer. The design shown in Fig. 102 is that executed for the play of *Pandoste*, written on the same theme as that which is used in *The Winter's Tale*. Whereas in Shakespeare's drama the scenes pass from Leontes' palace to Bohemian plains and wild sea-coasts, the French director places everything

Fig. 102. A SETTING FOR "PANDOSTE" AT THE HÔTEL
DE BOURGOGNE

At the actor's right are the sea and the Temple of Delphi; back stage is the
Palace of Epirus; at the actor's left is a prison.

upon the stage at once. To the left of the audience is a painted sea; immediately behind it appears the Temple of Delphi. The back of the stage is occupied by the Palace of Epirus, while the right-hand side contains a prison. In all probability the representations of these various *maisons*, or *case*, were angled, Serlio-wise, constructed of frames of wood covered with painted canvas, and some at least were practicable. "A window from which a letter is handed out" (Une fenestre où se donne une lettre) and "a tower, a knotted cord for descending from the tower, a draw-bridge which can be lowered when necessary" (une tour, une corde nouée pour descendre de la tour, un pont-levis qui se lâche quand il est nécessaire) prove that the houses were not merely symbolic. All sorts of buildings and of scenes were set on the stage in this manner, and there were even rooms, as if with a "fourth wall" knocked away. One "belle chambre" has in it "une table, deux tabourets, une écritoire." Quite clearly we are here at the meeting-point of classic and romantic, or, to be more precise, of medieval and Renaissance. We are near the stationary settings of the mysteries, yet we are in touch with Italian ideas. "Une perspective" is spoken of "où il y ait deux passages entre les deux maisons," —"where there are two passages between the two houses"—and the very word, 'perspective', tells its own story.

This impress made on the French stage by the medieval theatre, largely through the efforts of the Confrérie de la Passion, was thus destined to influence most of its endeavours well into the seventeenth century. It is true that when Henri II and his Queen, Catherine de Medici, visited Lyon in 1548, an Italian company performed *La Calandria* with a setting which must have been similar to those city-squares so well-known in Italy, but this production, although no doubt it played an important part in introducing the Serlian wings to France, seems to have had comparatively little effect in drawing that stage towards the unified setting.

We might almost say, therefore, that during a long period of years from the middle of the sixteenth century well on into the century following, France was pursuing a scenic path all its own in opposition to that taken by the Italian theatre. And the importance of the French practice is by no means confined to theatrical activities in Paris: without an understanding of the principles on which Mahelot worked we cannot fully understand the staging of plays at Court or by the boy companies in neighbouring London.

2. *The Elizabethan Stage*

During the earlier part of the sixteenth century, two quite distinct, yet nevertheless ultimately interacting, theatrical activities are apparent in England. First, there was the work of the small bands of professional actors, performing, as we have already seen, mainly on the plain floors of baronial halls or in market-squares or in halls of inns. For the interpretation of their interludes they needed no more than some means of entrance to the acting-area— whether doors or curtain-openings were used for this purpose, or whether the players thrust themselves into position by pushing through the audience, does not really matter. The basic fact is that, in general, the fictional localities were established by the words and actions of the performers, while an associated feature of interest is the close physical contact between spectators and performers. For all practical purposes these localities had little significance, and, when they did have to be made specific, a full understanding was reached—as it had been also in the performances of the *commedia dell'arte*—between the two participants: those who watched the production were prepared to use their imaginations, and those who interpreted the scenes were careful to make things clear. Fundamentally, the attention of the spectators was upon the actors and their words, not upon the place of performance.

In addition to the small groups of professional entertainers, however, there was another theatrical world in London and its surroundings. The choirboys of the Chapels Royal, the pupils at some of the more important schools, students at the universities, young amateurs belonging to the Inns of Court, all applied themselves to the production of plays, and these productions were usually given before audiences of a more select sort, with the Court as focus. Here many of those concerned with putting on the plays and of those who came to be entertained were educated "intellectuals," knowing at least something about the ancient classics, and numbers of them were aware of what was happening theatrically elsewhere, particularly in France. We have, unfortunately, no contemporary pictorial representation of any setting belonging to this period, but the invaluable Revels' Office accounts offer us at least the basis for conjuring up in our minds some kind of picture of the way in which numerous entertainments were put before Queen Elizabeth I and her circle. In these accounts two sets of items immediately attract attention. These are the various references to "houses" and to "great cloths." We hear of "sparres to make frames for the players howses," of "canvas to cover divers townes and howses and other devisses and clowds," of "hoopes for th' arbour and topp of an howse," of "nayles to strayne the canvas." As in early sixteenth-century Italy and as in France, apparently the stage was set with simulated buildings, made of laths, covered with painted canvas, and surmounted with fitting tops, while, above, cloud-borders masked the upper part of the acting-area. The number of these houses seems to have varied from two to six. A house and a battlement served for many dramas, but other plays demanded more; and the nature of the houses, of course, also varied. The ordinary dwelling-house is here, but there are also a "Pallace," "a gret Castell," battlements innumerable, cities, mountains; and we can assume only that these were placed, as required, on the stage in the French or medieval manner. The plays of John Lyly, for example, indicate that his scenes were constructed with such a multiple setting in view, and even Shakespeare's *The Comedy of Errors* (possibly because it was originally written for private performance) presupposes a similar arrangement of localities, either shown to the audience by means of painted houses or else indicated with title-boards.

About the use of the "great cloths" mentioned in the Revels' accounts we cannot be so sure, but it may well be thought that these were perspectively painted backcloths designed to close the stage at the back when only one or two houses were required. We have to bear in mind that "the chiefe busynes" of the Revels' Office was to have "skill of devise" and "iudgment . . . in sight of perspective and architecture." Nor can we tell with assurance what the "curteynes" or "greate curteynes" were, but, whether they were intended as front curtains or for use behind the actors, it is significant to observe that, instead of falling (as the early Italian front curtain had done) or rising, they were "drawn" by means of "lynes" and "ringes." That they may have served to open and close performances appears to be suggested by two contemporary allusions: "Now draw the curtens for our Scaene is done," writes the author of *Tancred and Gismond*, while some lines attributed to Sir Walter Raleigh evoke a metaphor out of the practice,

> *Our graves, that hyde vs from the all-seeing sun,*
> *Are but drawne curtaynes when the play is done.*

By means of these painted frames and backcloths, and with the addition of other three-dimensional properties—thrones, woods, rocks, wells, and caves—the Court and associated audiences had at least a modicum of visual display put before it—but it would seem that no more than in France was any attempt made to approach the Italian style.

The true glory of the Elizabethan stage, however, was connected not with these more aristocratic entertainments but with the theatres of the professional players. During the later sixties of the century we have evidence that their success with the public was such as to permit them to expand their acting personnel, and by 1576 they had reached a position when they could determine no longer to be itinerants but to have homes of their own. Thus came the epoch-making erection of The Theatre in that year, followed by the building of other and better playhouses up to the close of the century: the appearance of the Globe and the Fortune marked the climax of their efforts. Apart from several indications of the external shape of these buildings, shown in some panoramic maps of London, only one contemporary drawing, the famous De Witt sketch of the Swan, has come down to us, but a few other seventeenth-century prints, together with documentary material and stage-directions in plays,

Fig. 103. THE SWAN THEATRE

provide us with a fairly clear picture of their structure. Concerning particular details there still may be debate, but the principal features are certain.

All of them were round, octagonal, or square structures with thatched roofs covering the sides; in the centre they were open to the sky. Entering the playhouse, intending spectators would pay a small amount for the privilege of going into the yard, where, if they remained, they would be compelled to stand throughout the performance. If, however, they were able to pay for better positions, they could ascend stairs leading to galleries which swept round the greater part of the walls: there they might sit on benches. If they were men of fashion and money they could even penetrate further and occupy one of the "gentlemen's rooms," or else on occasion hire a stool and sit on the stage itself.

This stage was a great platform, as much as 40 feet square, jutting out into the middle of the yard in such a way as to have spectators almost, if not completely, surrounding it. A couple of stout pillars, set midway at the sides of the stage, supported a half-roof, partly concealing an upper area through a trapdoor from which objects could be lowered down or raised up.

7

Fig. 104. A SEVENTEENTH-CENTURY ENGLISH STAGE. DETAIL FROM THE TITLE PAGE OF W. ALABASTER, "ROXANA" (1632)

Fig. 104a. A SEVENTEENTH-CENTURY ENGLISH STAGE. DETAIL FROM THE TITLE PAGE OF N. RICHARDS, "MESSALINA" (1640)

Certainly in some playhouses the flooring of this upper area was painted below with a blue sky and stars—hence it was named the "Heavens." Above this rose a turret-like structure bearing, at the top, a flag with the theatre's emblem. At the very rear of the platform came a façade broken by doors of entrance, over which was a gallery forming a sort of "upper stage." In addition, we know that the players had at their command something in the nature of an inner stage: what this was, whether all theatres had inner stages of the same type, whether it was a back-stage area revealed by the opening of a central doorway, or some kind of movable structure set up in front of the middle of the façade, are questions which as yet have not been finally settled; but fortunately all that we are concerned with here is the existence of some acting-space which could be employed, when needed, to suggest an interior.

That scenic objects were occasionally brought onto the platform-stage seems certain from a list of properties belonging to the Admiral's Men at the close of the century; but the list is so short and other references to such objects so few that, for practical purposes, we may assume that these theatres were almost wholly lacking in any attempts to display painted or other scenery. Their actors carried into a later age the traditions which had been set by their forerunners, the "players of interludes." It must not be thought, however, that these play-houses were rough, primitive, and jerrybuilt edifices. Already in 1577 we are told of "the sumptuous theatre houses," and from the following year comes a reference to "the gorgeous playing place." When De Witt, a Continental visitor and by way of being a scholar, wrote a little description to accompany his text he spoke of their "beauty" and remarked that the Swan playhouse "is seen to follow the lines of a Roman structure." In 1600 another foreigner was using almost the same phraseology: the theatre, he said, was built of wood "in the manner of the ancient Romans" (theatrum ad morem antiquorum

Romanorum constructum ex lignis). And in the contract for the building of the Fortune it is insisted that the "posts" set upon the stage shall be "square and wroughte palasterwise, with carved proporcions called Satiers to be placed & sett on the topp of every one of the same postes."

All mental images derived from memories of Elizabethan black-and-white timbered houses must be laid aside and a reconstructed picture of these theatres must allow for interiors which might be styled "gorgeous," "beautiful," and "sumptuous" as well as for architectural features recalling classical styles. Whence came the form of the public Elizabethan playhouse we cannot tell: some have seen a model in certain street-theatres used in the Netherlands for royal and other entries; and it is difficult for us to believe that all the men associated with their planning were completely ignorant of what was being currently achieved in Italy. But such questions, perhaps, need not concern us. What is important is that here a special and peculiar type of theatre-building had been created, different from all others known at this period; and, moreover, a type of theatre-building which allowed full use of the traditional methods which had been evolving in England from the beginning of the sixteenth century.

Its essential feature may be described as flexibility. At a first glance, it might not have struck a continental visitor as markedly different from, let us say, some of the attempts which must have been made before the erection of the Teatro Olimpico to reconstruct a Roman *scaenae frons*: there was the façade behind the players, there were the doors of entry, the middle one larger than the others. What *is* distinct is the use made of this playhouse, with the possibility of movement in all directions. The wide, deep platform-stage, taking the place of the long, narrow Roman stage, allowed the actors to walk from side to side, from front to rear; they could come onto this stage by the doorways set in the façade or by entries at the sides, and maybe they might also make their appearances in the yard and thence step up upon the platform; they had an inner stage at their disposal, and even vertical movement was possible with the use of the upper stage. About the method of handling this playhouse we must be careful not to let modern ideas prejudice our judgment. There was, for example, a time when theatrical historians imposed on it an alternating-scene theory, presupposing that if one piece of action took place on the platform, then the next had to be enacted in the inner stage: but such a supposition had been conditioned by observation of the practice of the nineteenth-century stage wherein each scene was given its own setting. Nothing of the kind existed in the minds of the Elizabethan players: instead, we should do better to relate this playhouse with histrionic practices in medieval times. The inner stage did not stand, as it were, alone and separate: when it was required to suggest an interior, then it was put to service; but the performers could move out of the interior and still imaginatively carry their location with them onto the platform—which thus might be related to the medieval *platea*. In the same way, we must be careful not to assume that actions which, if they had taken place in actuality, would have been in an elevated position, always were carried out on the upper-stage or balcony. Everything depended upon dramatic effectiveness, and not on realistic concepts; and if a bedroom scene was important, then it would in all probability have been played on the lower-stage level. It is, indeed, worthy of observation that stage-directions in contemporary plays hardly ever show the upper-stage being used by itself; when actors appeared above, they almost always were associated with actors below them, the scene being presented, not horizontally on one plane or on two planes, but vertically from the stage-level to the balcony-level.

How precisely the actors interpreted their parts remains still a debatable question; but probably the truth lies in a recognition of two likely truths: (*a*) the existence of an earlier

Fig. 105. "TITLE ANDRONICUS" IN 1595

formal type of delivery overlapping with a later more natural style, and (*b*) the presence even in the latter of certain elements which we to-day would have designated as rhetorically artificial. It is extremely probable that the great actor of the Marlowe period, Edward Alleyn, was more bombastic than Richard Burbage, the player who seems to have interpreted Shakespeare's tragic heroes, but what appeared to Elizabethan spectators as natural or real may well have been highly coloured by formal gestures and delivery of lines. Such comments as we find in plays concerning the treatment of basic emotions seem to suggest that there were recognized stylistic movements to express the more common dramatic emotions—rage or fear or desperation or submission. Although there may have been nothing of the purely stylised actions so characteristic of the Chinese stage, nevertheless we may well believe that audiences were aided in following the rapid passage of the stage action by what might almost be described as a kind of histrionic shorthand.

These performers were certainly richly dressed, and Puritan opponents of the playhouses frequently directed their vitriolic attacks upon the "gorgious and sumptious apparrell" to be seen on the stage: "the very hyerlings of some of our players," we are told, "iet vnder gentlemens noses in sutes of silk." The colour and the beauty which Italian artists lavished on their settings were here presented in the rich dynamic costumes worn by the actors. Normally, it would seem, these costumes were of a contemporary sort; but sufficient evidence exists to indicate that out-of-the-way dresses, whether "historical" or fantastic, could freely be seen. In this connexion, it is interesting to note that the sole contemporary drawing of a scene in a Shakespearian play, that made by Henry Peacham of a performance of *Titus Andronicus* (Fig. 105), clearly shows an attempt to secure a Roman effect. Turks and Moors often had their turbans and scimitars; and among the costumes listed in a late-sixteenth-century theatre inventory we find several special attires for classical deities—Neptune had his own "sewtte," his "forcke" and garland; "Junoes cotte" is here, as well as "Dides robe"; Iris had some kind of a mask and, of course, bore a rainbow, Mercury had wings; ghosts wore particular suits and bodices. In the same inventory appear several animal disguises, for lions, boars, dragons, horses, and black dogs, in addition to what might be described as "professional" habiliments—friars' gowns and hoods; senators' gowns, hoods and caps; greenwood costumes for characters in Robin Hood plays; coats for shepherds and fools; a gown and cape for Merlin; a cardinal's cap. Danish characters had their own attire; popes wore their mitres and emperors their appropriate crowns. Considering even these few examples, it will be realized that hardly a play by Shakespeare does not contain some person or persons apt to wear a special dress. The assumption that by putting these plays into modern dress we come back to Elizabethan methods may be seen to be as false as the practices of Charles Kean, Irving, and Tree: apart from the fact that modern dress is usually drab whereas ordinary Elizabethan attire was colourful, we must remember that what the Elizabethan spectators saw was by no means a reproduction of what they would have seen on London streets or in their homes.

Finally, we must never lose sight of the fact that in this Elizabethan playhouse all the focus was upon the actors and the words given to them by their poets; and that focus was intensified by its association with the close contact between players and public. No doubt the Globe was a large theatre, capable of accommodating even thousands within its "wooden O"; yet this wooden O was so constructed as to bring all within the orbit of the play being enacted. Those standing in the yard were only a few feet from the players, and through them the whole body of the spectators was brought as a unit close to the place of action.

There was a time when attempts were made to depict the Elizabethan audience as a kind of restless, rowdy mob of unlettered louts; but when the evidence is looked at aright this picture is to be seen as coming far from the truth. These men and women had paid good money to watch their plays, and they were hardly likely to have indulged habitually in any practices apt to spoil their enjoyment of the afternoon's performance. They were hot-blooded, no doubt, and at times they were naïve; but there can be no doubt about the spell exerted on their minds by what the poets had to give them. A picture more correct may undoubtedly take as its central design the casual words written down by a distinguished foreign visitor in 1617, none other than Orazio Busino, the Venetian envoy. "To distract me," he says,

> they took me . . . to one of the numerous theatres here in London where plays are performed, and we saw a tragedy enacted there, which moved me little chiefly because I cannot understand a single word of English—though one may derive some little amusement from gazing on the sumptuous dresses of the actors and observing their gestures, and the various interludes of instrumental music, dancing, singing and the like. The best treat was to see and stare at so much nobility in such excellent array that they seemed so many princes, *listening as silently and soberly as possible.*

That Shakespeare possessed such a stage to work on and such an audience to enchant helps to explain the triumphant realization of what his genius had to offer.

3. The Spanish Corrales

By a strange coincidence, the playhouses which came into being in Renaissance Spain arose about the same time as the Elizabethan playhouses and assumed a form not dissimilar. In 1576 the first public theatre was built in London; three years later (1579) the first truly important Spanish theatre, the Teatro de la Cruz, was established in Madrid.

In both countries the arrangement of stage and auditorium which was finally adopted resulted from the experiences their actors had had in presenting plays during their earlier periods of itineracy. The English performers during the years before 1576 never possessed any one single type of building which they habitually used for their productions, and hence, when they came to build a permanent home for themselves, it had to take a shape unlike any other London edifice. The Spanish actors, on the other hand, had for years been accustomed to play in a *corral* or a *patio*, and therefore, when they eventually reached a position of security which permitted them to have a home of their own, it was to this that they turned. Already at the close of the fifteenth century a Patio de la Cancelleria at Granada was the place of several performances, and, as the sixteenth century advanced, we come across numerous records of playing in similar locations at many cities—for in Spain, unlike England, theatrical activities were by no means confined to a single metropolis. If Madrid had its Corral de la Cruz (1579) and Corral del Príncipe (1583), Seville could boast of no less than seven houses of entertainment, while divers other towns (in Portugal as well as in Spain) became close rivals.

Fig. 106. A MODERN PERFORMANCE OF LOPE
DE VEGA'S "EL ACERO DE MADRID" IN
AN ANCIENT SPANISH CORRAL

The *corral* may be defined as a court-yard formed by the walls of contiguous houses, not unlike in shape and size to the courtyards of English inns. At one end was set up a stage, a bare platform just as in the English theatres, although sometimes painted curtains might provide a background for the actors. Below, on the ground-level, benches were placed, while further advantageous positions for seeing the play were windows or small balconies (*célosías* or *aposéntos*) set in the containing walls of the houses. In addition, a special box-like gallery, called the *cazuela*, was assigned to women spectators. Often curtains were spread over the whole of the courtyard, and in later years permanent painted ceilings took their place.

By another strange coincidence, the staging arrangements were almost the same as those operative in London. Behind the platform was a dressing-room area which could, on occasion, be opened up as an inner stage, while an upper level, *lo alto del teatro*, might be employed for just the same purposes as the Elizabethan gallery, serving now as the battlements of a besieged city, now as the terrace of a house, now as a hill-top.

And regarding these theatres the same general comments may be made: they came at precisely the right time and their main features were splendidly qualified to encourage the Spanish dramatic genius. When Lope de Vega, born two years before Shakespeare and starting his career almost in the same year as his English counterpart, began writing his first plays, he found a newly established stage and inherited a lively tradition which still had to reach its culmination. His audiences were popular in the widest and best sense of the word, audiences eager to hear richly poetic dialogue well spoken, and presented within a theatrical structure excellently calculated to offer fullest opportunity for the delivery of such dialogue. In all essential theatrical conditions the Spanish playhouses were as fittingly equipped to meet the needs of their time as were the English theatres, and no doubt because of these circumstances her dramatists alone vied in Renaissance Europe with Shakespeare and his companions.

CHAPTER VII

The Baroque and its Legacy

1. Introductory

SHORTLY before the year 1594 an ardent group of enthusiasts in Florence were engaging in animated discussions concerning the way in which ancient Greek tragedies had been interpreted, and the focus of their attention was the musical element in these productions. At their head was the Count of Vernio, Giovanni Bardi, and among his associates were two musicians, Giulio Caccini and Jacopo Peri, and a poet, Ottavio Rinuccini. As a result of their deliberations came a drama written by Rinuccini and set to music by Peri, and this work, *Daphne*, was destined to have a mighty line of descendants: it was the very first real opera, in which the singing formed the core of the dramatic endeavour. Six years later, in 1600, a prominent geometrician, Guido Ubaldus, published a learned work, *Perspectivae libri sex*, in which one section was devoted to stage scenery. This study, the first truly basic investigation of the laws of perspective, opened up a new world of wonders for those concerned with stage affairs by suggesting a scenic method which, in its turn, was also destined to have many successors.

The combination of these two endeavours, the one in music and the other in perspective, ushered in and provided the foundation for the baroque theatre.

This term "baroque" offers almost as many difficulties and problems as the word Renaissance. In itself it cannot properly be applied to any one single restricted period of artistic activity, and therefore several historians have had to fall back upon the employment of such qualifying epithets as "early baroque," "middle baroque," and "late baroque"; and, in addition, considerable controversy has attended attempts to apply the term in any way to the artistic work of some European countries, notably that of England. Nevertheless, if we remember that its manifestations differed in different lands, and that dynamically it was in continual flux, the word may conveniently be employed to describe a general movement which extended from the first decades of the seventeenth century on almost to the close of the eighteenth.

In so far as the theatre is concerned, any study of baroque principles and practice must take account of some five cardinal facts. (1) During this period all countries, even conservative Spain, were brought into the same orbit, and although Italy remained always the true fount of inspiration, contributions, some of them very important, were made by architects and painters of other nationalities. Hence there was less cleavage of the sort which, during the sixteenth century, separated the English and Spanish and French playhouses from those of the Italian courts. (2) The central emphasis of baroque theatrical activity is to be found in its attention to scenery suitable for entertainments entirely different from the classically motivated sixteenth-century comedies and tragedies for which the earlier painters had executed their various city-scenes. Already in their days, as we have seen, the *intermezzi* had come to form increasingly attractive parts of stage performances as a whole, but in general the play remained the fundamental part of the evening's show, and the *intermezzi*, as their title implies, were *entr'acte* spectacles. Now, however, in many countries the *intermezzi* rose in stature to become the main or only ingredient in the productions: a great deal of baroque thought on the theatre was concerned with the presentation of ballets and masques, and when the opera expanded from its early beginnings it incorporated much of the material originally belonging to the "shows" introduced merely as supplementary to the drama. Of course, the methods devised by the later artists for spectacular display were still used, in simplified form, for the production of plays, but the main driving-force was directed towards the production of operas and associated works.

(3) As during the sixteenth century in Italy, the chief centres of activity were the playhouses connected with courts and given princely aid; at the same time, it must not be forgotten that this was a period when public theatres came to adopt the procedure invented and pursued in these palace appendages. The first opera-house opened to a paying public appeared in Venice in 1637, and it was followed by many others: when the English playhouses started once more after their eighteen years' suppression during the Commonwealth regime they abandoned the traditional Elizabethan shape and in their humble way sought to imitate the Italian style. Furthermore, in the later baroque period, the concept of national or civic theatres materially expanded the range of endeavour away from and beyond that of the private or courtly stage. (4) The baroque brought into being new means of securing spectacular effects, and it also encouraged the installation of machinery which went far beyond anything formerly imagined. The result of this was that spectacle, as such, dominated over all other considerations. The space which once had provided ample room for the actors now appeared ridiculously confined, and the stage boards which before had extended only a few yards back from the proscenium arch were stretched ever farther and farther from the auditorium. Towards such enlarging of the stage-area both practice and theory contributed. Ubaldus in 1600 had pointed out the way, and numerous treatises on theatrical affairs followed his direction, each one suggesting new and ever newer procedures, all directly or indirectly contributing towards the extension of the stage-space, in width and depth, in height and in that underground area which came to house so many of the machines necessary for the effecting of the spectacular display. (5) All of this in turn meant that the theatre architects were forced to adopt a fresh attitude towards the provision of seating for the audience. In many, indeed most, of the Italian sixteenth-century Court theatres all attention was directed towards the princely patron and his most favoured guests: frequently a daïs placed centrally on the auditorium floor was set up for this privileged party, and the artists planned their scenes in such a way as to make the perspective properly seen only from that position. Already towards the close of the century the disadvantages of directing all lines towards this central axis were being observed, and soon those responsible for the productions saw that other practices must be substituted for the old. The stress on operatic singing and upon extended spectacle alike brought problems of acoustics and sight-lines well to the fore.

2. The Scenic Spectacle

A consideration of these features of the baroque playhouse indicates clearly that this theatre, to be understood correctly, must be entered first through its stage-door, and also that, when this leads us up the acting-area, the first thing we should look at is the means of displaying the perspective setting.

Far back in 1545 a French scholar, Philander, had published a commentary upon the work of Vitruvius, and there, after describing the ubiquitous *periaktoi*, he turned to another device, the *scaena ductilis*, by which, he said, "through panels drawn to the side, this or that scene is revealed within" (quum tractis tabulatis hac atque illac species picturae nudaretur interior). For a long time no one seems to have paid much attention to this observation, yet it was to be this *scaena ductilis* which eventually seized hold of the modern stage—the *scaena ductilis* became the flat wing which remained for at least two hundred years as the fundamental means of securing scenic illusion.

Strangely, it was an-other Frenchman, Jean Dubreuil, who was the first theorist to describe and explain the working of this stage instrument; the third volume of his *Perspective pratique*, issued in 1649, thus anticipates by several years any discussion of its use by an Italian. Yet we know that it had been long put to service before the appearance of this work. In 1606 Giovanni Battista Aleotti employed it at the theatre belonging to the Accademia degli Intrepidi at Ferrara, and by 1640 it had become sufficiently well known for the English artist Inigo Jones (1573-1652) to apply it in the staging of a masque.

Since both Dubreuil and Inigo Jones present the device in its simplest form, a summary description of its operation may be taken from their designs. Figure 107 reproduces a plate from the former's volume, and this shows, at the

Fig. 107. THE SIMPLE USE OF FLAT WINGS FROM J. DUBRUEIL, "PERSPECTIVE PRATIQUE," 1649

top, the flat wing at its most primitive—just two perspectively painted representations of houses with a long painted back-shutter; the design below goes a little further in delineating a small courtyard, with columns and arches, all made up from a set of four flats in front and three behind. From these we may turn to the record of Inigo Jones' work in the production of masques during the first decades of the seventeenth century—a record which has the additional value of revealing a stage technician who might stand as a symbol of the whole movement from the old world into the new. In 1604, when he dealt with Samuel Daniel's *Vision of the Twelve Goddesses*, he almost certainly followed the style of simultaneous setting associated with the French Hôtel de Bourgogne; the next year, 1605, at Oxford he was experimenting with *peri-aktoi*, described by a contemporary as *peripetasmata*, which were turned to change the pros-

Fig. 108. FRONTISPIECE BY INIGO JONES FOR "ALBION'S TRIUMPH," 1609

pects. The following year the turning frame was used in *Hy-menaei*, while in *The Masque of Queens* (1609) it was employed to turn an "ugly Hell" first into "the House of Fame" and later into "fama Bona."

From these realms he soon moved to others more ambitious. All his later masques have frontis-pieces, or painted proscenium arches, designed to mask the sides and top of the stage (Fig. 108), and in this arch he often set a painted curtain which at the start of his career was of the falling variety but which later was made to rise. For our present purposes plans and designs for two of these later efforts are particularly important. For the first, a French pastoral called *Florimène*, in 1635 he prepared a plan of "that kind of sceane with triangular frames on yᵉ sydes where there is but one standing sceane and yᵉ sceane changes only at the back shutters" (Figs. 109-110), and, when we examine it, we realize that here we are dealing with a setting realized by means of four angled Serlian wings (which remained unaltered throughout the acting of the piece) and of four shutters at the rear, three of which could be drawn to the sides in two parts: there was scenic change, but this was restricted to the rear part of the stage; and the kind of wings that were used had been in existence for well over a century. The second masque, however, offers something entirely different and very much up-to-date. The plan for *Salmacida Spolia* (1640) is inscribed "Ground platt of a scaene where yᵉ side peeces of yᵉ sceane doe altogither change with yᵉ back shutters," and here Inigo Jones has moved forward into the world of the baroque playhouse (Figs. 111-114). Four sets of side-wings are placed on each side of the stage, each set consisting of four flats: behind are four shutters, each presumably in two parts to effect easy removal to the sides. In order to secure the perspective effect, the side-wings rapidly

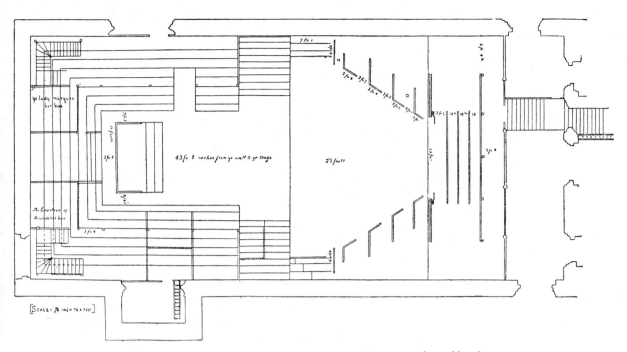

Fig. 109. PLAN BY INIGO JONES FOR "FLORIMÈNE," 1635

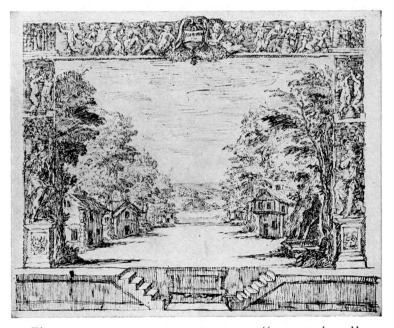

Fig. 110. THE STANDING SCENE FOR "FLORIMÈNE,"
1635. DESIGN BY INIGO JONES

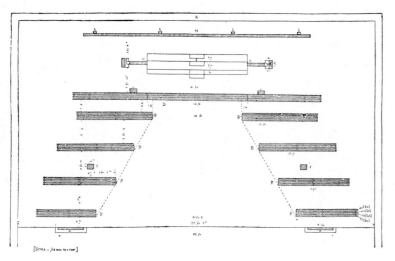

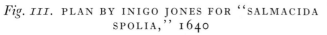

Fig. 111. PLAN BY INIGO JONES FOR "SALMACIDA
SPOLIA," 1640

Fig. 112. CROSS-SECTION OF THE STAGE BY
INIGO JONES FOR "SALMACIDA SPOLIA,"
1640

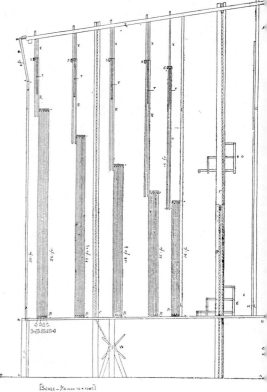

Fig. 113. DESIGN BY INIGO JONES FOR THE THIRD SCENE IN
"SALMACIDA SPOLIA," 1640

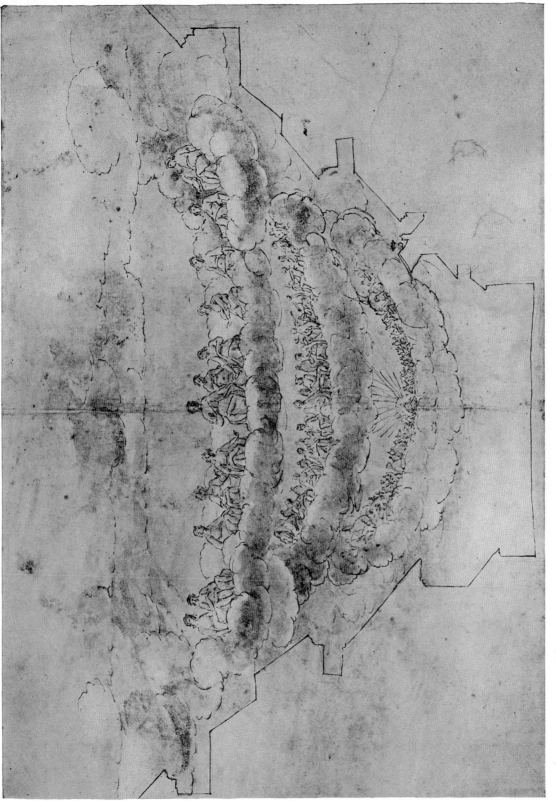

Fig. 114. DESIGN BY INIGO JONES FOR THE "WHOLE HEAVEN" IN "SALMACIDA SPOLIA," 1640

decrease in height, and for each of them there is a corresponding upper wing or a sky-border. From the plan and cross-section the arrangement becomes absolutely clear, although perhaps it may here be observed that the machine immediately behind the shutters has nothing to do with the scenery: this is a device for revealing, raising, and lowering the chief masquers as a glorious climax to the performance. The appearance of one of the scenes is shown in Fig. 113 and the "whole heaven" in Fig. 114.

Fig. 115. DESIGN FOR PERSPECTIVE SIDE-WINGS
Preserved among the drawings of Inigo Jones, these designs are probably of Italian origin.

Thus the simpler form of the wing-stage takes shape before us, and we may believe that in many productions, at Italian courts and elsewhere, the procedure adopted by Inigo Jones at Whitehall was practised. The very interesting series of pictorial records relating to "ballets" at the Turin Court, for example, may be regarded as typical (Figs. 116–123). Here most of the individual ballets had a pair of flat masking wings at the sides, not moved throughout the course of the action, while behind were four pairs of receding side-wings with changeable shutters beyond. As in the English masques, practicable scenic objects could be introduced, such as the ship on wheels (Fig. 119—the wheels no doubt being concealed by sea-borders); divinities could be seen on high (Fig. 120), and "whole heavens" displayed (Fig. 122).

It need not be said, however, that with only four wings on each side the producers remained fettered: they wished to present to the eyes of the audience ever more splendid effects, and yet even the most skilled perspective painting could not conceal the fact that they were working in an extremely restricted area. Still further, the necessity of sharply reducing the size of the flats as they receded made it essential that the performers should be made to maintain their positions well to the stage-front. Hence inevitably, as production succeeded production, attempts were made to deepen the stage-area and so to multiply the number of flats on each side. Figure 124, for instance, reproducing the plan of the reconstructed Teatro della Pergola at Florence, originally built for the Accademia degli Immobili by Ferdinando Tacca in 1656, shows ten pairs of wings, in addition to three cross-shutters which might be used as "cut-outs."

Fig. 116. SETTING FOR "IL TOBACCO," TURIN, 1650

Fig. 117. SETTING FOR "LA PRIMAVERA TRIONFANTE," TURIN, 1657

Fig. 118. CLOUD-MACHINE FOR "L'UNIONE PER LA PELLEGRINA," TURIN, 1660

Fig. 119. PRACTICABLE SHIP FOR "LA PRIMAVERA TRIONFANTE," TURIN, 1657

Fig. 120. SETTING FOR "LA PRIMAVERA TRIONFANTE," TURIN, 1657

Fig. 121. SETTING FOR "IL DONO DEL RE," RIVOLI, 1645

Fig. 122. SETTING FOR "IL GRIDELLINO," TURIN, 1653

Fig. 123. SCENE IN "L'UNIONE PER LA PELLEGRINA," TURIN, 1660

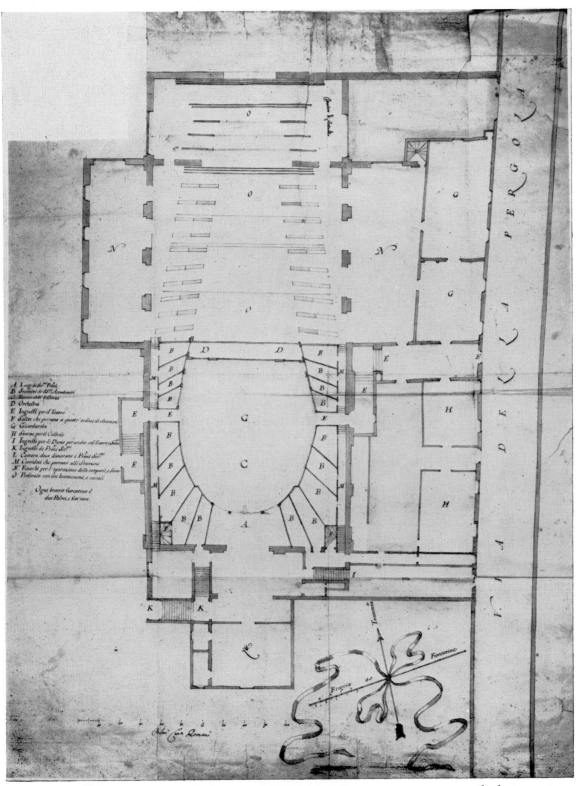

Fig. 124. PLAN OF THE TEATRO DELLA PERGOLA, FLORENCE, 1656

This design of the Pergola playhouse indicates another thing. The first five sets of side-wings are set diagonally to the stage-front, and such a disposition of the wings was an invention of the mid-part of the century, possible only when the art and science of perspective had moved far beyond that known in the century preceding. In 1672 Giulio Troili, familiarly called "Paradosso" from the title of his work, prepared his *Paradossi per praticare la prospettiva senza saperla*—which might be translated as "Paradoxes for practising stage perspective without

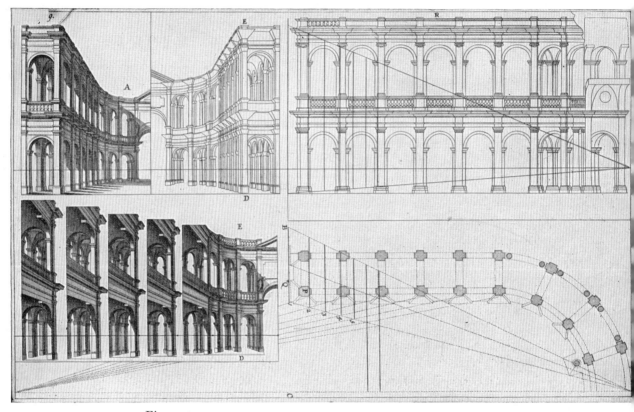

Fig. 125. THEATRICAL DESIGN BY ANDREA POZZO, 1700

really understanding its mathematical principles"—and for the first time provided theatre-workers with a handy manual which all could use for the painting of these diagonally placed wings. Then, in 1693 and 1700, came the learned volumes of Andrea Pozzo (1642–1709), *De perspectiva pictorum et architectorum*, dealing with still more abstruse matters and suggesting further means of securing the effects, while eleven years after the publication of Pozzo's second volume there was issued the exceedingly important *L'architettura civile pre-parata sulla geometria e ridotta alle prospettive* (1711) by Ferdinando Galli-Bibiena. Thus workers in the theatre possessed by the beginning of the eighteenth century invaluable aids for constructing settings of the most difficult kind, including, in Bibiena's words, "the manner of seeing scenic objects from an angle" (*maniera di veder le scene per angolo*) and the even more complex problem of showing curving streets and colonnades (Figs. 125–126).

Certainly with the aid of science and "engineering" they achieved wonders. One of the most active among them—Giacomo Torelli (1608–78)—was indeed named by many as *il gran stregone*, "the great sorcerer," and he helped to carry Italian theatre ideals and procedure

Fig. 126. THEATRICAL DESIGN BY ANDREA POZZO, 1700

to the rest of Europe. Starting in his native land and there making a considerable name for himself, he found his services eagerly sought for, and several of his greatest triumphs were associated with the ballets, operas, and tragedies produced at the Court of Louis XIV in France. Fundamentally, his work has three important features, one incidental, one structural, and one conceptual. The first is that through the publication of the spectacles with which he was concerned he has left behind him a rich array of engravings which grant us at least a general idea of his attainments: *Bellerofonte* (1642), as produced in Venice the preceding year, is a precious record of his earlier efforts, and similar volumes, *Apparati scenici per lo Teatro Novissimo di Venetia* (1644), *Feste theatrali per la Finta Pazza rappresentate nel Piccolo Borbone in Parigi* (1645), and *Scene e machine preparate alle Nozze di Teti. . . . rappresentate nella sala del Piccolo Borbone* (1654), are not only of very great historical value to us but were also of prime influence upon the later baroque stage.

The second feature of interest is that Torelli developed a new method of handling the side-wings. Before his time they seem to have been set in grooves (or *guide*, as they were known in Italy) through which they were drawn manually at the required moment of change—a method which remained standard in the English theatre up to within living memory. There were, of course, two disadvantages: many men had to be employed for the task and, however efficiently they might be drilled, the co-ordination of their movements could never be absolutely perfect. Then someone had the bright idea of cutting slits in the stage floor, attaching the wings to wheeled carriages placed under the stage, and by means of cables bringing all the side-wings under the control of a central winch. It is probable that this, or a similar, 'machine' was used by F. Guitti at the Teatro Farnese as early as 1628, but we may believe that Torelli was responsible for bringing it to perfection. "Marvellous indeed," says a commentator, "is the cleverness of this device, for a fifteen-year-old boy can work it by himself: he releases a counter-weight from a small iron rod and this causes an axle under the stage to revolve, thus drawing all the wings back or forward, just as required, simultaneously and in a flash." This instrument, variously constructed, came into very general use in the Italian, French, and German theatres, and it is needless to say that through its means the alteration of settings became much more easy to manage and much more effective.

The third feature concerns Torelli's basic objective. Until his time, theatre-workers had, for the most part, aimed at changing their settings from, let us say, the city-square used in a comedy to such a scene as might be demanded in the *intermezzi*: this might be put in another way by declaring that the alteration itself corresponded to a structural break between part and part of the entertainment. Because of the ease with which he could manage the changes, and perhaps with the aim of making them still more marvellous, Torelli did two things—he put aside all the methods advised by Sabbatini for momentarily distracting the audience's attention and he boldly introduced the changes within, instead of at the ends of, the scenes. At one moment the audience might be looking at a seascape; at the next, without being able to

Fig. 127. DESIGN BY GIACOMO TORELLI FOR "IL BELLEROFONTE," VENICE, 1641

Fig. 128. DESIGN BY GIACOMO TORELLI FOR "IL BELLEROFONTE," VENICE, 1641

fathom how or why, it found itself gazing at a scene of rocks and caverns—and yet all the time the action of the opera or the ballet proceeded without interruption. The arousing of wonder and admiration was part of the business of baroque art, and Torelli was its theatre prophet.

What he actually achieved is excellently suggested in the engravings to the several volumes illustrating his work. At the Teatro Novissimo in Venice in 1641 he was clearly working with a limited number of side-wings, apparently seven on each side: Fig. 127 shows the prologue with fortresses on one side and ships on the other, a seascape in the background; the side-wings remain in Fig. 128 but the further vista has changed and a cloud-machine appears in the sky; all disappears in Fig. 129, to be turned into a colonnaded square; and in Fig. 130 the architectural buildings have given place to a bosky setting with a palace in the rear. Something very interesting is introduced in Fig. 131: this is another woodland scene, a *delitiosa boscareccia*, in *Venere gelosa* (Venice, 1643), but the tree-wings on each side are of a novel sort, literally cut-outs, so that the audience can see not only along their inner lines but through them, looking, as it were, at two rustic paths. Bacchus' temple (Fig. 132) is a very formal courtyard

Fig. 129. DESIGN BY GIACOMO TORELLI FOR "IL BELLEROFONTE," VENICE, 1641

Fig. 130. DESIGN BY GIACOMO TORELLI FOR "IL BELLEROFONTE," VENICE, 1641

sharply contrasting with the first. Torelli himself has observed that the city-square (Fig. 133) was made up with no less than forty-eight pieces of scenery, and thus, although it reminds us of earlier city-squares, it exists in a new theatrical world. The variant city-square for *La finta pazza* (Fig. 134) happily gives us an idea of what these designs looked like when set in their appropriate frontispieces, while the engravings for *Les noces de Pélée et de Thétis* (Figs. 135–137) splendidly convey an idea of the later development of his art. Here, perhaps, it may be helpful to quote at least a few passages from the accompanying verbal descriptions. Concerning the first scene (Fig. 135) we are informed that

the first scene of Act I, which shows the Grotto of the Centaur Cheiron, is wholly composed of stones and fearsome rocks; this, being vaulted with stones, gives an impression at once of beauty and horror. Above, an aperture is seen whence the grotto receives its light, and through which is to be discerned a landscape with mountain paths which lead down to the entrance of the grotto. Two doors of rustic architecture open out on each side. There are to be seen many diverse tombs of a majestic type which enclose the remains of those Heroes who had been worthy to die disciples of so great a master. Beneath

Fig. 131. DESIGN BY GIACOMO TORELLI FOR "VENERE GELOSA," VENICE, 1643

Fig. 132. DESIGN BY GIACOMO TORELLI FOR "VENERE GELOSA," VENICE, 1643

Fig. 133. DESIGN BY GIACOMO TORELLI FOR "VENERE GELOSA," VENICE, 1643

Fig. 134. DESIGN BY GIACOMO TORELLI FOR "LA FINTA PAZZA," PARIS, 1645

125

the high opening is another which reveals the furthest parts of this dwelling. By ingenuity in the use of perspective the background seems very distant. There, a more superb tomb than the others can be seen. At the incantation of the sorcerers led by Cheiron a chariot bearing Peleus rises with thunder and lightning. This rises into the air in the midst of flames and smoke, crossing the grotto and departing through the aperture. The smoke vanishes into the air and the flames recede into the background.[1]

[1] La prima Scena dell' Atto primo rappresenta la Grotta di Chirone Centauro, è composta tutta di sassi, e scogli horridissimi, e coperta da vn vastissimo volto pure di sassi, rende insieme vaghezza, & horrore. Nell' alto si vede vn' apertura, per la quale la Grotta riceue il lume, e per doue si vedono le strade di vna montagna e paesaggio di fuori, che conduce all' entrata della sudetta Grotta, che aprono due porte di rustica architettura fabricate d'vna parte, e d'altra. Si vedono molti, e diuersi sepolcri di maestosa costruttura che chiudono quegli Eroi, che sono stati degni di morir discepoli di cosi grand maestro. Sotto la medesima apertura dell' alto, se ne vede vn' altra, che mostra i più intimi luoghi della sudetta habitazione ; e con ingegnosa regola di prospettiua appare di lontano il fondo, in cui vedesi ancora vn più superbo sepolcro de' gli altri. Quì all' incanto de' maghi, addittati da Chirone, frà tuoni e lampi sorge un carro, sopra di cui montata Peleo, si leua in aria in mezzo di fiamme, e fumosi vapori, che lasciati à mezzo corso, vola à trauerso della Grotta, vscendo per la sudetta apertura, il fumo suanisce in aria, e la fiamma ricade al fondo.

Fig. 135. DESIGN BY GIACOMO TORELLI FOR "LES NOCES DE PÉLÉE ET DE THÉTIS," PARIS, 1654

And, to describe Fig. 136, we read:

> Here all the perspective of the grotto changes. In place of a distant view of rocks there is to be seen a calm sea surrounded by lovely shores and gentle slopes and pleasant houses. On one side appears a great shell full of coral fishers who support in their midst a smaller shell which bears Thetis, the goddess of the sea. . . . Jove meanwhile appears in the air. . . . Juno, in a fit of jealousy, descends in her own chariot. . . . He flies off to heaven on his eagle, and causes the gods to close the great cloud. . . . Juno having called the Furies from hell, a head of a horrible monster rises from the earth and, with clouds of sulphuric smoke and flames, casts up four Furies.[1]

[1] Quì cangiata tutta la prospettiua della Grotta, in luogo di vna lontananza di scogli, si vede vn placidissimo mare, circondato di riue piaceuoli, de colli ameni, e deliziose habitazioni. Comparisce da vna parte vna gran conchiglia piena di pescatori di coralli, che sostenendone nel mezzo loro vn' altra più picciola, n'è portata Teti Dea maritima. Viene sorgendo dal mare di lei inuaghito Nettune, accompagnato da vn coro di Tritoni, e Sirene. . . . Gioue intanto apparisce in aria . . . mentre Giunone gelosa discende su 'l proprio carro . . . egli se ne vola al Cielo sù l'aquila, e fa chiudere Dei gran nuuola. Giunone intanto, chiamate dall' inferno le furie; sorge dalla terra vna testa di formidabil mostro, che esalando fiamme, e fumi sulfurci, vomita quattro furie.

Fig. 136. DESIGN BY GIACOMO TORELLI FOR "LES NOCES DE PÉLÉE ET DE THÉTIS," PARIS, 1654

Fig. 137. DESIGN BY GIACOMO TORELLI FOR "LES NOCES DE PÉLÉE ET DE THÉTIS," PARIS, 1654

Torelli, of course, was only one among many. The age teems with men who won fame for their work in the theatres—Alfonso Rivarola (known as "Il Chenda" or "Chendi,"*c.* 1591–1640), Gaspare Vigarani (1586–1663), Giovanni Servandoni (1695–1776), Stefano Orlandi (1681–1760), Vittorio Bigari (1692–1776), and numerous others, with the members of the Bibiena family towering above them all. This family started with Giovanni Maria Galli (1619–65), who, taking the name of his birthplace, Bibiena, as his own name, first laid the foundations of a style which was to become the hereditary property of his descendants. His sons, Ferdinando (1657–1743) and Francesco (1659–1739), both devoted themselves to scenic work, as did his grandsons, Antonio (1700–74), Giuseppe (1696–1756), Alessandro (1687–1769) and Giovanni (d. 1760): a great-grandson, Carlo (1725–1787), carried the family tradition on to the latter years of the eighteenth century—and that tradition, it should be remembered, passed far beyond the confines of Italy. The Bibiena magic was known southwards to Portugal and northwards to Russia. Between them, these artists executed a vast series of designs which can only amaze through their stupendous grandeur and charm, through their artistic proportion and innate beauty. And, as we shall see, their endeavours had the power of inspiring numerous distinguished followers.

Fig. 138. DESIGN BY FRANCESCO GUITTI FOR "LA CONTESA," FERRARA, 1632

Particularly to be noted are the steps leading into the auditorium and the painted panels above the proscenium frame.

Fig. 140. DESIGN BY FRANCESCO SANTURINI FOR "ANTIOPA GIUSTIFICATA," MUNICH, 1662

132

Fig. 141. THE IMPERIAL THEATRE, VIENNA, *c.* 1690, DESIGNED BY LODOVICO BURNACINI

Fig. 142. THEATRICAL DESIGN BY F. JUVARRA

Note should be taken of the permanent setting used apparently with a variety of back-cloths.

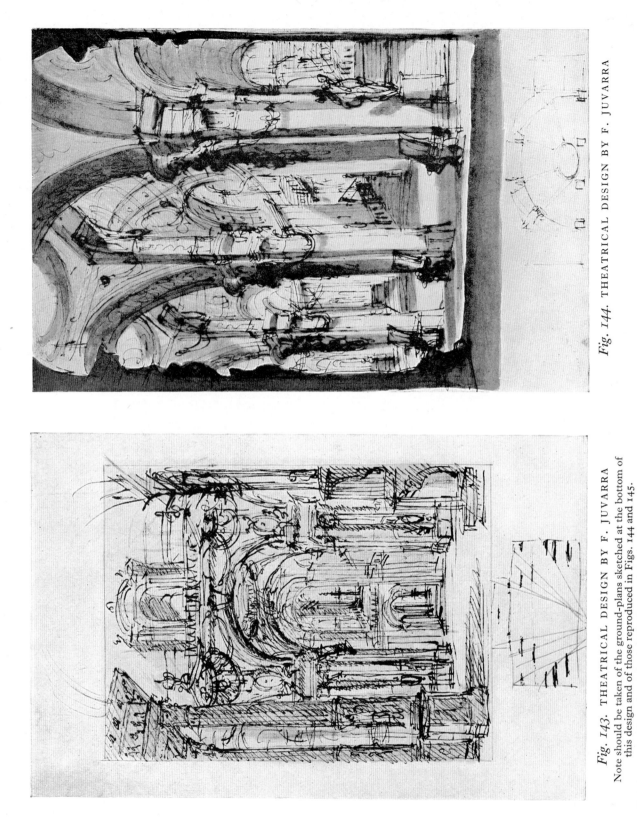

Fig. 144. THEATRICAL DESIGN BY F. JUVARRA

Fig. 143. THEATRICAL DESIGN BY F. JUVARRA
Note should be taken of the ground-plans sketched at the bottom of
this design and of those reproduced in Figs. 144 and 145.

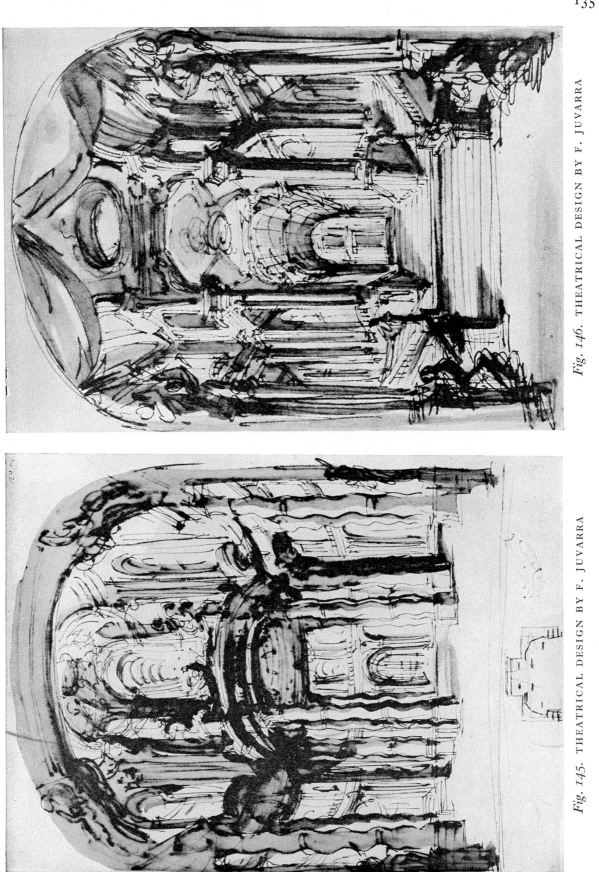

Fig. 146. THEATRICAL DESIGN BY F. JUVARRA

Fig. 145. THEATRICAL DESIGN BY F. JUVARRA

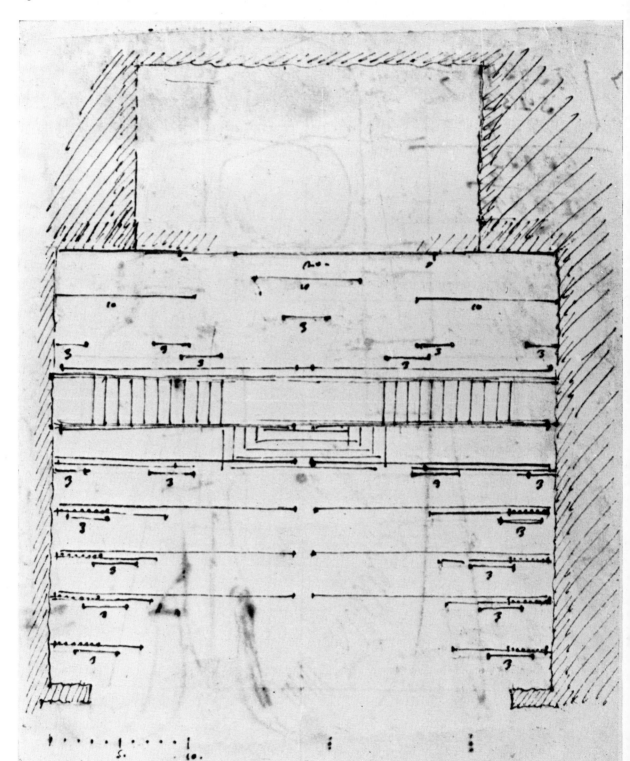

Fig. 146a SCENE PLAN BY F. JUVARRA, ABOUT 1710

Fig. 147. THEATRICAL DESIGN BY F. DA BIBIENA

Fig. 148. THEATRICAL DESIGN BY GIUSEPPE DA BIBIENA

Fig. 149. THEATRICAL DESIGN BY GIUSEPPE DA BIBIENA

Before looking at some examples of the work of the Bibienas and their companions, however, it may be profitable first to glance rapidly at the baroque proscenium frames which cannot be divorced from the magnificent settings they embraced and to which were devoted almost as much pains as were applied to the scenes themselves. One by Francesco Guitti (1605–45), planned for a production at Ferrara in 1632 (Fig. 138), illustrates well the care taken in planning these frontispieces, while Figs. 139 and 140 further illustrate how the Italian style was being carried freely abroad. Here something important must be noted. For the most part, the frontispieces designed in the sixteenth century had been merely two-dimensional and rectangular in shape: they were, indeed, just like flat picture-frames enclosing the stage proper. During the baroque period, on the other hand, they more and more tended to become three-dimensional, with decorations and figures in relief. Furthermore, although the rectangular form remained popular, a definite variant attracted many artists—the building up either of a formal arch or of a frame in which the cornice at the top was curved. When we note this development our attention must immediately be caught by still another feature. While many, indeed perhaps most, were simple openings masking the sides and top of the stage, with their main pillars set at each side of the stage-front, some at least were so deepened as to become parts of a façade leading the eyes of the spectators back to the scenes themselves. If, for example, we look at the plans of the Teatro alla Scala (Fig. 197) and the Turin royal theatre (Fig. 196), we see clearly what might be called the simple proscenium frame, whereas, if we turn to the plans of the Teatro Farnese at Parma (Fig. 186) and the Fano theatre

Fig. 150. THEATRICAL DESIGN BY GIUSEPPE DA BIBIENA

Fig. 151. THEATRICAL DESIGN BY GIUSEPPE DA BIBIENA

(Fig. 192), the recessed variety becomes immediately apparent. What the latter looked like in reality is shown in Fig. 187, revealing the interior of the Teatro Farnese, and in Fig. 141, depicting the interior of the Imperial Theatre at Vienna during the course of a performance.

Already it has been suggested that the original concept and the later development of the proscenium frame seems likely to have come from many sources; and certainly, in considering these baroque designs, we cannot escape the feeling that the recessed arch must have been largely conditioned by the classical example of such theatres as the Olimpico. This feeling, moreover, is strengthened when we encounter the further variant introduced into the plan for the Imola theatre (Fig. 198), where, although two pillars appear in front, the arch-façade has been carried round semicircularly and supported by two other pillars in the middle of the stage, thus actually providing not just one complete arch but three arches. Through the centre opening appears the chief scene, but flats and backcloths are placed also behind the other two, so that even the spectators at the sides of the house might have something wherewith to feast their eyes. What we encounter here is simply a further elaboration of the doorways of the Teatro Olimpico, with diverse settings instead of streets.

In approaching these baroque settings themselves, a useful guide comes forward in the person of Filippo Juvarra (1676–1736), an artist who was active theatrically both in Turin and Rome. The value of his sketches rests in the fact that many of them suggest or indicate the methods by which the grandiose columned courtyards and entries were realized on the stage (Figs. 142–146a). In the first of these Juvarra seems to have been thinking in terms of a kind of permanent set, with a great and noble archway opening up to a series of vistas, varying from a landscape to a perspective corridor. In others the

Fig. 152. DESIGN FOR A PROSCENIUM FRAME BY F. DA BIBIENA

Fig. 153. THEATRICAL DESIGN BY A MEMBER OF THE BIBIENA FAMILY

142

Fig. 154. THEATRICAL DESIGN BY A MEMBER OF THE BIBIENA FAMILY

arrangement of wings and free-standing frames is excellently delineated, while more than one offers a hint that parts of the settings may have been conceived in three-dimensional terms (Fig. 146*a*).

From these sketches by Juvarra we may be the better prepared to view and interpret the rich designs made by various members of the Bibiena family (Figs. 147–156), as well as by

Fig. 155. THEATRICAL DESIGN BY F. DA BIBIENA

Fig. 156. DESIGN BY FERDINANDO AND FRANCESCO BIBIENA FOR "L'IDEA DI TUTTE LE PERFEZIONI," PARMA, 1690

Fig. 157. SETTING BY DOMENICO MAURO, 1700

Fig. 158. "THEATRICAL" DESIGN BY G. B. PIRANESI

Fig. 159. "THEATRICAL" DESIGN BY G. B. PIRANESI

others among their immediate contemporaries and successors. The Bibienas may have been more productive, more bold and more famous than the majority of their companions, yet other families of scenographers came close to rivalling them. Thus, for example, the characteristic

Fig. 160. "THEATRICAL" DESIGN BY G. B. PIRANESI

style created by two gifted brothers, Bernardino (1707–94) and Fabrizio Galliari (1709–90), was carried on by the latter's sons, Giovanni (1746–1818) and Giuseppino (1752–1817), into the nineteenth century. Even further extended was the range of the family of the Mauro, the many members of which contributed largely to playhouses both in their native Italy and in countries abroad: here, spanning a clear century and a half, the line stretches out from an artist Gaspare Mauro (d. *c.* 1719) to an artist great-grandson Antonio (d. *c.* 1807). Gaspare had two brothers, Domenico (d. 1707), a scenic designer, and Pietro (d. 1697), a theatrical machinist. His two sons, Giuseppe (d. *c.* 1722) and Antonio (d. 1736), pursued the family craft, as did the four sons of Domenico—Gerolamo (d. 1719), Antonio (d. 1733), Alessandro (d. 1748) and Romualdo (d. 1756). Of these the third, Antonio, gained particular fame in Dresden, building the new opera-house in that city. These activities were continued, partly by one of Gerolamo's sons, likewise named Gerolamo (d. *c.* 1788), and, more importantly, by Alessandro's sons—still a third Gerolamo (1725–66) and a Domenico (d. *c.* 1780); while the last-mentioned was the father of that Antonio who died in 1807. Hardly any family record could more effectively demonstrate the long-enduring traditions so typical of Italian theatrical artistry during those years.

In considering such traditions we must also take into account two further things which contributed to the spread and development of the baroque scenic style. Gianbattista Piranesi (1720–78), for example, was an artist who did not particularly apply himself to the theatre, yet his magnificent designs of dark prisons and sunlit courtyards were paradoxically both inspired by contemporary stage settings and themselves the source of inspiration for others. We can see how a Pietro Gonzaga (1751–1831) carried memories of their bold light and shade to Imperial Russia, and how a Jan Bogumił Plersch (d. 1732), another of Piranesi's admirers, gave to his native Poland a characteristically local modification of the Italian mode.

3. *Theatres of the Baroque Age*

The early sixteenth-century artists who built their perspective city-squares obviously could without difficulty carry on their activities without permanent theatres of their own. Their sets, exceedingly shallow, were easily constructed within the bounds of a ducal hall and might as easily be dismantled. When, however, the baroque style had been developed, equally clearly the theatre magicians required to have buildings exclusively devoted to the production of operas and similar dramatic works. Furthermore, as has been seen, it was absolutely essential that these buildings should have very large and particularly very deep stages, with plenty of space above and ample room beneath. Hence the baroque age was one of active theatre planning and construction, with the consequent establishment of a basic pattern which with minor variations became universally accepted.

At the beginning, of course, certain deviations may be found, and even a few deviations may still be traced as we move into the later years, and perhaps it will be best to deal with these variants first. In England, for instance, the open-air Globe playhouse continued in regular use up to the closing of the theatres in 1642, and even although the indoor "private" house became more fashionable between 1600 and the end of the period, it seems to have followed, in general, the type of stage procedure familiar in the public theatres. A play which suited the Globe suited the Blackfriars as well. It is true that during the first half of the seventeenth

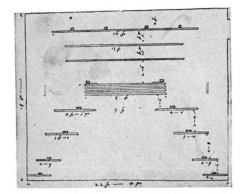

Fig. 161. PLAN OF THE RUTLAND HOUSE STAGE FOR "THE SIEGE OF RHODES," 1656, BY JOHN WEBB

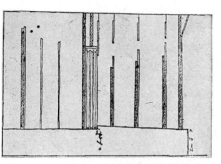

Fig. 162. SECTION OF THE RUTLAND HOUSE STAGE FOR "THE SIEGE OF RHODES," 1656, BY JOHN WEBB

century there are a few records of the utilization of scenery for the delight of the public, but not only do all of these come just before the closing of the theatres, they are also concerned with special occasions. In 1637, for example, the fact that Sir John Suckling's *Aglaura* "had some scenes to it, which in these days were only used at masques" called for contemporary comment, and all the other evidence relating to such practice before 1640 demonstrably points to something out of the ordinary. It may be said, therefore, that before 1642 the Italian-type perspective settings were known only in Court or similar special productions—mostly masques, although in the later years some plays also were decorated by Inigo Jones when given before royalty.

Fig. 163. FRONTISPIECE AND PERMANENT SIDE-WINGS FOR "THE SIEGE OF RHODES," 1656, BY JOHN WEBB

When acting started again, the tastes of the new audience, now largely composed of courtiers, led towards the installation of the scenic stage, yet even in these Restoration years, even, indeed, on to the beginning of the nine-

teenth century, the English theatres veered somewhat from the
norm current elsewhere. For an
understanding of the particular
peculiarity of the public theatres
erected after 1660 it is necessary,
first, to glance at a performance
which actually preceded the Restoration. Already in 1656, the en-
terprising Sir William D'Avenant
somehow succeeded in securing
permission for the performance of
an "entertainment," *The Siege of
Rhodes*, in the hall of Rutland
House, and for this John Webb,
the pupil of Inigo Jones, was commissioned to prepare some primi-

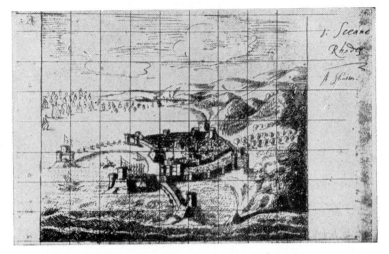

Fig. 164. DESIGN BY JOHN WEBB FOR THE SHUTTER AND
BACKCLOTH IN "THE SIEGE OF RHODES," 1656

tive scenery (Figs. 161–165). His plans show a tiny stage, with a fixed painted proscenium frame
and two sets of rocky side-wings, which were allowed to stand throughout the play. Beyond is
a set of back-shutters which could be drawn to indicate changes of scene. In effect, Webb was
here carrying on, in a very simple way, the style introduced by his master in *Salmacida Spolia*;
and, since *The Siege of Rhodes* was really an opera, and since Webb's designs, however primitive,
were in the Italian tradition, it might seem as though the English theatre, after its lengthy
suppression, was determined to start afresh with a complete break from its Elizabethan past.

This impression seems to be strengthened when we look at another, and equally interesting,
set of designs sketched by Webb nine years later (1665) for a Whitehall performance of
Mustapha, a drama written by the Earl of Orrery. The plan (Fig. 166) shows the "plane of the
sceanes." In front is a flat frontispiece, with a proscenium opening 25 feet wide. Behind
this are set the side-wings, four in all, and, as the section (Fig. 167) indicates, they run in

grooves: the smallest is 3 feet 6
inches wide, the rest, respectively,
5 feet 3 inches and 6 feet 6 inches.
Each pair is separated from those
behind by a distance of about 3
feet, and between the farthest pair
is a space of some 13 feet. All of
these wings are set on a heavily
raked platform, but beyond them
the stage floor is level. A special
feature of the design is that the
"Musick" was placed on a sloping
platform the fore part of which
rested on supports just behind the
last pair of wings and the back part
was attached to the wall beyond.
This orchestra was concealed by a
long sky-cloth, and the audience
must have looked underneath the

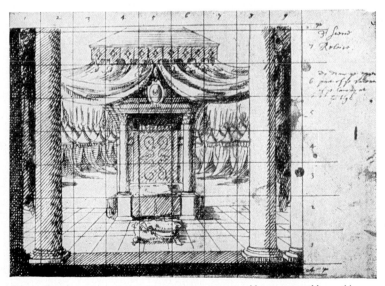

Fig. 165. DESIGN BY JOHN WEBB FOR A "RELEIVE" IN "THE
SIEGE OF RHODES," 1656

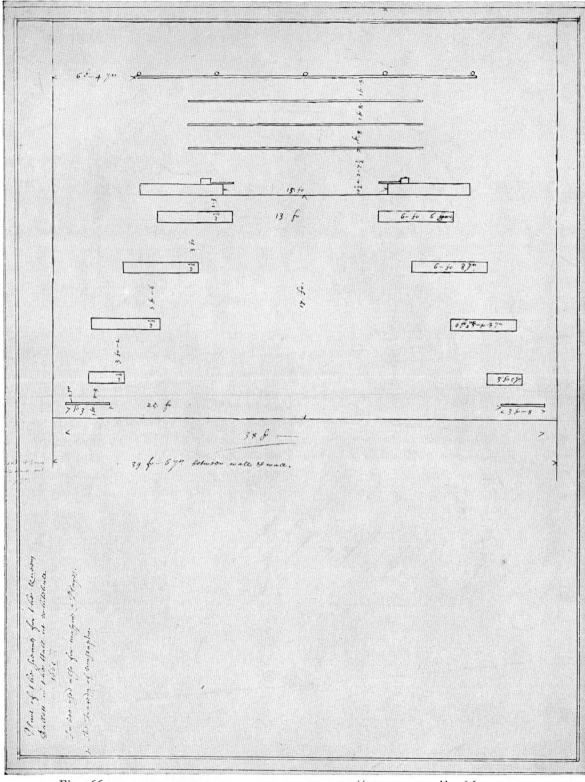

Fig. 166. PLAN OF THE WHITEHALL STAGE FOR "MUSTAPHA," 1665, BY JOHN
WEBB

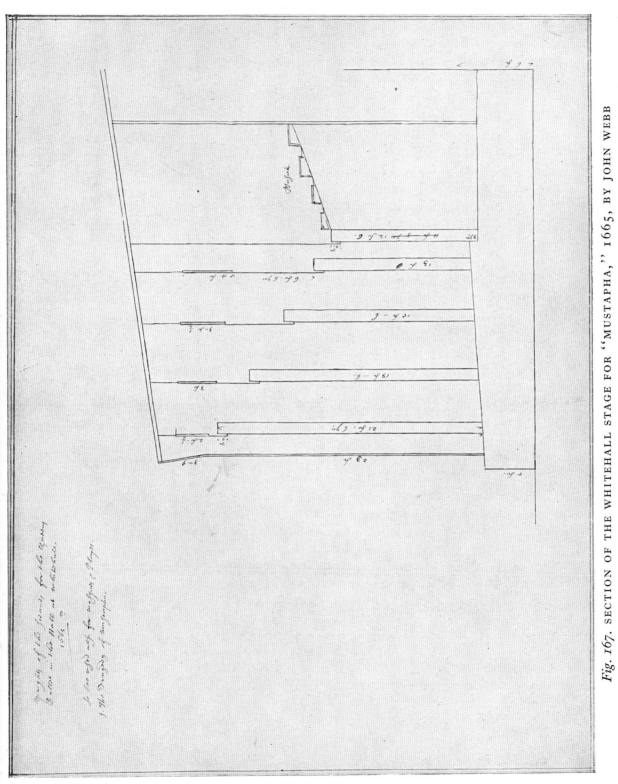

Fig. 167. SECTION OF THE WHITEHALL STAGE FOR "MUSTAPHA," 1665, BY JOHN WEBB

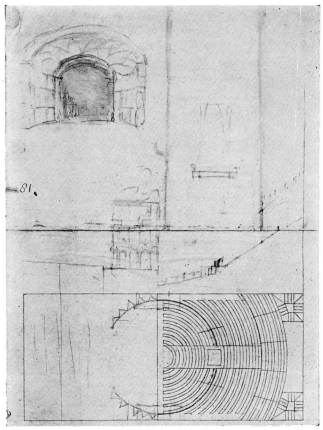

Fig. 168. THEATRE PLAN BY SIR CHRISTOPHER WREN

improvised gallery at the back-shutters shown in "releive."

Here again, therefore, except for the somewhat strange platform made for the musicians, we have a setting thoroughly in the Italian style. It must, however, be remembered that Webb's designs were both executed for private productions: *The Siege of Rhodes* was shown in a London mansion, *Mustapha* was being given a Court performance. Their close following of Italian practice is thus explainable by their direct association with the masque tradition set in earlier days by Inigo Jones. For what was happening in the realm of the public theatres we have to turn to some other designs by the great architect, Sir Christopher Wren. Of these two are of particular significance. The first (Fig. 168) shows a plan, a rough cross-section and a fragmentary elevation of a playhouse in which the auditorium seating is arranged in segments of circles struck from a centre almost in the middle of the long, narrow rectangular house. The segment which marks the seventh row of seats makes a complete semicircle as it approaches the side-walls and the line is carried on until it is cut at two-thirds of the radius by a straight line, which marks the position of the proscenium arch. The interesting point here is that the space from this arch up to the front seats provides a wide platform with entrance-doors and possibly stage boxes at its sides. This apron has a level flooring, but immediately behind the proscenium arch the stage is slightly raked. Still more important is the second design (Fig. 169), the cross-section of a playhouse which is almost certainly the Theatre Royal in Drury Lane, built in 1674. Here the whole stage floor is gently raked, with a platform some 17 feet deep and a portion behind the proscenium arch of 15 feet. In the rear portion provision is made for four sets of side-wings, with shutters beyond. Over the platform on each side are two boxes, beneath which are two doors. The pit slopes upward and there is provision for two tiers of boxes, four on each side being enclosed, the rest merely broken by dividing pillars. A top gallery faces the stage, although it is not carried round the sides of the house.

While unfortunately we possess no full contemporary picture of the interior of this theatre, a print illustrating an opera, *Ariane* (1674), gives some idea of what the proscenium looked like and also offers an interesting example of the freedom taken by many engravers of the period in dealing with their subject matter (Fig. 170). Although the proscenium frame seems to have been delineated here with fair exactitude, the platform is shown in severe foreshortening, by no means suggesting the depth which it actually had; and no side entrance-doors have been indicated. Furthermore, the set has been depicted as though it consisted of two lines of buildings painted upon frames joined together and running back diagonally to a back-shutter. In order to translate such an engraving into what really was seen on the stage we must expand the foreshortened apron in accordance with Wren's cross-section, and we must also see the

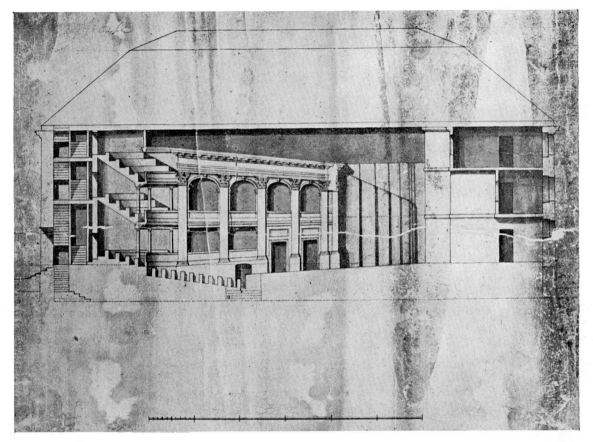

Fig. 169. SECTION OF A THEATRE, PROBABLY DRURY LANE, BY SIR CHRISTOPHER WREN

setting as composed of side-wings set parallel to the line of the proscenium: perhaps the kind of thing that audiences saw has been more clearly indicated in a somewhat primitive engraving of a German performance about the year 1655 (Fig. 171) wherein the appearance of the flats and the cloud-borders has been faithfully reproduced.

For the other important new English theatre built in the late seventeenth century, the Duke's Theatre in Dorset Garden (1671), we have a valuable set of engravings issued in 1673 to illustrate Elkanah Settle's *The Empress of Morocco* (Figs. 172–173). Once more, we may be reasonably sure that the delineation of the proscenium arch is close to the reality —a frame decorated with a formal pattern, and at the top a half-roof which presumably is a relic of the "heavens" in Elizabethan play-houses. Above this, two figures, evidently representing Thalia and Melpomene, stand on each side of a curtained window with leaded sashes opening inward. Similar windows appear in the curves to the right and left of the emblematic statues. On the ledges underneath these two side-windows

Fig. 170. FRONTISPIECE TO "ARIANE," DRURY LANE, 1674

are pictured a drum, a trumpet, and a violin, whence we may conclude that these were the windows of the music-room. The engraving cuts off all but a few feet of the apron, but enough is left to show the edge of the stage boxes and the beginnings of the proscenium doors. Within this frame the illustrator has placed five of the scenes, all to be interpreted in the manner suggested for the interpretation of the *Ariane* design.

Fig 171. A GERMAN SETTING, 1655

To be compared with the frontispiece to *Ariane* (Fig. 170). Here the side-wings are clearly shown, and note should be taken of the candelabra over the stage-front.

These plans and engravings reveal quite clearly the chief peculiarity of the late seventeenth-century English stages—the presence of a deep platform in front of the proscenium arch. It is true that occasionally theatres elsewhere had something of the kind, a narrow fore-stage which extends outward towards the audience. Typical examples are shown in the cross-section of the opera house at Versailles, with its deep proscenium frame (Fig. 175), and in the view of the Hôtel de Bourgogne (Fig. 176). So common, indeed, was its use that Francesco Algarotti, writing his *Saggio sopra l'opera in musica* (1762), devoted some considerable space to arguing for its abolition, since, in his opinion, it destroyed visual illusion by removing the actor too far from the setting. Nevertheless, this European *avant-scène* must in no wise be confused with the Restoration English platform; whereas the former had but little depth, the latter extended far into the auditorium; and on the continent of Europe, except in Holland, there are no signs of the proscenium doors so characteristic of the English model.

Without doubt, this English model derived from the old platform of the Elizabethan public playhouses, and its native power can be gauged by the length of time it took to disappear. About 1696, according to Colley Cibber, the manager of Drury Lane first tried to nibble away a part of the fore-stage. "It must be observ'd," he says, that up to this date

the Area or Platform of the old Stage projected about four Foot forwarder, in a Semi-oval figure, parallel to the Benches of the Pit; and that the former lower Doors of Entrance for the Actors were brought down between the two foremost (and then only) Pilasters, in the place of which Doors now [i.e., in 1740] the two Stage Boxes are fixt. That where the Doors of Entrance now are, there formerly stood two additional Side-Wings, in front to a full Set of Scenes, which had then almost a double Effect in their Loftiness and Magnificence.

By this Original form the usual Station of the Actors, in almost every Scene, was advanc'd at least ten Foot nearer the Audience than they now can be, because, not only from the Stage's being shorten'd

Fig. 172. THREE SETTINGS IN "THE EMPRESS OF MOROCCO," DORSET GARDEN THEATRE, 1673

in front, but likewise from the additional Interposition of those Stage Boxes, the Actors (in respect to the Spectators that filled them) are kept so much more backward from the main audience than they us'd to be.

"When the Actors were in possession of that forwarder Space to advance upon," Colley Cibber continues, "the Voice was then more in the Centre of the House, so that the most distant Ear had scarce the least Doubt or Difficulty in hearing what fell from the weakest Utterance."

Fig. 173. TWO SETTINGS IN "THE EMPRESS OF MOROCCO,"
DORSET GARDEN THEATRE, 1673

We may easily see what happened. The manager wanted more space for spectators, so he cut off part of the platform (thus allowing a greater area for the pit) and he made the lower doors at the side into stage boxes. The significant thing, however, is that the force of tradition was such that he was compelled to sacrifice part of the scene space for the placing of two doors immediately behind the proscenium arch. A further fact worthy of comment is the obvious dissatisfaction of the players at being removed from the "Centre of the House": they had inherited from their Elizabethan forerunners a love of close contact with the audience.

As years went by, the new upper pair of doors tended to vanish, but the lower doors, with or without stage boxes at their sides, remained standard: they were incorporated into the still-existing Theatre Royal at Bristol (1766); they are to be seen in the Royalty Theatre in 1787

Fig. 174. MODEL OF DORSET GARDEN THEATRE,
BY HERBERT NORRIS

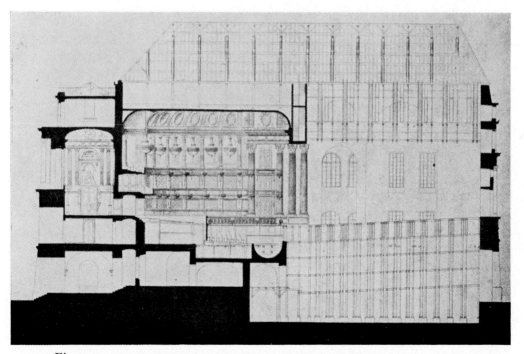

Fig 175. CROSS-SECTION OF OPERA HOUSE AT VERSAILLES, 1753

Fig. 176. THE HÔTEL DE BOURGOGNE, *c.* 1765

(Fig. 177) and in the Haymarket twenty years later (Fig. 178). By the end of the century, how-ever, their days were becoming numbered, and soon the last poor remnants of the old platform were to disappear. In 1843 a Haymarket advertisement informs us that,

during the recess, the theatre has undergone Extensive Alterations, the Proscenium has been entirely remodelled, and the whole of the Interior decorated in the most Costly and Elegant Style. By a cur-tailment of the useless portion of the Stage in front of the Curtain, and advancing Orchestra and Lights near the Actors and Scenic Effects, the Lessee has been enabled to appropriate the portion so obtained, to form a certain number of Orchestra Stalls, which can be retained for the parties taking them the whole of the Evening.

Fig. 177. THE ROYALTY THEATRE, LONDON, 1787

Thus a native Elizabethan tradition, which had withstood the pressure of the European baroque stage throughout the whole of the eighteenth century, finally departed during the Victorian era.

It is, therefore, necessary to regard the English theatre form as a national aberration from the Italian baroque model, and at the same time to recognize that its presence imposed its own conventions upon the actors. Normally the players went on and off the stage, not through the wings, but by the doorways; and sometimes these doorways had to be interpreted imagina-tively by the spectators as indicating particular localities—once more a relic of Elizabethan practice. Behind the pro-scenium arch there were the painted settings, but, in spite of some special spectacular productions, these must commonly have been indicative and general rather than speci-fically and naturalistically particular. Here conven-tionalism ruled. For trage-dy there was a Grove, a Palace, a Temple; for com-edy a Room, a Hall, a Garden, a city Park or Square. Such stock scenes no doubt appeared in play after play. Through the

Fig. 178. CROSS-SECTION OF THE HAYMARKET THEATRE, LONDON, 1807

Fig. 179. THE FITZGIGGO RIOT AT COVENT GARDEN
THEATRE, 1763

combination of platform and pro-scenium-arch stage, moreover, a peculiar procedure appears to have been common. In numerous plays we find actors, standing on the forward area, bidden to move back "within the scene"—that is to say, behind the proscenium arch. Then two things happen. Shutters click together, hiding the players who have thus stepped to the rear, and other actors come onto the platform through the doorways. Thus, the forward area itself, which might almost be regarded as though it were an ancient *platea*, in a flash changes its fictional locality.

Fig. 180. STAGE OF THE SCHOUWBURG, AMSTERDAM, 1638

Much the same retention of older native traditions may be observed in the growth of the Spanish theatre during the same period, although there the gradual introduction of scenery was slower even than in England. One other country, too, exhibited an interesting theatre plan all its own. In 1638 Jacob van Campen designed and built a Schouwburg at Amsterdam in a style which can be paralleled nowhere else (Figs. 180–181). The auditorium, in the shape of an ellipse, had two tiers of boxes, and the other half of the ellipse was, as it were, carried on in a kind of variegated stage façade with open balconies over the two sides. This façade itself consisted mainly of pillars, with cornices above them, and within the open spaces flat painted panels could be set. The panels, however, were not intended to give the appearance of any unified setting; rather, they represented diverse localities, and thus their conception is seen to derive from the medieval simultaneous stage.

Nothing quite like the Dutch plan exists elsewhere: obviously some of its features remind us of the Teatro Olimpico; others recall the contemporary English playhouses; others clearly stem from earlier Dutch theatrical performances by the so-called "Chambers of Rhetoric"; and others have direct connexion with the methods employed at the French Hôtel de Bourgogne.

Apparently this interesting combination of various different elements was not copied in other Dutch theatrical buildings, so that the Schouwburg of 1638 remains unique: when a new Schouwburg was built in the third quarter of the eighteenth century the old structure was entirely remodelled in the familiar Italian baroque style (Fig. 182).

Fig. 181. THE AUDITORIUM OF THE SCHOUWBURG, AMSTERDAM, 1638

Fig. 182. THE NEW THEATRE IN AMSTERDAM, *c.* 1774

Finally, before turning to consider the prevailing movement in the establishment of this Italian-type baroque theatre, one other thing may be noted. From the time when, between 1588 and 1590, Vincenzo Scamozzi planned and built the theatre at Sabbioneta, we may trace in several countries the erection of a series of small private royal or ducal playhouses which in many respects retained features borrowed from the experiments in the reconstruction of Roman playhouses such as find their prime expression in the Teatro Olimpico. In these private

Fig. 183. AUDITORIUM OF THE PRIVATE THEATRE AT KRUMLOV CASTLE, CZECHOSLOVAKIA

Fig. 183a. STAGE OF THE PRIVATE THEATRE AT KRUMLOV CASTLE, CZECHOSLOVAKIA

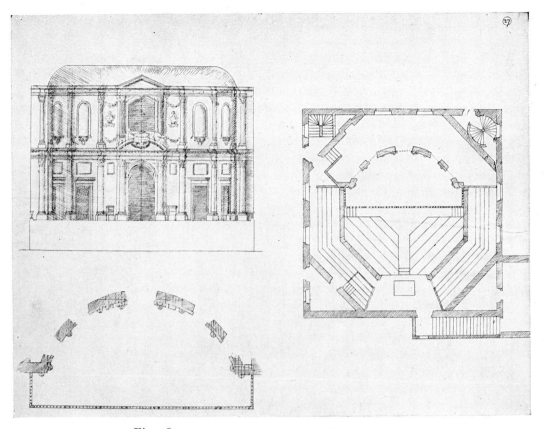

Fig. 184. PLAN FOR THE COCKPIT-IN-COURT

theatres, precisely because their privileged audiences were extremely small, the auditorium could often be of a very simple semicircular shape, generally backed by a colonnaded corridor runnning round the house, and the stage itself could be meagre in size. As at Sabbioneta, frequently the proscenium arch and the walls were decorated with *trompe d'œuil* frescoes, showing galleries or boxes with painted figures conversing, looking down or leaning over— artists' tricks to catch the eyes of nobility and royalty. The line which leads from Sabbioneta onward to the little theatre in the Łazienki park at Warsaw, the theatre in Krumlov Castle (Fig. 183), the theatre in the Swedish Gripsholm Castle, and that in Russia's Hermitage is clear. With these may be associated two interesting designs executed by Inigo Jones or by his assistant John Webb (Figs. 184–185). The first sketch no doubt shows the Cockpit-in-Court, although whether the original building as it existed in 1632 or as it was later reconstructed is not sure. The ground-plan of the small house, almost square, has the seating arranged in a manner reminiscent of the more common semicircular style, while the stage-area, 35 feet wide by 16 deep, has its forward part enclosed by a curving architectural façade pierced by five doors—a patent modifica-tion of the *scaenae frons* in the Teatro Olimpico. The second drawing is of a rectangular theatre in which the seating is set in concentric curves, while the stage, 43 feet wide, has a façade in which the central doorway has been mightily enlarged so that it becomes in effect a proscenium arch revealing a perspective set behind, built up by means of Serlian angled wings. It may further be observed that in this design Jones has backed the auditorium by columns reminiscent of those placed by Scamozzi in his Sabbioneta playhouse.

The existence of these structures, some inspired by native traditions in the countries of their origins and some following the earlier Italian academic form, must be carefully borne in mind as we look at the growth of the baroque stage during the seventeenth and eighteenth centuries; but obviously that which was most characteristic of the age and that which laid the foundation for the nineteenth-century playhouse was the series of large edifices built in Italian style for the exhibition of operatic and similar spectacles before larger audiences.

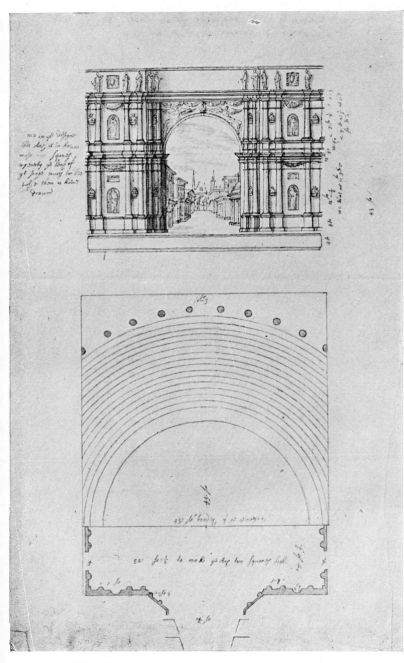

Fig. 185. THEATRE PLAN BY INIGO JONES

The story may start with the famous Teatro Farnese at Parma, constructed by Giovan Battista Aleotti (1546 –1636) in 1618 and formally opened some ten years later (Figs. 186–187a), a building peculiarly interesting because of its transitional form. Fundamentally, it displays within itself a fresh treatment of several largely distinct traditions: here there is something of the style which led towards the Teatro Olimpico; here are suggestions taken from earlier academic theatres; here are features taken from the old tourney-halls; and at the same time here are elements which make the Teatro Farnese stand at the head of a long line of baroque playhouses. The building itself, once part of the palace, is a rectangle much longer than it is wide. For the spectators there are rows of benches, surmounted by two rows of arches, topped by a small gallery with statues. At the furthest end of the hall, these benches are set semicircularly, but they are then continued at right angles to the diameter of the semicircle until they meet the front portion of the decoration associated with the stage. The stage itself is framed by a very wide, deep

166

Fig. 187. THE TEATRO FARNESE, PARMA

Fig. 186. PLAN OF THE
TEATRO FARNESE,
PARMA

Fig. 187a. THE TEATRO FARNESE, PARMA

proscenium, formed by an architectural *scaenae frons* with a large square opening. Behind this opening extends a deep stage-area with two half-walls in the middle almost separating it into two parts: in the forward portion there is provision for three sets of side-wings and a back-shutter, and the rear portion has space for four sets of wings on each side or for sets of shutters. What we have in the Teatro Farnese, therefore, is a combination of diverse elements fashioned so that the structure could be used both for play productions and for aristocratic tourneys; in this sense it must be regarded as transitional. But the fact that it was designed as a permanent building, conceived as a single architectural whole, for a deep baroque stage, allied to the other fact that its auditorium assumed a new form in the shape of an elongated U, makes it the ancestor of scores of playhouses immediately to follow.

The deep stage, suited for long perspective vistas and spectacular scenic changes, is clearly the first characteristic feature of the baroque playhouse, and its second feature depends upon that. A hall with a shallow stage at one end presents no difficult seating problems in the auditorium, especially when the spectators, generally limited in numbers, belong to a single social group, the prince, his guests, and courtiers. But the deepened stage almost inevitably means an enlarged auditorium, and it demands careful planning if most of the spectators, at least, are to be placed in positions where they can see something of the stage effects; moreover, since the performances put upon this stage are mostly operatic in character, these spectators have to be considered as auditors, so that good acoustics and good sight-lines become equally important. And the whole architectural problem grows more complicated when the theatres

Fig. 188. THE TEATRO S. SAMUELE, VENICE, 1656

The setting, by Antonio Codognato, was made for Carlo Goldoni's *Il mondo alla roversa* in 1753.

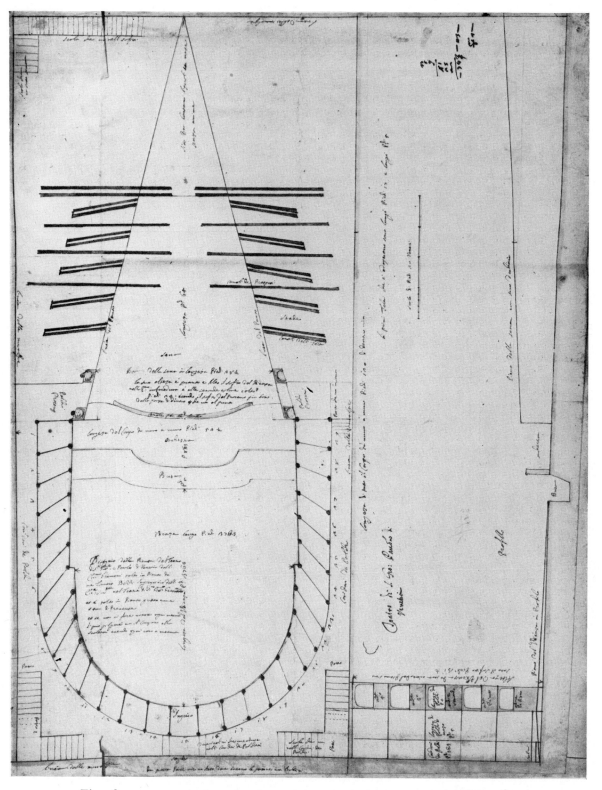

Fig. 189. PLAN OF THE TEATRO SS. GIOVANNI E PAOLO, VENICE, 1639

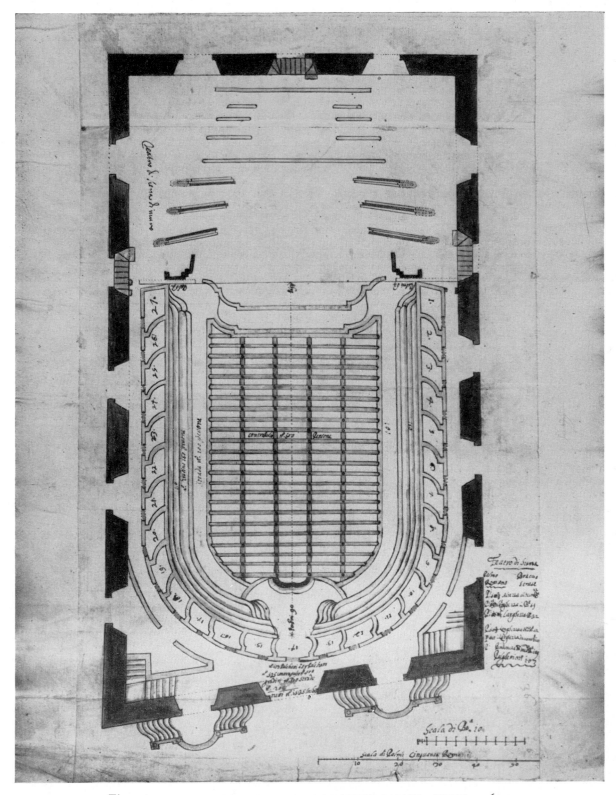

Fig. 190. PLAN OF THE TEATRO DEGLI INTRONATI, SIENA, 1670

begin to admit larger publics, consisting of different social strata: the princely audience could be conceived in very simple terms, whereas in these playhouses the spectators have to be offered seating accommodation which separates one class from another, and for the higher classes such comforts have to be provided as may allow them to visit the playhouses without coming into contact with others of lower rank.

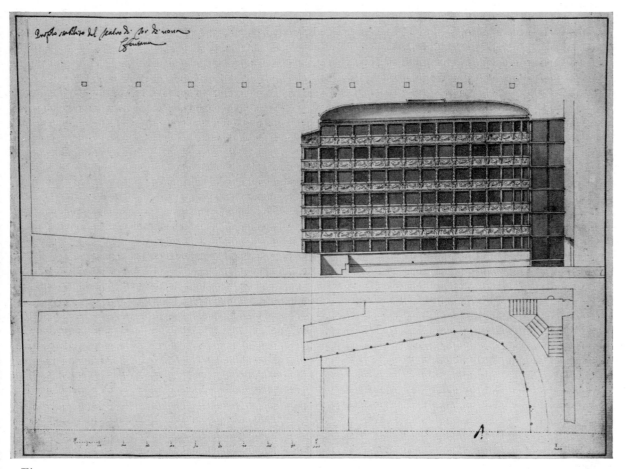

Fig. 191. PLAN OF THE TEATRO TOR DI NONA, ROME, DESIGNED BY CARLO FONTANA ABOUT 1660

With these problems in mind, we may quite easily travel on our way from the first half of the seventeenth century onward, observing two contrary impulses—on the one hand, a steady baroque tradition which gives these theatres a form immediately recognizable, and, on the other hand, a continual experimentation which offers distinctive special form to each. So the passage can be made from the early theatres of the century, such as the Venetian SS. Giovanni e Paolo (1638–39: Fig. 189), through the S. Samuele (1656: Fig. 188), also at Venice, the Teatro Falcone (named after its architect) at Genoa, erected shortly after 1650 and reconstructed by Carlo Fontana in 1703, the Teatro degli Intronati at Siena (1670: Fig. 190), the Tor di Nona in Rome, as designed by Carlo Fontana in 1660 (Fig. 191), the Teatro della Fortuna at Fano, built by Giacomo Torelli in 1677 (Fig. 192), the Argentina in Rome, built by G. Teodoli in 1732 (Fig. 193), the San Carlo at Naples, designed by G. A. Medrano and Angelo Carasale in 1737 and rebuilt by Antonio Niccolini in 1817 (Figs. 194–195), the

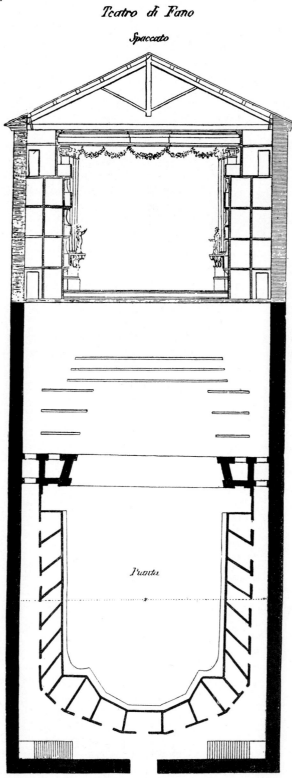

Teatro di Fano

Spaccato

Pianta

Fig. 192. PLAN AND PROSCENIUM OF THE
TEATRO DELLA FORTUNA, FANO, DESIGNED
BY GIACOMO TORELLI, 1677

Theatre Royal at Turin, built by B. Alfieri
in 1738 (Fig. 196), on to the project for the
Imola theatre by Cosimo Morelli (1779:
Fig. 198), the famous Scala of Milan,
designed by G. Piermarini in 1778 (Fig.
197), and the Venetian Fenice, designed by
A. Selva in 1792 (Fig. 199).

The list of Italian theatres might be
multiplied many times over; and in addition
to these there were scores of playhouses
contributed by other countries. By 1668
Vienna had its opera-house (see Fig. 141)
and Munich its Salvatorplatz (Fig. 139):
these were followed by similar structures
in almost every court and cultural centre—
such as Dresden (1718), Berlin (1742),
and elsewhere. In France, the Grand
Théâtre at Lyon was opened in 1756; in
Sweden, C. F. Adelcrantz built the
Drottningholm theatre in 1766 and the
Stockholm Kungliga Operan shortly after
(1782). Prague had its theatre in 1783;
at Warsaw in 1748 the opera-house had
what seems to have been the first round-
horizon in Europe.

Even in England, where, as we have
seen, a native tradition gave to eighteenth-
century playhouses several features which
rendered them distinct, the same general style was obviously at work (Figs.
201–204).

4. The Theatre Plan

Already, the deepened stage in these
buildings has been discussed; now we must
turn to the auditorium and its relation to
the acting-area (although the term scenic-
area might better express what dominated
the minds of the architects). Here, perhaps,
a start may be made with a brief consideration of a plan and cross-section of a
kind of ideal but simple baroque playhouse
designed by Andrea Pozzo and published in
1693 (Fig. 205). The stage itself is fairly
elaborate, offering space for two sets of six

Fig. 192a. DESIGN BY GIUSEPPE MITELLI FOR A DUCAL THEATRE AT MANTUA, 1674

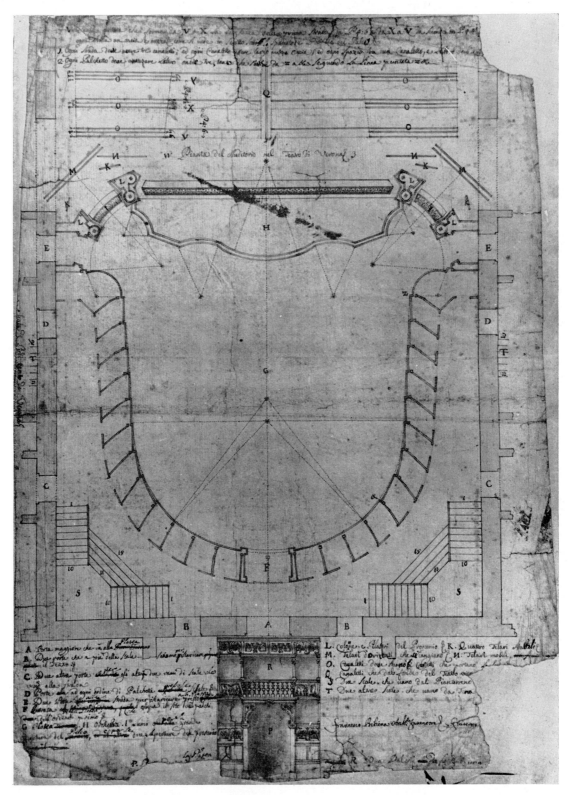

Fig. 192b. PLAN OF THE TEATRO FILARMONICO, VERONA, DESIGNED BY FRANCESCO DA BIBIENA, 1720

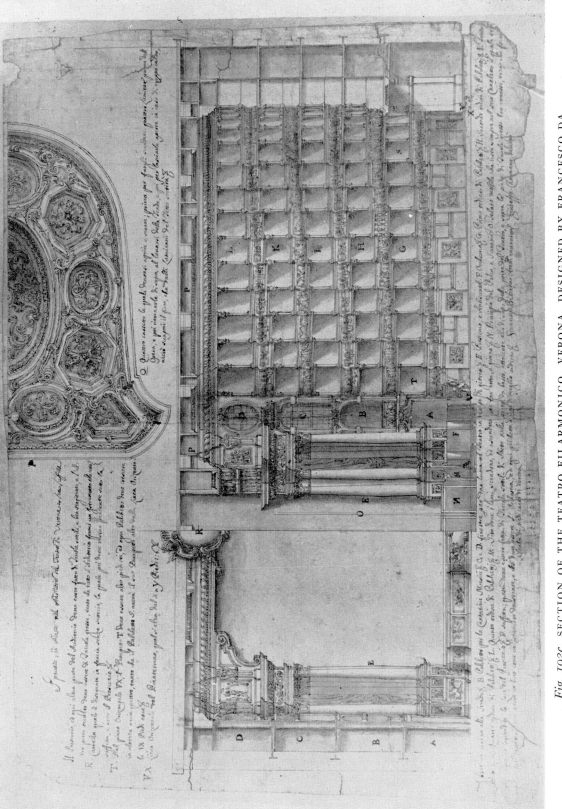

Fig. *192c.* SECTION OF THE TEATRO FILARMONICO, VERONA, DESIGNED BY FRANCESCO DA
BIBIENA, 1720

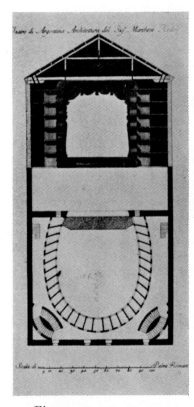

Fig. 193. PLAN OF THE
TEATRO ARGENTINA, ROME,
DESIGNED BY GIROLAMO
TEODOLI, 1732

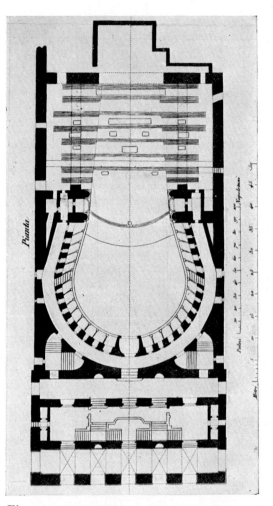

Fig. 194. PLAN OF THE TEATRO S. CARLO,
NAPLES, DESIGNED BY G. A. MEDRANO
AND ANGELO CARASALE, 1737

Fig. 195. THE TEATRO S. CARLO, NAPLES, AS RECONSTRUCTED BY ANTONIO
NICCOLINI, 1817

side-wings placed obliquely to the stage-front and decreasing in height as they reach the rear; farther back are two sets of shutters, with a space behind for still more perspective effects. This is perfectly normal. The auditorium, however, reveals something different from anything that may be met with up to and sometimes even beyond the building of the Teatro Farnese: instead of graduated tiers of benches, instead of open balconies, there are five galleries divided up into boxes by pillars and arches.

Now boxes in themselves were no new things. The "gentlemen's rooms" in the Elizabethan theatres formed separate compartments of such a kind, and in Italy we hear of galleries with at least some boxes as early as 1608. What, however, is both new and thoroughly characteristic of the baroque theatre design is the breaking up of all the galleries into separate compartments, so that the auditorium assumes what has aptly been called a "bee-hive" appearance. Because they served to give spectators the comfort and privacy they sought for, these serried ranks of boxes soon became standard in all Italian playhouses, and their relics are still to be seen among us to-day, not only in opera-houses but in ordinary theatres as well. They linger on in many European houses; they have not completely disappeared in several English theatres; and even in New York their shadows are to be discerned in the bird's-nest projections which, although opened up, clearly derive from this baroque tradition.

At the start we may believe that most of these compartments were inconveniently separated from each other by wooden partitions set at right angles to the balcony front; but very soon the

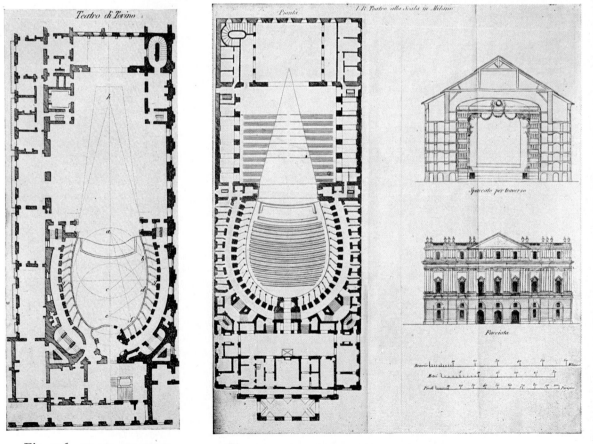

Fig. 196. PLAN OF THE
TEATRO REGIO, TURIN,
DESIGNED BY B. ALFIERI,
1738

Fig. 197. PLAN OF THE TEATRO ALLA SCALA, MILAN,
DESIGNED BY G. PIERMARINI, 1778

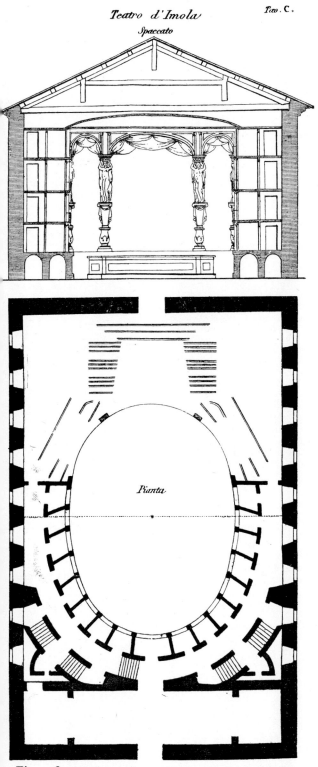

Fig. 198. PLAN AND PROSCENIUM OF THE THEATRE AT IMOLA, DESIGNED BY COSIMO MORELLI, 1779

partitions were angled towards the stage, thus giving the spectators better visibility, and in many houses (notably the new ducal theatre at Mantua (1706), designed by Ferdinando da Bibiena, the Teatro Filarmonico (1729) at Verona, designed by Francesco da Bibiena, and the Teatro Falcone at Genoa) the boxes were made to project slightly in strict order so that necks might not be unduly strained in watching the pirouettes of the dancers or the wonders of the changing scenes.

In spite of its plan based on the galleries of boxes, however, Pozzo's auditorium is shaped in a form rarely to be encountered save in the smallest of baroque playhouses. The semicircular arrangement, ultimately taken from the attempts to reproduce or reconstruct the Roman theatre, was perfectly satisfactory when audiences were restricted in number; except at its extreme edges its sight-lines were reasonably good. But for larger audiences clearly it was quite unsuited, and already in the Teatro Farnese we see the audience-space being deepened to match the deepness of the stage, with the simple semicircle extended until it assumes the form of a U (Fig. 186). The same arrangement was used at Siena (Fig. 190) and at Venice (Fig. 189), while a slight variant, with a modification of the semicircle at the back, appears in the Fortuna theatre at Fano (Fig. 192). It need hardly be said, however, that this shape was by no means one calculated to give good sight-lines, and for the most part it was rarely employed. Much more common was a series of variations on shapes which may be styled as "horseshoes" and "bells." The former, already employed in the Argentina at Rome in 1732 (Fig. 193), has its most famous examples in the Scala at Milan (Fig. 197) and the Fenice in Venice (Fig. 199); the latter may be illustrated by the plan of the San Carlo at Naples (Fig. 194). Still other architects preferred to work on the basis of an ellipse cut at the end by a proscenium arch, in the manner employed at the royal theatre of Turin (Fig. 196). Especially interesting, although somewhat eccentric, is the plan for the theatre at Imola, where, as we have seen, the ovoid is cut lower down its length and,

Fig. 199. THE TEATRO LA FENICE, VENICE, DESIGNED BY A. SELVA, 1792

as it were, carried onto the stage. Instead of an ordinary proscenium, two pillars appear upon the curving line, so that in effect there are three scenic openings: that in the centre has the main scene, but subsidiary side-wings and shutters give the opportunity of introducing two other sets (Fig. 198).

In Italy, for the most part, the theatre planners inclined to lengthen their auditoria, but, somewhat strangely, opposition to this kind of design began to develop in eighteenth-century France, where least it might have been expected. From the latter part of the sixteenth century Parisian theatres had been greatly influenced by the elongated rectangular shape of the indoor tennis-court: the Hôtel de Bourgogne was a narrow and lengthy structure; the hall converted into a theatre at the Petit Bourbon was 108 feet in length and 48 feet wide; the Théâtre du Marais (1634) was, in fact, a remodelled tennis-court; and the same plan can be seen influenc- ing the Palais Cardinal (1641) and, even more, the Salle des Machines (Fig. 206), built by Gaspare Vigarani (1586–1663) in 1662, with its stage 141 feet deep and its long, narrow auditorium. During the eighteenth century, however, two forces came to work in opposition to this style. Many great civic playhouses were commissioned outside of Paris—at Lyon, Caen, Brest, Montpellier, Nancy, Bordeaux, and elsewhere; and at the same time various French architects came to feel a new classically inspired impulse which resulted in their

Fig. 200. A PRODUCTION OF "ARMIDA" AT THE THÉÂTRE RUE ST HONORÉ. PAINTING BY
G. DE SAINT-AUBIN

deviating from the prevailing baroque plans. At Bordeaux, for example, in 1780 Victor Louis (1731–1800) designed an edifice on a circular foundation, with an auditorium 64 feet wide at the diameter and 52 feet from the stage-front to rear wall; the stage was just over 37 feet wide and had a depth of 78 feet. The result of this was that in France men began to think of the possibility of widening instead of lengthening the auditorium; and the fact that they were thus gripped by a fresh idea rapidly led to a vigorous combination of theory and practice. Instead of an emphasis, as in Italy, upon the stage, there was stress upon audience demands for seeing and hearing. The destruction of the Académie Royale de Musique in 1763 brought forth a stream of projects for a new structure to take its place as well as studies such as Chevalier de Chaumont's *Véritable construction d'un théâtre d'opéra à l'usage de France* (1766). The famous *Essai sur l'architecture théâtrale* (1782) by Pierre Patté[1] together with the line of theatres from that at Lyon (1756) on to the Théâtre Feydeau (1791) at Paris, clearly shows the fresh impulses at work. Perhaps partly because of the classical inspiration, moreover, the plans executed by these French architects generally moved considerably from the beehive arrangement of boxes

[1] This work remained for decades a study familiar to architects and theatre planners. As late as 1830 G. Ferrario issued an Italian version augmented with "erudite osservazioni" by Paolo Landriani; it was also largely responsible for the preparation of numerous volumes in various countries, such as Francesco Riccati's *Della costruzione de' teatri secondo il costume d'Italia* (1790), wherein the multiplication of boxes was deplored.

182

Fig. 201. DRURY LANE IN 1775

This shows the interior as it was redesigned by Robert Adam. The three galleries should be contrasted with the five of the later Drury Lane (Fig. 203).

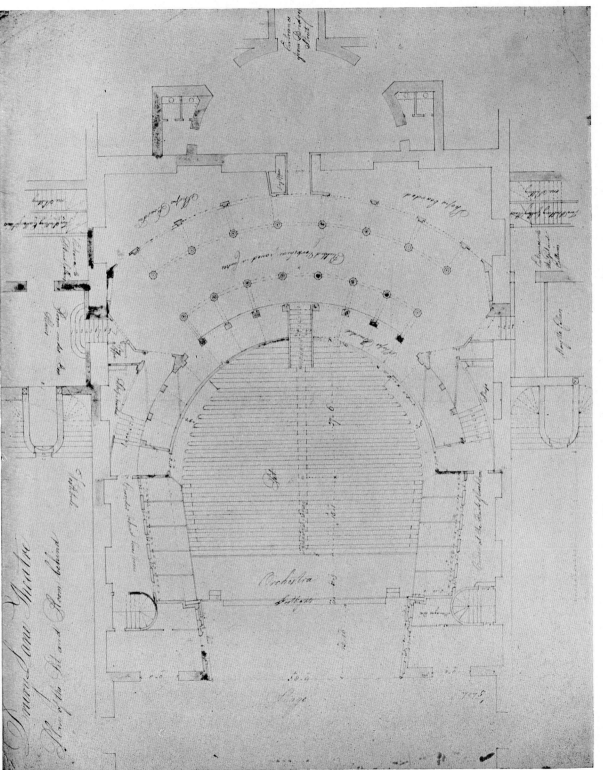

Fig. 202. PLAN OF DRURY LANE IN 1809

Fig. 203.
DRURY LANE IN 1808

Fig. 204. COVENT GARDEN IN 1810

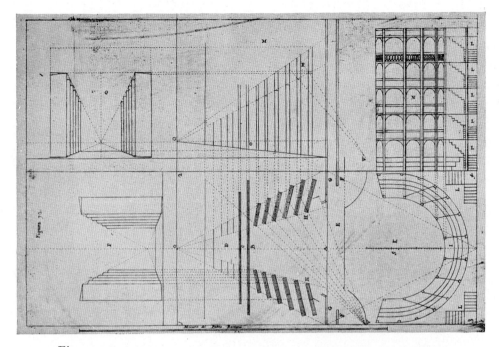

Fig. 205. PLAN AND CROSS-SECTION OF A THEATRE BY ANDREA
POZZO, 1693

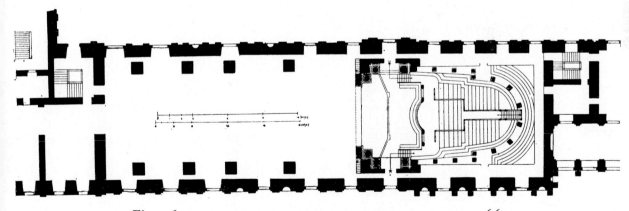

Fig. 206. PLAN OF THE SALLE DES MACHINES IN PARIS, 1662

so characteristic of the Italian houses: boxes, indeed, were provided, but the parterre was given due attention, and the upper gallery was arranged in amphitheatrical form.

A further part of the road leading towards the modern playhouse was thus being laid.

5. Costume: Theatrical and Realistic

Fig. 207. COSTUME OF A KNIGHT MASQUER IN ''OBERON,'' 1611, DESIGNED BY INIGO JONES

This is a typical example of the fanciful, semi-Romanized costume of the seventeenth century.

In all these theatres the costumes worn by the actors and singers tended on the whole towards a formalism in keeping with the grandeur of the settings. Tragic heroes and heroines stalked about in heavy garments, their heads surmounted by plumes of feathers; and the operatic performers were even more heavily clad. And when the spirit of the rococo induced designers such as François Boucher (1703–70) and Louis-René Boquet (1717–1814) to bring in something new, the fantastic merely took the place of the laboriously formal. Nevertheless, the same neo-classic movement which can be seen in the French playhouse design was already apparent by the middle of the century, and with it, somewhat peculiarly, came another movement towards historical realism. Nowhere did these operate so actively as in England, and it is in the theatres of that country we can see their effect most clearly.

The English stage was not a wealthy one sustained by grants from ducal and royal treasuries, and consequently both settings and costumes were less rich, less elaborate than those generally to be found abroad. No doubt the players wore on occasion formal, befeathered baroque dresses so exaggerated as to become ridiculous (Figs. 214–217), but the tradition of modern dress for many characters in Shakespearian plays was one freely accepted by the audience. The spectators were quite content to see Romeo, Macbeth, and Hamlet (Figs. 218–222) clad in their own garments, and when they watched *Othello* they asked for no more

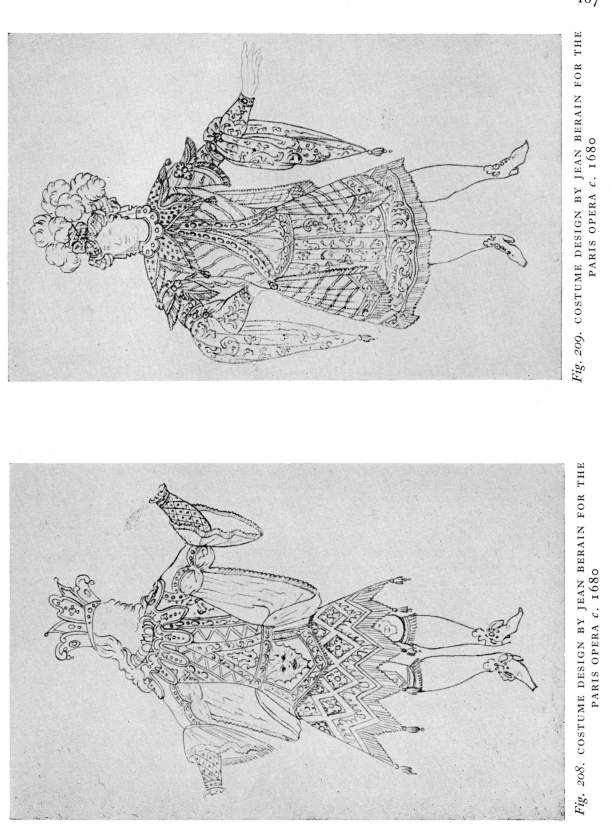

Fig. 209. COSTUME DESIGN BY JEAN BERAIN FOR THE
PARIS OPERA *c.* 1680

Fig. 208. COSTUME DESIGN BY JEAN BERAIN FOR THE
PARIS OPERA *c.* 1680

Fig. 211. COSTUME DESIGN BY JEAN BERAIN FOR THE
PARIS OPERA *c.* 1680

Fig. 210. COSTUME DESIGN BY JEAN BERAIN FOR THE
PARIS OPERA *c.* 1680

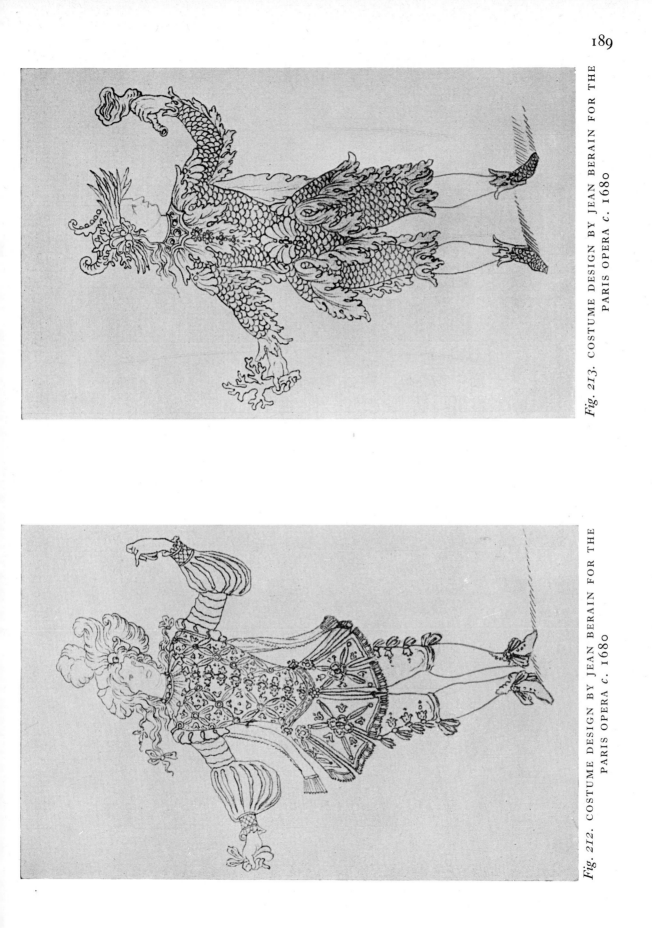

Fig. 213. COSTUME DESIGN BY JEAN BERAIN FOR THE
PARIS OPERA *c.* 1680

Fig. 212. COSTUME DESIGN BY JEAN BERAIN FOR THE
PARIS OPERA *c.* 1680

Fig. 215. DAVID GARRICK
AS DEMETRIUS, 1777

Fig. 214. JAMES QUIN AS CORIOLANUS, 1749

Fig. 216. CHARLES MUR-
RAY AS DEMETRIUS,
1797

Fig. 217. SPRANGER BARRY AND MRS BARRY AS BAJAZET
AND SELIMA, 1776

than a kind of oriental transformation of these garments into something vaguely suggesting the costumes of the East (Fig. 223). In addition, the popularity of Shakespeare's plays, which carried with them a long stage tradition, had accustomed them to see at least a few characters, such as Falstaff, in an attire based on the Elizabethan (Figs. 224–225). Indeed, there is good reason for believing that when London spectators looked upon their stage Falstaffs, they saw before them actors dressed in a manner fundamentally akin to that of the original creator of the rôle. Among Inigo Jones' costume designs is one which he has described as

> a roabe of Russet Girt low w^t a great belley like a swoln man long mistchaheos [moustaches] the sleeues shorte . . . buskines to shew a great swolen lege on his head a capp comming fourth beefore like a peake . . . a hood gatherd behind a great head and balde.

This description would, in general, fit such illustrations as we have of the eighteenth-century Falstaffs; and in view of this fact there is indeed very special interest in observing that Jones has added a final note—"like a Sr Jon fall staff." Very probably the later stage-costume was a traditional one handed down from the last years of the sixteenth century, when, perhaps, it had already a certain touch of the historical about it.

Everything, therefore, combined to make London audiences more willing than most to accept a break from the prevailing baroque operatic style. As early as 1723 Aaron Hill had suggested that for a play on Henry V the costumes worn by the actors ought to be like those actually worn in that monarch's reign; and no one was particularly offended by the suggestion. It is true that a similar proposal had been put forward about the same time in the preface to Antonio Conti's *Il Cesare* (1726), that somewhat later Pier Jacopo Martelli expressed similar views, and that in 1741 Johann Christoff Gottsched in Germany actually persuaded the actress Carolina Neuber to present *Der sterbende Caton* with strictly "classical" costumes. But the reception of these innovations was different from what it was in England: the German public merely laughed, the London public was definitely interested. It did not jeer when Aaron Hill, in 1731, sketched "a few light drawings," beautiful and inexpensive, offering "a novelty in the old *Saxon* dresses." Nor did many jeer when Charles Macklin dared to appear as Macbeth in "the old Caledonian habit," or when Garrick introduced old English costumes into a production of *King Lear*. At Covent Garden the spectators seem to have approved of Mlle Sallé when, in 1734, she appeared in *Pygmalion et Ariane* in a real Greek tunic. Gradually, the same approach was certainly being made, as in this last instance, on the French stage, so that Mlle Clairon wore the simple dress of a slave in *Electre* (1752), and Le Kain abandoned the formalized costumes in favour of others more authentic: at the same time, it seems obvious that the drive towards historical realism, whether in the adoption of genuinely classic models for plays set in Greece or Rome, or of Saxon and Caledonian habits, found a warmer reception in the country of Shakespeare than it did anywhere else.

The significance of this impulse goes, of course, far beyond the realm of costume. The next step after putting Henry V into an attire somewhat like that which the real Henry V had worn is to think of providing a background reproducing the buildings of that past age. And this step was actually taken by William Capon at the very close of the century. A scenic artist who doted on the antiquarian, he prepared in 1794 a number of scene-designs which incorporated the results of his researches. One of these may be regarded as typical: it showed the "Ancient Palace of Westminster," described as a delineation of the edifice as it had been at the close of the fifteenth century. He was not satisfied simply with displaying a scene of the

Fig. 218. ROMEO AND JULIET ON THE
EIGHTEENTH-CENTURY STAGE

Fig. 219. DAVID GARRICK AND MISS BELLAMY AS
ROMEO AND JULIET, 1763

Fig. 220. DAVID GARRICK AND MRS PRITCH
AS MACBETH AND LADY MACBETH, 177

Fig. 221. DAVID GARRICK AS MACBETH

Fig. 222. JOHN HENDERSON AS
HAMLET, 1779

Fig. 223. SPRANGER BARRY
AS OTHELLO 1770

Fig. 224. JOHN HENDERSON
AS FALSTAFF, 1778

Fig. 225. FALSTAFF IN 1709

Tower of London; his Tower appeared as it had been in the reign of Richard III. And, if he had to design a composite street scene (Fig. 226), the buildings in it were carefully copied from existing Elizabethan houses. Most of these settings were intended for revivals of Shakespearian dramas, but the significance of his work is revealed when we observe that various contemporary dramatists provided him with ample opportunities of showing his skill. George Colman the Younger thus gave him *The Iron Chest* (1796) and James Boaden *Aurelio and Miranda* (1799), based on M. G. Lewis' novel *The Monk*. The public once more was prepared to welcome his efforts, and when J. P. Kemble took over Covent Garden in 1809, Capon was engaged as his scene-designer.

Here the baroque age is clearly passing into the age when the "Gothic" was admired and when historical realism was gradually being associated with a realism of still wider scope.

Fig. 226. ANCIENT STREET SCENE FOR JOHN KEMBLE'S SHAKESPEARIAN REVIVALS AT COVENT GARDEN, 1809. DESIGN BY W. CAPON

CHAPTER VIII

The Theatre during the Nineteenth Century

1. *Realisms and Lights*

WE have seen the eighteenth century, during its last years in England, moving steadily towards historical realism; and perhaps the best way of approaching the following decades is to carry this movement forward. Capon's antiquarianism had been rather lightly founded, but soon others more learned than he began to apply themselves to the theatre.

The next stage is reached in 1823, when J. R. Planché, an enthusiastic antiquary as well as an indefatigable playwright, persuaded J. P. Kemble to permit him to design the costumes to be used for a new production of Shakespeare's *King John*. With the assistance of a number of scholarly enthusiasts, and fortified by a close study of illuminated manuscripts, Planché put on what was undoubtedly the first completely "historical" production of Shakespeare's drama, for he paid attention not only to the hero's costume but to those of the meanest underlings. The result was that "receipts for 400 to 600 pounds nightly soon reimbursed the management for the expense of the production," and, this being so, quite naturally "a complete reformation of dramatic costume became from that moment inevitable upon the English stage." From now on the revivals of Shakespeare's plays are billed as dressed in correct, authentic garments, and in the advertisements the various "authorities" are duly printed. The crisis, if not the catastrophe, is reached in the versions prepared for the stage by Charles Kean. Plentiful record remains in the newspapers of the time regarding these revivals, but we need do no more, in our endeavour to estimate the tendencies of the time, than turn to the printed texts of the plays. How erudite are the notes to difficult passages in the dialogue, and how anxious the actor-manager is to convince his public that he has consulted all the possible sources of information, and that his settings and costumes do not conflict with historical fact! The preface to *The Merchant of Venice* (Princess's, 1850) informs us that

> the costumes and customs are represented as existing about the year 1600, when Shakespeare wrote the play. The dresses are chiefly selected from a work by Cesare Vecellio, entitled "*Degli Habiti Antichi e Moderni di diverse Parti del Mondo*. In Venetia, 1590": as well as from other sources to be found in the British Museum.

The procession which opens the comedy "is copied from a print in the British Museum, by Josse Amman, who died in 1591," while the text is generously padded out with a series of lengthy "Historical Notes."

For *The Merchant of Venice*, for the tragedies and for the histories, of course, all was plain sailing. The manager had merely to look up the historical sources for the reigns of King John or of Henry VIII and reproduce "the costumes and customs" on the stage; but a difficulty obviously arose when *The Winter's Tale* was revived. Kean's preface to this play as performed at the Princess's in 1856 is so illuminating that parts of it may be quoted in full.

196

Fig. 227. A DANCE OF FAIRIES IN CHARLES KEAN'S PRODUCTION OF "A MIDSUMMER NIGHT'S DREAM." DESIGN BY GRIEVE

While recognizing the "charming" nature of the drama, the actor-manager grumbled loudly at the fact that Shakespeare had

> left the incidents of the play . . . alternating between Sicily and Bohemia, without assigning any specific date to the time of action. Chronological contradictions abound throughout the five acts; inasmuch as reference is made to the Delphic oracle, Christian burial, an Emperor of Russia, and an Italian painter of the sixteenth century.

Surely this was a hard nut for an antiquarianly minded manager to crack. Typical is the manner in which Kean solved his difficulty. He may be allowed to tell his own tale:

> It is evident that when an attempt is made to combine truth with history, conflicting epochs cannot all be illustrated; and I have therefore thought it permissible to select a period which, while it accords with the spirit of the play, may be considered the most interesting, as well as the most instructive.
>
> The pivot on which the story revolves, is in fact the decision pronounced by the oracle of Delphi; and taking this incident as the corner stone of the whole fabric, I have adopted a period when Syracuse, according to Thucydides, had, from a mere Doric colony, increased in magnificence to a position in no way inferior to that of Athens herself, when at the summit of her political prosperity. An opportunity is thus afforded of reproducing a classical era, and placing before the eyes of the spectator, *tableaux vivants* of the private and public life of the ancient Greeks, at a time when the arts flourished to a perfection, the scattered vestiges of which still delight and instruct the world. Assuming that the civilization of Athens was reflected by Syracuse, I feel that no period could have been selected more interesting and suggestive, or more likely to give additional zest to those who wish to contemplate the manners and habits of a country once "the centre of ancient civilization, and the fruitful mother of so many illustrious sons," but which can now, alas! boast of nothing beyond its history and its ruins.
>
> To connect the country known as "Bohemia" with an age so remote, would be impossible: I have therefore followed the suggestion of Sir Thomas Hanmer, in his annotations on Shakespeare, by the substitution of *Bithynia*. The difference of name in no way affects the incidents or metre of the play, while it enables me to represent the costume of the inhabitants of Asia Minor at a corresponding period, associated so intimately with Greece, and acquiring additional interest from close proximity to the Homeric kingdom of Troy.
>
> The Phrygian dress presents a marked distinction between the two races that constitute the chief actors in the drama, while at the same time scope is afforded for the introduction of customs common to both. A leading instance is furnished in the pastoral scene of the fourth act, where the festivities applicable to the season of sheep-shearing take place, and in which Shakespeare brings in, for the purpose of a dance, twelve rustics, "who have made themselves all men of hair, and call themselves Satyrs." I have here ventured to introduce one of those festivals in honour of Bacchus, known under the title of "Dionysia," wherein similar disguises were used, while the actors indulged in mad enthusiasm and extravagant merriment.
>
> For the purposes of presenting with closer accuracy the domestic manners of the period, Leontes and his Queen Hermione, together with their Kingly guest, are first discovered towards the termination of a *Feast*. . . . As dancing and music invariably formed a portion of such entertainments, a representation of the celebrated *Pyrrhic Dance*, so popular throughout the principal states of Greece for its martial character, has been attempted.
>
> Later in the play, "TIME, as CHORUS," has been restored, in accordance with the poet's conception. By this restoration, the lapse of sixteen years, supposed to have taken place from the birth of Perdita until she is seen as the shepherdess in the fourth act, is rendered more intelligible. To carry out the idea, a classical figure, more in accordance with the character of the play as now represented, has been preferred to the ordinary old man with his scythe and hour glass, who was unknown in classic ages. CRONOS, the ancient representative of Time, has been chosen, and I have ventured to associate him with an allegorical tableau of Luna and the Stars (personified), sinking before the Car of Phoebus, which rises with all its attributes of splendour. Each figure is taken from an antique, or from the works of Flaxman.

Kean has obviously "ventured" much, but he has done so in good company. "Eminent Professors" are referred to; the architecture has been superintended by George Godwin, F.R.S.; thanks are given to "George Scharf, Esq., F.S.A. (author of the Hand-book to the Greek and Pompeian Courts at the Crystal Palace)"; the "vegetation peculiar to Bithynia is adopted from his private drawings, taken on the spot"; "James A. Davies, Lecturer on Ancient Music," has given his valuable aid; while a host of artists, including Grieve, Telbin, W. Gordon, F. Lloyds, Cuthbert, Dayes, and Morris, were responsible for the scenery. Truly an awe-inspiring production, beautiful perhaps in some ways, but not Shakespeare, not even genuine theatric art, something which, to use Kean's own words, is "an exhibition of pageantry appealing to the eye" and "an illustration addressed to the understanding." Pageantry is not scenic art, and historical instruction—what on earth is it doing in this galley?

It is hardly necessary to state that these historical efforts of Kean, which he had inherited from Macready, who in his turn had them from Capon and Kemble, were passed on to Tree and to Irving.

These are English examples, but they may stand as representative of what was happening elsewhere.

Quite clearly, this antiquarianism, this passion for the historically correct, is associated with two forces which seem at first sight diametrically opposed. The first of these is well illustrated by the endeavours of Charles Kean: the audience would not have been attracted simply by the historical; it was attracted by the historical when it became combined with the spectacular, and spectacularism flourished during the nineteenth century just as it had in the baroque period. It was, however, a new kind of spectacularism, even although it had been adumbrated in the latter half of the century preceding. At Drury Lane Capon had been a realist who founded his work upon careful scrutiny of past records; some twenty years before his time another designer had been engaged at the same theatre, and his efforts, also realistic, were directed towards a realism of a different sort. Philippe Jacques de Loutherbourg (1740–1812) was a native of Alsace, and David Garrick was responsible for giving him an opportunity to work on the English stage. While it must be confessed that much of his scenic art was devoted to 'shows' rather than to play performances, his influence was widespread, and in himself he may be taken as representative of a movement which touched or transformed the settings presented in theatres almost everywhere. In effect, he was a romantic realist who sought to base his stage scenes upon nature and who, from the practical point of view, tried his hardest to simulate atmospheric effects upon the boards. Thus, for example, his show, *The Wonders of Derbyshire*, produced at Drury Lane in 1779, was conceived in terms of sketches which he had himself made during a tour of that district; and, as the scene from another show, *A Christmas Tale* (1773), demonstrates, this was not a unique experiment (Fig. 228). Everything in picturesque nature that was out of the common became grist to his mill. In 1775 a Polynesian native had been brought to London, and there was much talk of Captain Cook's expedition, talk which was stimulated by the publication in 1784 of an account of the voyage. Promptly a "pantomime" libretto was composed, entitled *Omai: or, A Trip around the World*, and de Loutherbourg applied himself eagerly to designing scenes from Kamtchatka to Tongatabu. It was not, however, his skill as a draughtsman alone which brought him fame; his atmospheric effects appealed because of their novelty. John O'Keeffe, author of *Omai*, informs us that, before this production, "he had previously invented transparent scenery—moonshine, sunshine, fire, volcanoes, etc," and that he was responsible for "breaking the scene into several pieces by the laws of perspective, showing miles and miles distance." The setting for *A Christmas Tale* could not have been executed by means of the usual wings, and the impression

Fig. 228. SCENE FOR "A CHRISTMAS TALE," 1773,
DESIGNED BY P. J. DE LOUTHERBOURG

it made on the spectators must have been based very largely on its deviation from the usual means of lighting the stage. Indeed, so much was this artist interested in simulating the light and shade of nature, and so much were audiences delighted in what he could achieve, that he actually set up a show called an "Eidophusikon" which relied solely upon such spectacles displayed one after another. That the appeal of this show was not merely a temporary one is proved by the fact that in 1820 a production of *King Lear* had in it "A Land Storm. After the manner of *Loutherbourg's Eidophusikon,*" in which a most realistic storm howled round the head of the aged king.

This kind of realism and the means by which it was secured obviously might veer far from de Loutherbourg's landscape effects, and it was freely applied in many countries to entertainments exhibiting the purely fantastic. The French *féeries*, the fanciful shows which were so popular in Vienna, and the English extravaganzas alike frequently appealed precisely because they applied the realistic methods to things of the capricious imagination. J. R. Planché was responsible for the historical realism of the *King John* production, but he was also responsible for such light entertainments as *The Sleeping Beauty in the Wood* which Covent Garden advertised in 1840 as "An Original, Grand, Comic, Romantic, Operatic, Melo-Dramatic Fairy Extravaganza," the settings for which included

PART FIRST.—Period 1583.
BOUDOIR OF THE FAIRY BANEFUL....
Banquet Hall in the Castle of the King of Noland.

PART SECOND.—Period 1601.
VESTIBULE IN THE ROYAL CASTLE.
APARTMENT OF THE PRINCESS IN THE OCTAGON TOWER. ...
Lobby and Lumber Room at the very Top of the Castle.
STATE BED CHAMBER.

PART THIRD.—Period 1701.
MAGIC FOREST
CASTLE GATES. MOAT AND DRAWBRIDGE. OLD PALACE YARD,
And Re-view of a Company of the "Old Guards."
Quick-set Hedge, and a merry Green Wood in the Spring-time of the year.
THE STATE BED CHAMBER (Exactly as before.) ...
Illuminated Palace and Gardens of the Fairy Antidota.
FETE AL-FRESCO. ...
DEPARTURE OF THE SEVEN FAIRIES, in a Patent Safety "Fly,"
constructed by Mr. W. Bradwell, "time out of mind the Fairies' Coachmaker."

Although this is confessedly an absurdity, the dates given to the various parts—1583, 1601, and 1701—and the references to forests and illuminated palaces all connect it with the trends adumbrated by Capon and de Loutherbourg.

During the century there were many other "realisms" besides these. Even the melodrama often captured public attention by the introduction of commonplace objects on the stage—cabs, carts, lamp-posts, living animals such as hens and geese—and in the sixties in England Tom Robertson won fame for his attempts to introduce scenery of a more "realistic" sort. Instead of an interior presented by what were palpably side-wings, the box-set was coming into favour; instead of doorknobs simply painted on the flats, real, tangible doorknobs were screwed upon doors which were stoutly fashioned; instead of sky-borders, veritable ceilings were set upon the walls of a room.

In most countries the passion for the real and the actual was taking the place of delight in the theatrically splendid, and soon it moved towards a fresh kind of realism which not only sought to ape the real but which also aimed at depicting the sordid. Indeed, many of the younger enthusiasts reached a position whereby the term "realism" had lost much of its original stage significance and was being interpreted ideologically.

When we consider these various tendencies, which paradoxically at once conflict with each other and yet lead towards the same objective, we realize that the aims of the new theatre-men could not have been achieved in earlier years, that one innovation was required to make them all possible. One and all they depend for their success upon a new means of illumination. It is perfectly true that even during the early Renaissance considerable attention was given to the illumination of the sets; the contemporary descriptions of *Mirame*, the opening play at the Palais Cardinal in 1641, amply testify to the care taken with the lights; de Loutherbourg could not have produced his effects without painstaking care in the placing of his lamps and candles. Lamps and candles, however, no matter how painstakingly manipulated, could not provide a means of realizing what was in the minds of the designers and producers if only because they were not susceptible to easy control. No doubt the footlights could be lowered by means of simple mechanisms, and no doubt the battens of lamps set behind the side-wings could be covered by shades or coloured glass, but these devices inevitably left much to be desired. And when the time for the box-set arrived, it is clear that this could be effectively illuminated only by some instrument which might be regulated from a position outside the set itself.

It would not, therefore, be going too far to say that on the material plane the most significant and the most characteristic innovation in the nineteenth-century playhouse was the introduction of a new means of illumination. First came the employment of gas lighting, already introduced at the Paris Opéra in 1822, installed at the Lyceum in London eight years later, and by 1850 almost universal in all European and American theatres. Next came the utilization of limelight; and, finally, during the second half of the century, illumination by means of electricity gradually brought an even more supple means of lighting the stage. New effects were thus easily obtained. The stage might be brilliantly illuminated or it might be completely darkened, not by a laborious process of kindling and quenching hundreds of candles but by the mere turning of a tap or the flicking of a switch. Partly at least, the development of the nineteenth century's spectacularism may be explained by this substitution of gas jets for the old candles and lamps. Settings which had seemed perfectly satisfactory when dimly lit now appeared to be tawdry, and consequently a fresh start had to be made. Managers were forced to provide entirely different backgrounds for the actors and at the same time to gratify the spectators with magnificent scenes which, adequately lit, could produce a sense of delight and wonder.

2. The "Mystic Gulf"

One further result of this innovation was, however, even more important, and in order to appreciate its force it is necessary to turn for a moment from a consideration of the new means of illumination to a rapid survey of what was happening in the theatres of contemporary Germany. In 1802 Franz Ludwig Catel published a study entitled *Vorschläge zur Verbesserung der Schauspielhäuser*, designed to offer suggestions for the improvement of theatre-planning: in this he argued that all the vices and evils of the playhouse of his day derived from the deep, flat-wing baroque stage. Influenced profoundly by the philosophies of his age, he claimed that the association of three-dimensional actors and those perspectively painted settings was ridiculous, precisely because it was unrealistic. In place of such absurdities, he argued that the sets ought to be as "plastic" as possible, and he further averred that, with such scenes, the auditoria of theatres could effectively be built in an amphitheatrical form which had been proved to be unsuited for the deep, flat-wing stage.

This, of course, was all theory; but there were practical men prepared not only to plan such theatres but to carry their inherent objectives to a logical conclusion. A start was made by Karl Friedrich Schinkel (1781–1841); most of his designs, certainly, remained projects merely, but he did succeed in having some of his ideas incorporated in the reconstruction of the Neues Schauspielhaus of Berlin (1818–24), and these ideas were to have an effect on the minds of others. Fundamentally Schinkel was a classicist, and as such he was opposed to the perspective illusionism of the baroque stage. His auditorium was an amphitheatrical one, and he proposed the banishing of the wings in favour of a large single painted back-drop set a considerable distance behind the actors, so that the three-dimensional and the two-dimensional should not be brought into direct contact with each other.

One of this man's pupils was Gottfried Semper, and Semper's true significance is that he was closely associated with Richard Wagner. When the Festspielhaus at Bayreuth was opened in 1876, Oscar Brückwald and not Semper was its architect, but the completed plans were based on the latter's studies. Here the orchestra pit was abolished; the audience were seated in a vast amphitheatrical array of seats with no marked sub-divisions. Democracy had finally triumphed. Most important of all, however, were Wagner's own "philosophical" ideas, made possible only because he now had a lighting instrument which could be exactly controlled. So far, we have considered only the control which could alter the illumination on the stage; but clearly both gas and electricity could do much more than that—they could control the lighting of the auditorium as well. Up to this time, no effective darkening of the auditorium could be conceivable: the great branches of lights hanging over the parterre might be raised through a trap in the ceiling, but even so the candles or lamps in the wall sconces would remain. Hence for all practical purposes we may say that theatres up to the nineteenth century had the audience almost as brightly lit as—sometimes, perhaps even more brightly lit than—the actors on the stage. Now, however, at the commencement of a performance the former could be plunged into darkness, and this is precisely what Wagner, in his folly, desired. In characteristic Germanic manner he even gave a philosophical and metaphysical aura to the device, speaking dimly about the "mystic gulf" between performers and viewers. Thus the true peepshow-stage, never quite possible before, came into being.

While we must recognize that Wagner's philosophy had comparatively few sympathetic readers, his aim has to be seen as the culminating, and indeed logical, result of what was happening generally in the nineteenth-century playhouse. For the most part, all theatres took to darkening their auditoria before the beginning of a performance, and with this came an employment of the front curtain such as had hardly been dreamed of before. It has been seen that Giacomo Torelli actually wanted his scenic changes to take place in full view of the spectators, and in this he might be regarded as the prime example of the baroque scenic artist. Now, the theatre-men kept the curtain lowered until the beginning of the play and dropped it at the end of acts or scenes. The "pictures" were conceived of not as dazzling kaleidoscopic transformation scenes but as images of reality revealed one by one by the rising of the curtain. We may put this in still another way by saying that the concept of the "fourth wall," although it was not much talked about during this century, was being firmly established.

3. Mechanical Theatres

In this new world of the theatre the realistic-spectacular settings which so fascinated audiences raised problems of their own. Certain effects were not so difficult of realization on the stage, since the baroque playhouses had had such a long time to perfect their methods of dealing with large-scale scenes and actions. Ships could be tossed about in what their directors hoped would be taken as true-to-life storms; horse-races could be simulated by means of a little ingenuity; and so could train-wrecks. In order to show an army on the march, no more was required than to have a short column of men become visible through a window and the open door in the back wall of a room: this trick was tried in numerous playhouses and everywhere spectators were thrilled. When Irving introduced it into *The Lady of Lyons* an English commentator spoke for all:

> It seemed as if the line would stretch out till the crack of doom! . . . They would march into the wings with set pace, but the instant they passed out of sight of the audience they would break into a run; in perfect order they would rush in single file round the back of the scene and arrive at the other side just in time to fall into line and step again. And so the endless stream went on.

But other effects proved not so easy. When audiences were prepared to imagine the solid walls of a room although all they saw was a number of painted side-wings placed parallel to the proscenium arch, the directors' task presented few problems. In most larger European theatres, and in the newly built theatres of the United States of America, the wings were handled mechanically from below; but even when they had to be run on grooves there was no real difficulty in dealing with them expeditiously; and in any case, except for the transformation scenes in pantomimes and fairy plays, the spectators did not ask for sudden alterations of setting executed without concealment in front of them. In this new world, however, what they sought was an appearance of solidity: "Belasco realism" appealed everywhere.

Now, if three-dimensional "plastic" scenes are to be used there are really only two ways of changing them. The first method is to drop the curtain and get a large team of scene-shifters to move the component parts of the set as rapidly as they can, followed, of course, by a scurry back with the components for the second scene. Unless the unsatisfactory device is adopted of having a front cover-scene take place in front of a drop, clearly awkward intermissions must result. It is true that spectators became trained to accept these intermissions in, for example, the historically "accurate" and spectacular productions of Shakespeare's plays, but no director in his senses could ever regard intermissions as good things in themselves.

Consequently, in this age of the mechanical, numerous theatre-workers began to think of means of effecting a second kind of scenic change. That obviously could not be carried out unless the playhouse was equipped with sufficient mechanism to move the three-dimensional components or the box-sets bodily away from behind the proscenium frame. As far back as 1879, in America, the inventive Steele MacKaye filed a patent for a "double stage," a project realized when he introduced it into the Madison Square Theatre. Driving the orchestra to the top of and behind the proscenium arch (the position it had occupied in London's Dorset

Garden Theatre two centuries before, although there, characteristically, it was in full view of the audience), MacKaye built an elevator platform so planned that while a scene was being played below, a new scene might be set above, all ready for being bodily lowered, together with its own stage floor, to the appropriate level. From this time on, mechanical devices multiplied, with Germany tending to take the lead. Sometimes the stage was made to slide to either side; sometimes the sliding device was combined with an elevating one. In 1896, moreover, Karl Lautenschläger (1843–1906) seized upon a feature of the Japanese Kabuki stage and built a revolving platform for use in the Munich theatre (Fig. 230): by its means one three-dimensional set could be shown on half the circle while a second remained concealed beyond its contours.

Fig. 229. THE MADISON SQUARE THEATRE NEW YORK, 1879

The mechanical theatre thus evolved continued on through the present century, so that, for example, the Shakespeare Memorial playhouse, now the Royal Shakespeare Theatre, completed at Stratford-upon-Avon in 1932 might well have been designed and constructed thirty or forty years previously.

New improvements in lighting, the substitution of three-dimensional for prevailingly two-dimensional sets, all devised to satisfy the craving for realism, had the result of placing still more stress

Fig. 230. MODEL OF THE REVOLVING STAGE AT THE DEUTSCHES THEATER, BERLIN

upon the proscenium arch. It has been said that the concept of the Fourth Wall is inherent in Wagner's theatrical philosophy: that is true, but, quite apart from any philosophical considerations, the framework and the curtain, for purely practical reasons, had now become absolute essentials. If the director was to have a chance of making his scenes life-like he had to have this frame, sharply separating the stage picture from the spectators, so that these spectators might, from their darkened seats, enjoy a peep-show view of the solidly set and naturalistically illuminated spectacle put before them. Still further, external conditions forced its retention. Up to the latter half of the nineteenth century nobody worried much about theatrical fire hazards, so that hardy audiences cheerfully and unthinkingly accepted the risks attendant upon watching play performances. By the 1880's the danger of fire was becoming a subject of frequent debate, and the result was the settling upon the theatre of numerous regulations, in some countries less strict and in others more strict, a prime element in which was the compulsory use of a fire-curtain. Now, the effectiveness of a fire-curtain depends upon a solidly built wall between the stage and the auditorium, and hence the framing arch, besides being a necessity for the achievement of naturalistic and spectacular effects of the kind then desired, virtually became a necessity under law. The new fire regulations, too, insisted upon more solid playhouse structures than many playhouses had boasted in the past, and solidity had to be paid for by greater and ever greater outlays. During earlier years numerous houses perished in vast conflagrations, and consequently there was considerable opportunity for experimentation in theatrical design, particularly when solidity was not always demanded; but the solidity of the late nineteenth century, soon to be accentuated by the use of reinforced cement, tended to make theatrical architecture more and more set. Some experimental structures were designed and built, but the pattern established during the two last decades of the earlier era was largely followed during the opening decades of our present century.

CHAPTER IX

Theatres of the Twentieth Century

1. Theatrical Revolt

THE years immediately before 1900 and the years immediately after, in spite of, or perhaps because of, this mechanical stage, were strangely studded with revolutionary organizations set up in opposition to what now was being called the "commercial" theatre; but by no means were the revolutionary aims inspiring these groups all the same. During the last years of the nineteenth century the revolutionary aims tended to be ultra-realistic, sometimes placing the stress on productional method, sometimes on the content of plays, sometimes on both. Ibsen's star was beginning to rise above the horizon, and numerous enthusiastic groups anxiously hitched themselves to it—the Théâtre Libre of Paris, under André Antoine, Berlin's Freie Bühne, under Otto Brahm, Konstantin Stanislavski's Moscow Art Theatre, and (far less important) London's Independent Theatre. Such enthusiasts were not, in effect, reacting against any current trend in theatrical presentation; they were intent merely upon further refining the realism of the commercial theatres and upon channelling it in directions which they regarded as socially significant—for this was the time when a new definition of realism was being shadowed forth.

Fig. 231. SETTING FOR CHEKHOV'S "THE THREE SISTERS" AT THE MOSCOW ART THEATRE

During the first decades of the present century the number of these organized groups multiplied rapidly, and for the most part their objectives went absolutely counter to the ideas animating their predecessors. There were still some which rather depressingly clamoured for more and more social realism, but the general trend was definitely towards an escape into a truly theatrical world. The activities of these groups rarely succeeded in giving them strength to build theatres of their own: indeed, some devoted the greater part of their time to plans and projects merely; but certainly in the field of scene-design some notable results were achieved. Diverse in their proposals for reforming the playhouse, and often clashing with each other, they yet found a sense of common purpose in their detestation of realism and in their desire for an entirely fresh approach towards stage production. To outline here all the manifold

Fig. 232. SETTING BY M. G. DOBUJENSKI FOR TURGENEV'S "A MONTH IN THE COUNTRY"
AT THE MOSCOW ART THEATRE

Fig. 233. ALEXANDER TOLSTOI'S "TSAR FEODOR IVANOVITCH" AS PRESENTED BY THE MOSCOW ART THEATRE, 1922

concepts and experiments which extended over the entire Western world during this time would be impossible, but at least a few of the more important trends may be briefly surveyed.

(*a*) First may be taken the theatre philosophers. There were numbers of these, and perhaps it will be advisable to start with the satiric logic that Nikolai Evreinov applied to the stage of his time. In effect his thesis goes as follows. If you wish for realism, if you set this up as your aim, for heaven's sake be reasonable and carry your practice as far as it can go. Never let a play be acted in English or in Russian when its characters are supposed to be Swedes or Germans. Never employ a careful reproduction of a fourteenth-century oak table in an historical play: realism demands that you should purchase a genuine original. Don't bother about the audience: the Fourth Wall presents a problem; all right, be logical and build up that wall.

Fig. 234. DESIGN FOR IBSEN'S "THE PRETENDERS" BY GORDON CRAIG

Then, and then only, will your play, your acting, come close to actuality. Luigi Pirandello, in Italy, penetrated a trifle farther still. Even with all this, he declares, your play will not be realistic. Your actors, after all, are only actors pretending to be something they are not. Nay, more, even if you were to dismiss these actors and employ a labourer, a clerk, and a typist for their "real" parts they could not produce in absolute sincerity the words, intonations, and passions which they might have uttered or experienced at some particular crises in their careers. The only "realistic" play, it would seem, is to be found in the ordinary conversation and customary actions of daily life. Here indeed is a *reductio ad absurdum*, and one not lightly to be dismissed.

Fig. 235. A SETTING FOR GLUCK'S "ORPHEUS" BY ADOLPHE APPIA

(*b*) Associated with such views are the concepts of those who recognized that stage realism, in order to be thoroughly "dramatic," tends towards the use of violence and brutality. The greater masters, such as Ibsen, may escape this taint, but every one who is familiar with the range of plays in this style, from those of the 1890's on to the present day, must recognize that their authors are inclined to interpret "reality" as the dark, the sordid, or the abnormal, and to create dramatic episodes out of the sensationally crude. During the early years of this century, however, several writers, such as Maurice Maeterlinck, began to plead for a quieter neo-romanticism which might offer opportunity for the dramatic exploitation of less crass emotionalism. Their campaign was not directed against realism as such, yet their indirect influence

14

was undoubtedly strong among the disparate movements inspired by dissatisfaction with the current theatrical mode.

(c) In the theatrical rather than in the dramatic sphere, more powerful were the innovations of Gordon Craig and Adolphe Appia. The essence of Craig's artistic endeavour is to be found in a revolt against the falsity of the realistic method, in a determination to dismiss the cluttering trivialities which only too often do service for art on the stage. For those falsities he would substitute symbolic form, and in order to cast out the trivialities he would make the theatre once more a temple. Mass of light and shade he substitutes for naturalistic detail, imaginatively conceived shapes of a statuesque kind he brings in place of illusionistic interiors, and for the more adequate display of the actors he provides various planes on the stage. Easily is it to be seen that with these ideals Craig draws inspiration from the theatre of the Greeks; from it he derives strength, and to its majestic shapes he endeavours to give modern interpretations. Designing a set for the *Electra* of Sophocles, he fills his stage with "a vast and forbidding doorway"—hardly more than that, reality reduced to its simplest terms. To evoke the mood of *Hamlet* he gives us great sweeping curtains to establish a sense of loftiness, and, to suggest the outer world, a glimpse of sky seen through parted folds with the faint image of a wandering moon.

Craig thus uses curtains on occasion, but in his work the prevailing element is three-dimensional form. He attacks the realistic theatre, but he also attacks the painted theatre. There is virtually no "decoration" in his designs: his effects are created wholly by the employment of simple mass-forms. In this he allies himself to another pioneer, the Swiss Adolphe Appia, whose work, although usually emphasizing the horizontal in place of Craig's typically vertical lines, resembles his in its rejection of detail and of painted ornamentation. In both, to secure variety, light

Fig. 236. A SETTING FOR "KING LEAR" AT THE DEUTSCHES
THEATER, 1908, BY KARL CZESCHKA

plays an important rôle, striving to create mood quality, and not merely to illuminate the actors and to simulate natural phenomena.

The Craig-Appia method is of fundamental import, since its system of three-dimensional simple masses, with ample space for the actors, has formed a basis on which many artists have founded their work. In such a design as Karl Czeschka's palace for *King Lear* (Fig. 236), as produced at the Deutsches Theater in 1908, there is evident the same use of severely unadorned masses of light and shade, the same elimination of detail, the same endeavour to evoke mood and to arouse imagination by formal shapes. Far removed from this is Ernst Stern's doorway for *The Miracle* (Fig. 237), with its stained-glass windows; yet here too an identical force is at work. The plain walls, the vastness of proportion, are similar in aim. Still other artists, who otherwise deviated far from Craig's method, found inspiration in his various planes of action. The notorious stage steps of Leopold Jessner at Berlin's Schauspielhaus were a direct result of his ideas.

(*d*) Craig dreamed of a modern theatre which should once more have taken on the spiritual atmosphere of a temple, and this ideal of his may lead to consideration of yet another aspect

Fig. 237. A SETTING BY ERNST STERN FOR "THE MIRACLE," 1911

Fig. 238. THE GROSSES SCHAUSPIELHAUS, BERLIN

of dissatisfaction with the typical theatre of 1900. To many men's minds came a vague realization that the peep-show theatre had lost in soul far more than it had gained in body. In the
past, and particularly during those ages when drama most powerfully flourished, there was
little or no separation between the actors and the audience. In the Greek playhouse the citizens
sat in the open air, almost embracing the orchestra and the histrionic platform; the townsfolk
mingled with the performers in medieval days; the Elizabethan theatre, like the Greek, was
an open-air structure wherein the audience almost surrounded the stage; and even when
indoor houses took the place of those unroofed, the inadequate means of artificial illumination
kept a feeling of intimacy between those presenting and those watching the productions. All
of this was lost in the new theatre, and gropingly some men sought to find ways of escape.
Quite clearly, Max Reinhardt's Grosses Schauspielhaus in Berlin (Fig. 238), with its carefully
planned stage and orchestra, its towering dome of innumerable lights, its vast seating
accommodation, springs from study of the Dionysian theatre at Athens. All that remains of
the old proscenium arch is a wide rectangular frame serving to mask what now is a mere
background for the actors. Audience and players are once more being united.

It is obvious, however, that this is only one way of achieving the desired objective, and the
same inventive director, Reinhardt, himself showed another approach of an entirely different
kind. In Vienna he converted the beautiful ballroom called the Redoutensaal, once the delight
of Maria Theresa, into an intimate theatre of purely formal design. The proscenium frame here
was moved back of the actors; and the central aperture (with four other doors, reminiscent of
the Teatro Olimpico) became a setting for all kinds of plays. Locale, instead of being illusionisti-
cally displayed, found suggestion merely by the placing of a few properties on the stage—
chairs, tables, trees in tubs, screens serving to indicate for the audience the surroundings of
the actors. A somewhat similar stage resulted from the efforts of Jacques Copeau at the Parisian
Théâtre du Vieux Colombier (Fig. 239). From a relatively small acting-area steps lead down
to the floor-level. A wide aperture is at the back, doors give exits left and right, and the whole
is framed within a series of three arches. Again a few properties—the use of a screen or a
curtain—serve to indicate the locality and the atmosphere. Still a further move was made by

Fig. 239. JACQUES COPEAU'S STAGE AT THE VIEUX COLOMBIER, PARIS

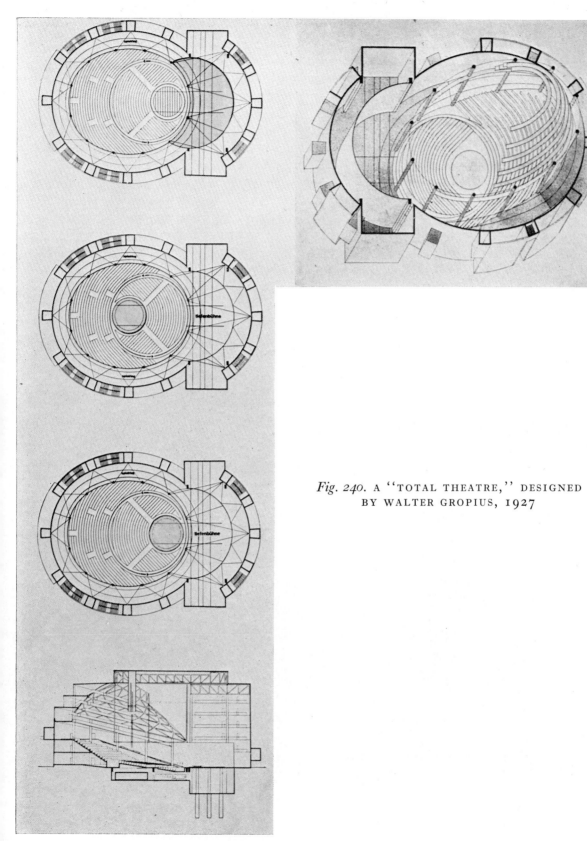

Fig. 240. A "TOTAL THEATRE," DESIGNED
BY WALTER GROPIUS, 1927

Terence Gray when he created the Festival Theatre at Cambridge, since here the whole planning of the interior was designed to bring audience and actors into a single unity, while almost the only concession to scenery was a set of cubes of different sizes, so constructed that they might be fitted together into any desired patterns. In a sense the use of these cubes derived from Craig's emphasis on formally conceived masses; in another sense their employment sprang from a fundamentally different concept. For Craig the setting had to be an artistic unity wrought to evoke a mood, even when no actors appeared before or within it. In Terence Gray's hands the masses of simple planes became for the most part merely acting-space; the set as such had lost its independent meaning and, like the stage façade in the Globe, could be vested with significance only when the business of the stage was associated with it. Animated by a kindred spirit, although vastly different in scope and calculated for the use both of three-dimensional settings and projected scenery, was Norman Bel Geddes' design for a theatre in which audience and actors were placed in a large rectangular hall roofed by an all-covering dome, with the stage located in one of the corners and hence assuming a triangular shape. In this way and that men sought novel expedients and created plans of a kind undreamed of before. Besides the project just described, for example, Bel Geddes also published another in which his audience was arranged in two sections, the one facing the other, with a long narrow platform-stage stretching lengthwise between the two. And Walter Gropius, clearly inspired by contemplation of the Greek stage, published a vast project for a "Total Theatre" (Fig. 240) in which the audience circle round a centrally placed ring.

Fig. 241. "PRINCESS TURANDOT" AS PRESENTED BY THE THIRD STUDIO OF THE MOSCOW ART THEATRE

(*e*) Meanwhile, in the midst of this ferment, the theatre came under the influence of various modernist movements in the world of art. The years just before and immediately after the First World War were enlivened and distracted by numerous schools of painting and sculpture, all of which set their minds firmly against representationalism and the majority of which sought to achieve new effects by stripping off the inessential. Inevitably these led to similar attempts being made in the theatre: Cubism and many other related -isms led onward to Constructivism. These -isms flourished particularly in Russia and in Germany during the twenties, before the U.S.S.R. and Hitler's Reich both decided that art's ideal was to be found in Victorianism. Alexander Tairov's productions in the Kamerny Theatre, Vachtangov's work in the Third Studio of the Moscow Art Theatre, Mardshanov's project for a "synthetic" stage, Meyerhold's experiments in bio-mechanics, Foregger's emphasis on acting as acrobatics, Eisenstein's various experiments in the Proletkult Theatre—these developments and many more were born of the same spirit. Fundamentally all believed that the theatre, remaining true to its essential being,

Fig. 242. CONSTRUCTIVIST SETTING BY ALEXANDRA EXTER FOR CALDERÓN'S ''LA DAMA DUENDE''

must strive to be conventional, that its work must be based on the skill of its actors, and that its settings must become dynamic in the sense that their significance should derive solely from the movements of human actors associated with them. Within this general atmosphere, however, much diversity was to be found. Meyerhold, for example, tended to be suspicious of anything more in the way of scenery than a few pieces of property or mechanically conceived structures, mostly introduced for the sake of gymnastic display (Fig. 243); Tairov regarded scenery as in itself important and valuable; while other artists, such as Alexandra Exter in her constructivist design for Calderón's *La Dama Duende* (Fig. 242), obviously were primarily intent on adding 'decoration' to planes for acrobatic action.

Fig. 243. OSTROVSKI'S "THE FOREST" AS PRESENTED BY THE MEYERHOLD THEATRE, 1924

Cubism suggested the emphasis upon planes; Italian Futurism encouraged the simple massing of form; the anticipatory movements leading to later Surrealism suggested the use of symbols. In all, dynamic vitality was stressed, and theatrical Constructivism, by presenting an unadorned stage set with scaffoldings which supported platforms and raised passageways, sought at once to stress the mechanical quality of our age and to present opportunities for revealing the active human in the midst of the machines. This active human, as has been indicated, was made to express himself through a method of acting almost acrobatic—Mardshanov's ideal player was singer, actor, dancer, gymnast—and it is by no means surprising that, in addition to seeking inspiration in current artistic schools, the revolutionary theatrical enthusiasts should turn back to find support in the ancient *commedia dell'arte*, some of the performers in which were gymnasts, contortionists, and jugglers as well as artists in the realm of improvisatory prose and operatic aria.

(f) The *commedia dell'arte* performers characteristically presented their shows on bare

Fig. 244. A SETTING BY ERNST STERN FOR "DIE WÜPPER," 1919

217

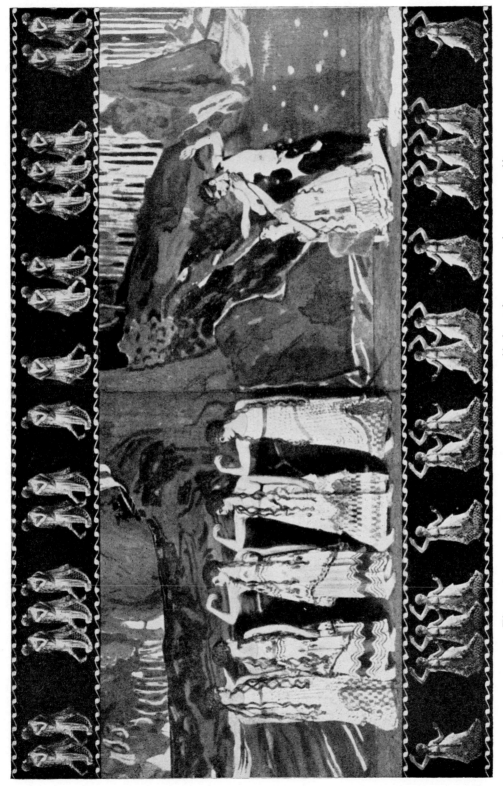

Fig. 245. A SETTING BY LEON BAKST FOR "L'APRÈS-MIDI D'UN FAUNE"

stages, and their influence, together with the allied influence of other theatrical ventures of the past, helped to encourage the tentative endeavours designed to banish the cluttered stages of realism, to bring the actors into close touch with their public, and to proclaim the frank theatricalism of the theatre. About 1900 the word "theatrical" had acquired the meaning of "false" and consequently was used to describe what ought not to be permitted in a production; now "the theatre theatrical" became a battle-cry. The support given by study of the *commedia dell'arte* was strengthened by increasing attention on the part of scholars and theatre-men to other periods of stage history. Knowledge of the Elizabethan playhouse had been markedly advanced by the discovery in 1888 of the De Witt drawing of the Swan (Fig. 103), and already in 1889 Jocza Savits had presented *King Lear* at Munich in what purported to be a reconstruction, or adaptation, of an early seventeenth-century setting. The Elizabethan Stage Society,

founded and directed by William Poel, sought not merely to rebuild the shape of the early stage but also to establish a new method of interpreting Shakespeare. At the same time others began to explore the medieval theatre, and still others penetrated to the far Orient, sometimes intent solely on historical investigation but often seeking either for fresh ideas or for such support as the past might give to concepts of their own.

(*g*) This, however, is not the whole story, since we must also take into account still another movement which, in general, ran directly counter to many of the others, even though in one basic particular it harmonized with them. Quite evidently reaction to the realistic stage picture could take one of two directions. On the one hand, men might seek to simplify, to render symbolic, or utterly to banish the ordinary elements of the set; on the other, they might try to get back to conventionalism by frank painting in two dimensions, perhaps deliberately emphasizing the artificiality through false perspective and bizarre exagger-

Fig. 246. A FIGURE STUDY BY LEON BAKST FOR
"L'OISEAU DE FEU"

Fig. 247. A SETTING BY NATALIE GONCHAROVA FOR "L'OISEAU DE FEU"

Fig. 248. A FIGURE STUDY BY NATALIE
GONCHAROVA

ation. Shortly before and after the First World War the Russian ballet came as an exciting shock to the Western world, and men were introduced to the extraordinary genius of Leon Bakst. Bakst's inspiration went directly back to early Byzantine art. From it he took his rich colours, his grotesque conceptions, his formalism. Greece influenced him too: but the gods of ancient Athens he caused to relive their existence in a light tinged always with the hues of the ikon; perhaps we might say that the element which most appealed to him in Grecian art was precisely that formalism which, when carried to extremes, grew into the unreality of the Byzantine religious painting. At the same time Bakst possessed a deep knowledge and love of the stage, so that his interests in art were transformed into designs eminently fitted for the theatrical world—and that passion for the stage he handed down to his immediate associates and followers, in particular to Natalie Goncharova, like him animated by inspiration from Byzantium, and to others, such as Larionov and Poshedaiev, who transformed the elements of his art into more abstract and bizarre forms.

So long as the painted set remains vitalized by truly theatrical aims it is a worthy and a stimulating contribution to the stage, but when it is applied without such innate theatrical aims its dangers are great. When Diaghilev came to Paris he brought with him the work of those who had been associated with him in Russia; but only too soon he started to encourage French artists—Picasso, Braque, Matisse, and others—to provide scenes for new ballets. Many of these men had been trained and had hitherto practised simply as easel painters, and often their conception of a theatrical setting was no more than a canvas enlarged to a sufficient size for a backdrop. Huge shapes of animals and humans were made to hang in devastating immobility behind the dancers, with a consequent clash between the painted design and the movements of the human performers.

The result of this invitation to well-known painters, however, was that numbers of artists who otherwise might never have thought of applying themselves to the stage began to concern themselves with theatrical designing, and, although many of those who turned from the easel to scenic art failed to make any significant contributions, the new atmosphere had the

221

Fig. 249. A SETTING BY PAUL SHELVING FOR "THE INTERLUDE OF YOUTH," AS PRESENTED AT MALVERN, 1934

222

Fig. 250. A SETTING BY AUBREY HAMMOND FOR "ACROPOLIS" BY R. E. SHERWOOD

Fig. 251. A SETTING BY LEE SIMONSON FOR "MARCO MILLIONS" BY EUGENE O'NEILL

224

Fig. 252. A SETTING BY DONALD OENSLAGER FOR "THE EMPEROR JONES," BY EUGENE O'NEILL

Fig. 253. A SETTING BY JO MIELZINER FOR "WINTERSET" BY MAXWELL ANDERSON

226

Fig. 254. A SETTING BY ROBERT EDMOND JONES FOR "MACBETH"

227

Fig. 255. A SETTING BY NORMAN BEL GEDDES FOR "KING LEAR"

further effect of encouraging various talented younger men to think of expressing themselves primarily in terms of the theatre. For the most part, the stage of the past had been furnished with scenery by men of lesser genius, the major painters either ignoring it completely or coming to it only for occasional productions. Now there was opened up a great new opportunity for the scenic artist, and the stages of many lands were thereby enriched and made more colourful. In England men such as Lovat Fraser, Paul Shelving, Aubrey Hammond, Norman Wilkinson, George Sheringham, and Albert Rutherston materially enlarged and vivified the stage of the twenties. In the United States, too, a remarkable group of young designers— Robert Edmond Jones, Lee Simonson, Norman Bel Geddes, Jo Mielziner, Donald Oenslager, and others—brought to the stage artistic gifts which under different conditions they would almost certainly have applied in other ways. Their approach was thoroughly theatrical, yet they might never have worked for the stage had their efforts in that direction not been encouraged—perhaps we might even say made possible—by the circumstances of the time.

2. *The Theatre of the Thirties*

One of the most potent consequences of all this varied endeavour was that the public, which had been taught to think only in terms of the realistically appointed set, was gradually trained to accept both long-forgotten conventions and conventions of a novel sort. From 1880 to 1910 this public had been accustomed to think of a curtain rise at the beginning of a new scene, to demand that that scene should have an appearance as like to reality as possible, and to interpret a curtain fall as the ending of the scene. By the twenties the younger generation at least were viewing, without conscious surprise and without embarrassment, stage methods based on an entirely different principle. Bernard Shaw, it is said, was deeply upset when he went to see the Pitoev production of *Saint Joan*, where the scenery consisted of curtains drawn in a line directly at the rear of the actors, with the outlines of Gothic arches simply sketched in by means of coloured ribbon; but Shaw's younger contemporaries found no difficulty in accepting the symbol for what it was intended to convey. These spectators took many things in their stride: they went to see Werfel's *Bocksgesang* at the Theatre Guild in New York, and expressed no wonder when the curtain rose to exhibit the interior of a hut, not framed by the arch but set in the middle of the stage, with a cyclorama suggesting vast open space around it; they correctly interpreted a pillar or two as a symbol of Athens, and a few folded curtains let down from the flies as the trunks of trees in a forest; they even found themselves able, like their forefathers, to imagine a setting when all that appeared before them was a bare, unadorned stage. As a result, such hitherto strange-seeming conventions as those of the medieval mysteries or of the Restoration theatre, where actors could move from one locality to another without stepping an inch from their stage positions, became perfectly understood and appreciated. Even while the majority of commercial theatres still clung to the realistic idea, the way towards other things was opened, and the theatre theatrical had been fully re-established.

Fundamentally, the thirties may be regarded as a period when earlier experimentation was toned down and the opportunity was seized for the fuller and deeper exploitation of what the preceding decade had (often crudely) suggested. In two countries, Hitler's Germany and the U.S.S.R., the earlier eccentricities came to be heavily frowned upon by the ruling powers, and in effect a brusque return was ordered to a nineteenth-century style—not the less anti- quated because it was now dignified with the title of "Socialist Realism." Elsewhere, for entirely different reasons, the constructivist and related efforts became rarer; occasionally there might be an aberration, such as Theodore Komisarjevsky's "aluminium" *Macbeth* at

Stratford-upon-Avon, but in general productions of a similar kind were rare. If we cast back our minds to the thirties, or turn over volumes of photographic records of performances given during those years, what appears as a characteristic pattern is a varied movement within fairly well prescribed limits—the older realism on the one hand (although usually much more selective than it had been in the past), and an unaggressive formalism on the other. Even among the many independent acting groups which sprang up, mushroom-like, at this time the more erratic and grotesque styles were comparatively rarely to be seen. Nevertheless, this decade demonstrated emphatically that the fight for theatricalism had been (except for the two countries already mentioned) securely won. Even in lands such as Denmark, Norway, and Argentina, where the older realism had been firmly set, the newer aims came to be accepted by the public at large.

One thing characteristic of the thirties was the rapid popularization of the theatre festival, and this, of course, arose from a desire on the part of the enthusiasts to extend and enlarge the scope of the playhouse. Salzburg led the way with its combined programmes of music, opera, and plays; Sir Barry Jackson's Malvern Festival soon followed, and that in turn was the inspirer of similar ventures in many countries. In effect, the festivals could not be said to have had any marked influence on theatrical styles since they never, or at least rarely, were attached to any single theory of production, nor did they originate any theatre forms of their own; but the opportunities thus offered for intercourse between those interested in the stage undoubtedly played a very significant part in creating that atmosphere of confidence and determination which was prevalent when war broke out afresh in 1939.

3. Post-War Endeavour

The Second World War had effects on the theatre different from those created by the First World War, and it soon became evident that its impact and the consequent general heart-searching was causing many among the most serious and talented theatre-men anxiously to re-examine their philosophies of the stage, in preparation for the work to come after the cessation of hostilities. This was the foundation on which most of the experimental work from 1946 to 1964 has been based.

In an attempt to outline the nature of this latest theatrical thought perhaps we may take as our cue the discussions at a conference in 1950, when numerous leaders of the stage in half a score of countries gathered at Paris to consider the theme of modern theatre architecture. On this occasion, as was natural, much attention was paid to practical, technical matters; but over and beyond these practical and technical affairs loomed something much more fundamental. Speaker after speaker demonstrated in his address that he was teased and harassed by issues of a deeper sort, issues which concerned the whole philosophical and sociological import of the playhouse. Among such issues two assumed particular weight; and, although both have already been found disturbing theatrical activity during the twenties and the thirties and thus have summarily been examined above, it seems necessary once more to take them under review in the light of modern experience and present-day conditions. These two issues are (*a*) the rôle of the theatre in our society, and (*b*) the fundamental ideal in stage production.

Underneath all our ponderings about the playhouse of to-day and to-morrow rests the thought of cinema and television. It is true that even towards the beginning of the present century the rivalry of the film had been recognized as an ominous force, and that during the twenties and thirties much reflection was given to the question of how this rivalry might best be met; but only in these most recent years has this same question assumed real urgency. Naturally this leads to consideration of the public to whom the theatre appeals or should appeal. Cinema and television obviously attract the masses; for most people to-day "theatre" means a place with a screen, and the hideous appendages, row upon row, on the roofs of suburban semi-detached and council houses drearily testify to the power of the screen at home. The query at once arises: ought we to declare that the living theatre is likely to appeal in the immediate future only to a very small section of the community, and that hence we should concentrate on holding its attention, or ought we to make a bold endeavour to compete with these rivals and seek, in vast productions, to combat with Cinemascope on its own terms? Should our efforts be based on the Grosses Schauspielhaus or on the Redoutensaal? In general, our tentative considerations of the problem appear discordant, with a hesitant decision to try to make the best of both worlds—or at least not to abandon either. The year before the International Conference in Paris, Gaston Baty, in his *Rideau baissé* (1949), was saying:

> Le théâtre actuel est sous le signe du chaos. De celui de demain, nous ne savons rien. Il n'y a place, là, que pour des vœux platoniques. Je serais tenté de penser que le théâtre se divisera de plus en plus en deux formules: l'une pour les masses dans les constructions qui viseront à fondre les spectateurs entre eux et avec l'action présentée—l'autre pour une élite de plus en plus restreinte, avec des salles intimes.

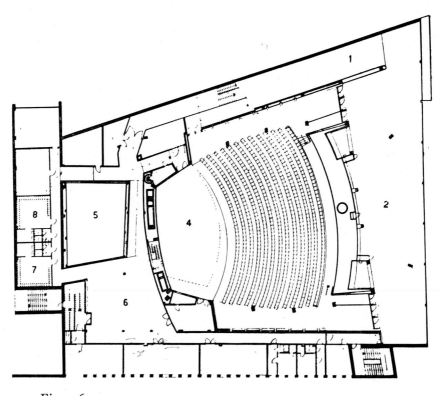

Fig. 256. PLAN OF THE CULTURAL CENTRE AT TURKU, 1952
1. ramp 2. foyer 4. stage 5. upper part of chorus hall 6. hall for personnel.

In one of the very few theatres built during the war, that at Malmö, in Sweden, sliding walls were incorporated into the structure, so that the auditorium could be made to seat about seventeen hundred persons, or twelve hundred, or seven hundred, or five hundred. And constantly when new theatre plans are discussed those concerned tacitly assume that either two stages and two auditoria must be included in the building or that there should be some device whereby audiences of different sizes might be accommodated. At Limoges, for example, the new theatre (1963) has an auditorium with fifteen hundred seats in stalls and two galleries, but when desired the whole ceiling, weighing 40 tons, can be lowered so as to cut off the topmost tier—thus diminishing the capacity of the house to 960 places. At the very start, therefore, the modern playhouse world finds itself facing two ways.

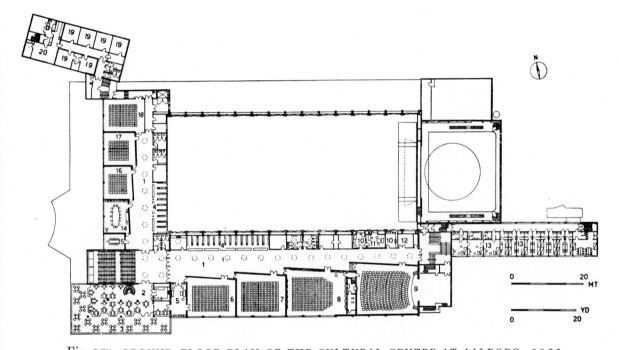

Fig. 257. GROUND-FLOOR PLAN OF THE CULTURAL CENTRE AT AALBORG, 1953

1. foyer   2. restaurant   3. terrace   5. Burgomaster's hall   6. guest hall   7. concert hall   8. wireless hall   9. small theatre   13. dressing rooms   14. farmers' room   16. merchants' room   17. room of the Aalins' Association   18. hall of the guilds   19. offices and sitting room.

Reference to the theatre at Malmö reminds us of something else. The designing of new playhouses in Europe and to a certain extent in the United States has frequently been associated during recent years with the thought of civic centres wherein much more than provision for play performances would be sought for. In practice this has meant that the particular part of the structure intended for the performances is constructed in such a way as to make it suitable for many other non-theatrical activities. At Mannheim (1957), it is true, there is a larger theatre, with a capacity of some thirteen hundred, reserved in general for operas and ballets, but the smaller house, with a capacity of five hundred, is intended not only for plays but also for film shows, concerts, and the like. R. V. Luukkonen has conceived the theatre in the Turku "Cultural Centre" (1952) in the same way: at Aalborg (1953) Otto Frankild,

Preben Hansen, and Arne Kjaer, besides incorporating two separate stages and auditoria in their building, have adopted in their main theatre the sliding-walls device (here weighing nearly 70 tons) in such a way as to offer facilities for everything from play productions to cinema shows and sporting events. All of this sounds most modern and up to date, and yet to a large extent it means putting the clock back. As long ago as the days of Julius Caesar, two identical wooden theatres were built, in conjunction with each other, and fitted with "machinery" by which they might be turned round. Thus separately they could be used for the performance of plays, or else, when brought together and made into an amphitheatre, they could provide the space necessary for the presentation of gladiatorial shows. Seventeen

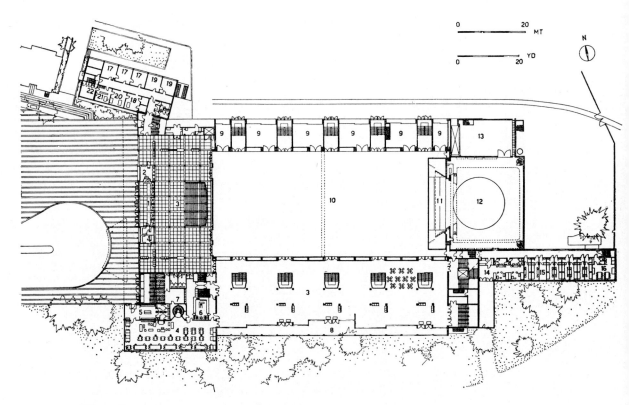

Fig. 258. FIRST-FLOOR PLAN OF THE CULTURAL CENTRE AT AALBORG, 1953
1. entrance   3. foyer   4. restaurant   8. balcony   10. main hall   11. orchestra pit   12. stage   13. scene shop   14. green room
15–16. dressing rooms   17. musicians' rooms.

odd centuries later, the Teatro Farnese at Parma gained its peculiar shape from the fact that the architect wished to construct a building suitable both for the exhibition of plays and for the exercise of tournaments. And, a few years afterwards, for a similar purpose, the Stallone theatre at Padua was actually equipped with some kind of machinery by which whole sections of the seating could be moved bodily into different positions. From these modern and ancient examples it is obvious that attempts to establish adaptable theatres can be inspired by very different objects: they may aim simply at making a large theatre small; they may be designed to provide a theatre which may be suited for non-theatrical displays; and, as will be seen, they may go further and seek to offer a series of stage arrangements which reproduce the main types of theatres of the past. More must be said of them later; but for the moment it may be suggested that the endeavours of classical Rome and Renaissance Italy in this direction did not prove very fruitful, and that present-day designs calculated to offer full facilities for screen-projection, concert platform, and theatre-projection risk failure of a like kind. No doubt modern machinery is vastly superior to the machinery of earlier times, but we are concerned here, not with the means of achieving a pre-determined end, but with the validity of that end in itself.

A further conflicting element in the designing of modern theatres arises from two chief tendencies to be observed in their conception. One of these tendencies may be regarded as both negative and positive: negatively it takes shape as a reaction against the proscenium-arch "peep-show" stage of the nineteenth century; positively it generally exhibits a direct or indirect influence of the ancient Greek theatre. Obviously, the proscenium arch may be done away with in different ways. Sometimes, for example, in less elaborate structures or in play-

Fig. 259. THE THEATRE AT RED ROCKS, COLORADO, 1942

houses which, for one reason or another, have had to be built in a long narrow space, no more is needed than simply to remove it altogether—thus creating what is now being styled the "open-end" stage. Much more commonly, however, the spirit of the Athenians descends upon the new playhouses. At times, as in the startling open-air theatre at Red Rocks, Denver (designed by Burnham Hoyt in 1942: Fig. 259) or in the charming "garden" theatre of San Giorgio in Venice (designed by Luigi Vietti and Angelo Scattolin in 1954: Fig. 260), the classical form cannot be overlooked. Nor could anyone avoid seeing the Athenian inspiration in Vietti's earlier project, executed in 1935 (Fig. 261), or in the plan of the Teatro S. Erasmo at Milan, designed by Antonio Carminati and Carlo De Carli in 1952 (Fig. 262). In both these last-mentioned theatres, however, we realize that the spectators, instead of merely going part-way round a circular orchestra, actually embrace that orchestra within their folds: and here we come to what may perhaps be regarded as one of the most characteristic of

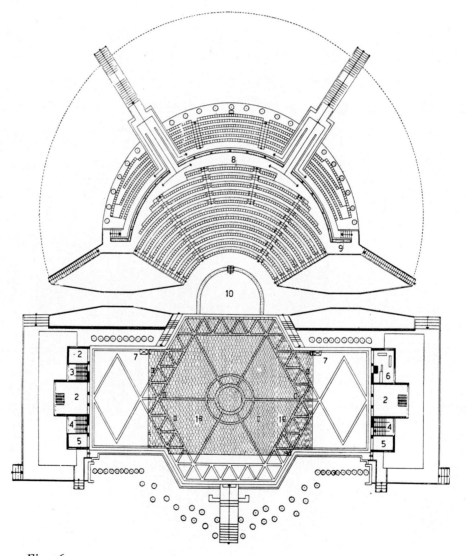

Fig. 260. PLAN OF THE THEATRE AT SAN GIORGIO, VENICE, 1954

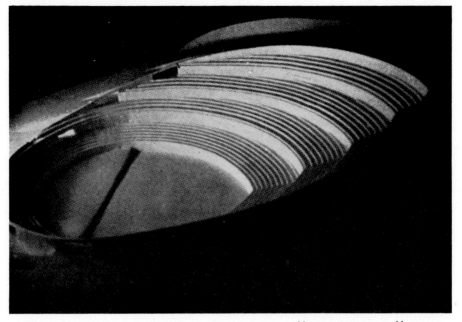

Fig. 261. PROJECT BY LUIGI VIETTI FOR A "MEGATEATRO," 1935

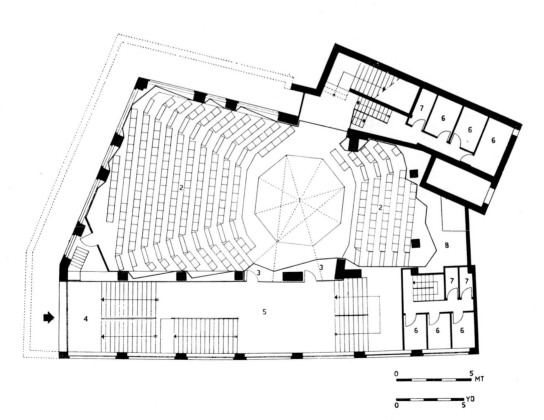

Fig. 262. PLAN OF THE TEATRO S. ERASMO, MILAN, 1952
1. stage   2. tiers of seats   3. foyer   4. bar   6. dressing rooms   7. manager's office.

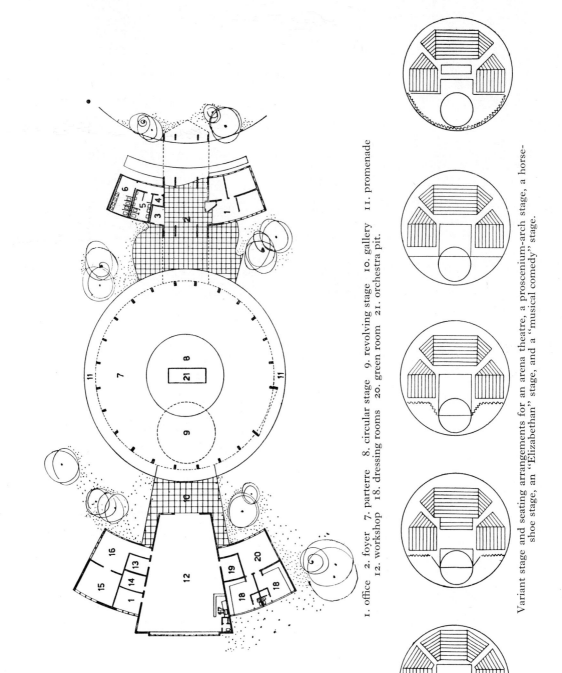

1. office 2. foyer 7. parterre 8. circular stage 9. revolving stage 10. gallery 11. promenade
12. workshop 18. dressing rooms 20. green room 21. orchestra pit.

Variant stage and seating arrangements for an arena theatre, a proscenium-arch stage, a horse-
shoe stage, an "Elizabethan" stage, and a "musical comedy" stage.

Fig. 263. PLAN OF THE EXPERIMENTAL THEATRE AT THE UNIVERSITY OF MIAMI, 1950

modern theatrical experiments, "theatre-in-the-round." Already in the thirties the Pasadena Playhouse had had small, intimate arena productions alongside its larger conventional ones, and by 1940 Glenn Hughes' Pentagon Theatre at Seattle, Washington, had established itself as the first structure specifically constructed for this type of theatrical presentation. Nevertheless, it is only in recent years that this concept has spread beyond the occasional private performance and the college atmosphere into a larger world. A professional company under the direction of Margo Jones won esteem for performances in this style in the United States; several local organizations in England, such as John English's "Arena" company in Birmingham, have applied themselves to the same method; and in Europe there are many directors, such as Jan Doat and André Villiers in France, who find the central ring potent in its appeal.

At the same time, in considering this tendency, we must not lose sight of the second tendency, which in a sense runs directly counter to the first. Never, in the long record of the stage, has so much attention been given to the history of the theatre and to the connexion between particular theatres and the plays which had been written for them. Societies for theatrical research have been established in many countries, and an international organization now binds them together. All aspects of the stage, from classical days down to the nineteenth century, are being explored, with peculiar emphasis both upon the details of playhouse practice and upon what may be called the philosophical basis of theatre endeavour during the various periods concerned. As a result of this, the terms "adjustable theatre" or "adaptable theatre" are ones which have been much bandied about during recent years. Already we have encountered the terms in the sense of providing means for making a particular auditorium larger or smaller, and also in the sense of creating a hall which might be considered suitable for both theatrical and non-theatrical performances: but here they are being given a different significance. Such great stress has of late been laid on the desirability of producing older plays more or less in the theatrical styles for which they had been composed that numerous theatre-workers and architects have come to assume that new theatres must include mechanical means of altering the stage-forms and, particularly, of giving different adjustments to the relationship between spectators and players. "Adaptable Theatres" was, thus, the theme of the 1961 conference of the Association Internationale des Techniciens de Théâtre; and several of the designs for an "Ideal Theatre" sponsored by the Ford Foundation Program for Theater Design (1962–64) in one way or another are dominated by this concept. Already, numbers of existing playhouses have gone some way towards realizing such an object, and others are actively planning structures of the same kind. As examples, we may take the Experimental Theatre of the University of Miami, built in 1950 by Robert M. Little and Marion I. Manley (Fig. 263) so as to permit the stage and the actor-audience relationship to assume almost any form desired, the projected plan, by W. S. Hattrell, for the Ealing Questors' Theatre (Fig. 264), designed with a similar aim in view, and London's latest playhouse, the May Fair (1963). As Sean Kenny puts it:

> It is necessary to have the baroque proscenium stage, just as it is necessary to have theatre in the round. But please let us have all kinds of theatres. Square, round, triangular, oblong, and whatever you like. A completely flexible theatre giving all forms of staging.
>
> With the minimum of scenery and machinery one could present different styles of play by altering the interior relationship of the house to the relationship required between actor and spectator for the particular play, the writer and director creating the space they need to work in.

Thus, in reality, we are confronted by two things at once—the strong influence of the Greek-type stage and an eager searching for a theatrical form which may escape from the

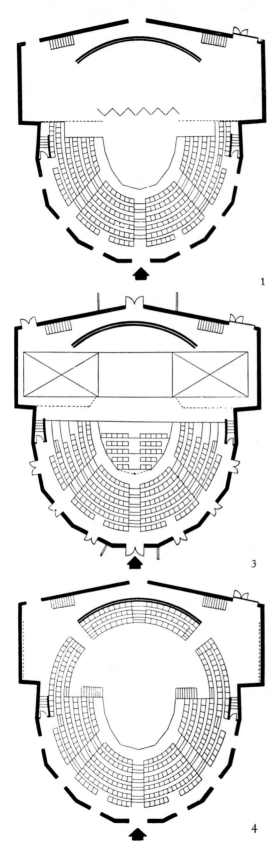

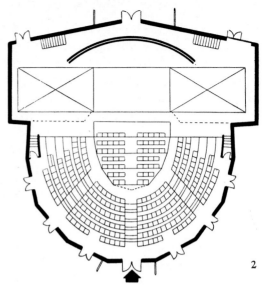

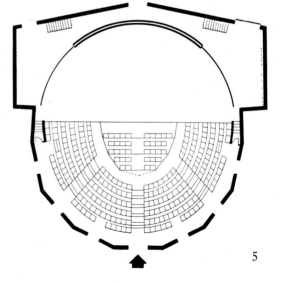

Fig. 264. ARRANGEMENT OF SEATS AND STAGE, QUESTORS' THEATRE, EALING

1. open stage 2. picture-frame stage with cyclorama
3. proscenium-arch stage with adjustable forestage
4. arena stage 5. "space stage".

Greeks. In reflecting upon these "adaptable theatres," obviously, a distinction ought to be made between two distinct types of playhouse—the university theatre and the theatre designed for a more general public. The former, quite obviously, has every right to ask for a building which may allow it to display, at least in general outline, theatres of varying kinds; this will add to its educational value and it may also offer opportunities, in the field of research, of testing theory by practice. Hence the "adaptable theatre" is, within such a sphere, entirely proper, if not positively necessary. On the other hand, grave doubts may enter in when adjustability is sought for in a playhouse designed for a general audience. Adaptability may have its advantages, but too much adaptability may well have a dulling effect both upon creative writing and upon production. Unquestionably Charles Kean, Sir Henry Irving, and others ruined the structure of Shakespeare's plays by forcing them, mutilated, into a kind of theatre for which they had never been intended; and yet we must agree that some of the most exciting presentations of these plays during recent years have been given on stages entirely unlike the Globe stage for which they had originally been conceived.

There is, therefore, the basic necessity, when we are thinking in terms of the general audience, of making a sharp distinction between the "adaptable theatre" and what for convenience may be called the Greek-type theatre. The former may well prove disturbing, precisely because it has no central idea save its adjustability. The other, because it has an

Fig. 265. A SETTING BY TANYA MOISEIWITSCH FOR "HENRY V," 1951

aesthetic objective, may well prove inspiring. And here, of course, one must enlarge the concept of the Greek-type stage to include several other forms related in spirit although variant in form. The Elizabethan Globe theatre, for example, was by no means "Greek," but in essence modern theatres designed on the Elizabethan model, as well as productions in Elizabethan style within theatres of nineteenth-century shape, have to be considered alongside both the classically inspired models and the associated arena playhouses. In all of these the attempt is made, by dispensing with ordinary scenery, to stimulate the imagination of the spectators, and also to bring about an actor-audience relationship which is the very opposite of that once desired by Wagner. Thus, the theatre constructed under the direction of Sir Tyrone Guthrie at Stratford, Ontario, was planned not only to reconstitute "the physical relation between actor and audience which prevailed in the Elizabethan Playhouse" but also to allow of "the ritual as opposed to the illusionary quality of performance." For the series of history plays at Stratford-upon-Avon in 1951 Tanya Moiseiwitsch, although bound by the permanent structural shape of the Memorial Theatre's stage, designed a simple structural set (Fig. 265), allowing for action on several levels, which served as a neutral area on which not merely one but various dramas were enacted. At Chichester the new theatre took shape as a modified open-stage structure. And elsewhere many experiments of a similar kind have been made during recent years. All of these efforts might be said to reflect a theatrical philosophy which had been adumbrated as early as 1941 by the great American scene-designer Robert Edmond Jones. "The theatre we knew," he wrote then,

> the theatre we grew up in, is dwindling and shrinking away, and presently it will be forgotten. It is essentially a prose theatre, and of late it has become increasingly a theatre of journalism. The quality of legend is almost completely absent from contemporary plays. . . . Of late years realism in the theatre has become more and more closely bound up with the idea of the "stage picture." But now it would seem that this idea is to be done away with once and for all. The current conception of stage scenery as a more or less accurate representation of an actual scene—organized and simplified, to be sure, but still essentially a representation—is giving way to another conception of something far less actual and tangible. It is a truism of theatrical history that stage pictures become important only in periods of low dramatic vitality. Great dramas do not need to be illustrated or explained or embroidered. . . . The reason we have had realistic stage "sets" for so long is that few of the dramas of our time have been vital enough to be able to dispense with them. . . . Actually the best thing that could happen to our theatre at this very moment would be for playwrights and actors and directors to be handed a bare stage on which no scenery could be placed, and there told that they must write and act and direct for this stage. In no time we should have the most exciting theatre in the world.[1]

In spite of this movement, however, another very strong modern trend has been towards the pictorial, leading frequently towards over-ornamentation and an undue emphasis on the setting as opposed to the play. In England many Shakespearian productions have suffered from over-decoration, and it is of significance that numerous younger designers and directors have approached their stage plays from the worlds of revue and ballet, or have had their ideas dominated by non-dramatic pictorial art. It is truly extraordinary how many of the designers whose names loom large in the theatre of the forties and fifties—Rex Whistler, Cecil Beaton, Oliver Messel, John Piper, Leslie Hurry, William Chappel—were trained in the schools of revue and ballet, how many have moved from the world of ballet into dramatic theatre, and how heavy is ballet's impress on other directors and designers who have not actually been concerned with dance productions. The result is that only too often the stage has been over-loaded and that plays have been sacrificed to spectacle and supernumerary "groupings"—not,

[1] "Towards a New Stage" in *Theatre Arts Monthly*, March 1941.

Fig. 266. A SETTING BY ARNE WALENTIN FOR
"MIDSOMMARDRÖM I FATTIGHUSET," 1951

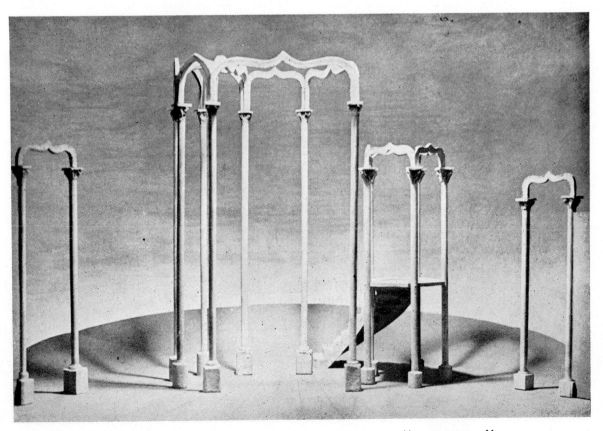

Fig. 267. A SETTING BY MICHAEL WARRE FOR "RICHARD II"

as in the times of Charles Kean and Irving, for the sake of giving historically correct pictures of past ages, but for the sake of colourful visual effects. This tendency has further been encouraged by the rapid development of a new fashion—the presenting of plays by Shakespeare and other classic dramatists in the styles of famous painters, not necessarily contemporaneous with the dramas themselves. Thus have we seen Watteau, Titian, and Breughel brought into service. In this approach perhaps there is nothing basically wrong, provided that the director bears in mind the essential fact that he has been engaged not to reproduce on the stage paintings by gallery masters or to display his own cleverness, but to bring out what is best in the dialogue set before him; yet it is very easy to ignore the drama for the sake of improving the stage picture. It is tempting, for example, when producing *Romeo and Juliet*, to permit the visually decorative in set and action to swamp the impact of imaginative words, or, in *Othello*, to lose the impression of urgent haste and alarm in the senate scene by attempting to provide the audience with a three-dimensional representation of a Titian canvas; it is tempting to vary the scene and so to exhibit more pictures. It is tempting, too, for the sake of novelty, to impose an alien artistic style on a classic play, as was done at Stratford-upon-Avon in the "Japanese" *King Lear*.

Something of the same development in the exploitation of the pictorial is to be seen in France, where numerous young painters have been drawn into the theatre's orbit, with a consequent elaboration of decorative and colourful elements; in Italy kindred conditions have led to the arising of a new kind of baroque, based ultimately upon the grandiose designs of the great eighteenth-century masters in that style; and in Germany much the same movement is to be traced, stemming partly from the romantic stage of the nineteenth century and partly from the constructivist experiments of the twenties. In the United States no such strong

Fig. 268. A SETTING BY OLIVER MESSEL FOR "THE SLEEPING PRINCESS"

native traditions have laid their impress on the designers, in whose work, accordingly, appears a more eclectic style, displaying many different Continental influences; but the fundamental pictorialism is here as well. Among these American designs, however, varied as they may be, there is one trend which deserves particular attention. Many years have passed since Lee Simonson, for the production of *Bocksgesang*, placed a small interior set stage-centre, with a vast cyclorama behind it suggesting space around and beyond; but for some reason this device has caught the imagination of the New York scenic artists. Jo Mielziner's design for *Death of a Salesman* (1949) shows us the skeleton of a house, with several opened-up rooms, against a distorted vista of bleak tenements; Mordecai Gorelik's set for *Desire under the Elms* (1952) very similarly reveals a house section, framed by two arching trees, against an open sky, and the same artist's design for *Thunder Rock* (1939) is basically the same; Robert Edmond Jones has something akin to this for *A Moon for the Misbegotten* (1947), and Leo Kerz for *A Long Way from Home* (1948); while Oliver Smith varies the plan in his sketch for *Fall River Legend* (1949, Fig. 269) by completely stylizing the skeleton framework.

It is easy to see that this recurrent model serves both to stress the artificiality of the stage setting and to render nugatory the force of the proscenium arch as a frame. It is thus but one among several expedients currently being employed by modern designers to escape from the trammels of the playhouse structure in which they are forced to work. The long-discarded wings, for example, are coming back into favour again, and with them many conventions which the later Victorians fondly thought they had banished for ever. Apart from this, how-

Fig. 269. A SETTING BY OLIVER SMITH FOR "FALL RIVER LEGEND," 1949

ever, the American centrally placed set and the vast background has another, and deeper, significance. During the realistic period the whole endeavour of the producers was to confine the imagination of the audience to the picture framed in the arch. Nowadays the conscious or unconscious desire is generally to suggest expansion—to make the spectators think of a world outside the boxed interior. No doubt this is why, when presenting *The Comedy of Errors*, Guy Krogh in Norway places behind the actors a stylized structure suggestive of the little houses of an Italian hillside town clambering up the slopes (Fig. 270), why Leslie Hurry in England gives to *Cymbeline* a deep perspective vista leading to what appear to be towering buildings in the rear, why in Italy Franco Zeffirelli gives another hillside effect to *Troilus and Cressida* (Fig. 271).

Interesting and effective as many of these designs may be, however, we must in the end come back to a recognition of the fact that the Greek-type or Elizabethan stage forms are intrinsically at odds with practically all kinds of pictorial settings, and that in this dichotomy, no less than in the struggle to develop "adaptable theatres," we have another example of this age's eclecticism. Perhaps we may go even further. One of the latest pleas put forward is for a playhouse which, instead of being called an "adaptable theatre," might be styled an "adapted theatre"—a playhouse having an architectural design which should offer the opportunity of "combining in one stage the essential qualities of each" of the several stage forms observable in the historical past, even, as has been further suggested, of making room for cinematic devices within the scope of play production. Peter Moro, for example, asks, "Is the proscenium obsolete?": he observes how some persons argue for it precisely because it is artificial and formalized, hence distinguishing the theatre from the cinema, while others argue against it on the grounds that it presents simply a framed almost two-dimensional picture, and he proceeds to suggest that

Fig. 270. A SETTING BY GUY KROGH FOR
"THE COMEDY OF ERRORS," 1947

Fig. 271. A SETTING BY FRANCO ZEFFIRELLI FOR "TROILUS AND CRESSIDA," 1949

architects should turn their attention to finding a new conception altogether where the action takes place on some form of open staging partly surrounded by the audience in a wide fan but much less than 180°, where three dimensional scenery and scene changes are possible and where lighting can be easily controlled; where a large number of spectators can be brought close to the stage, but where the acoustical difficulties of the three-sided stage arrangement are minimised. Such a theatre would combine all that is valuable in the two basic forms as we know them and would go a bigger step towards revolutionising theatre than either form could ever hope to do by itself.

And René Allio proposes a fresh architectural approach in which a centrally placed stage-area would be confronted, as it were, by two fan-like auditoria facing each other: these might be separated so as to form a large theatre and a small, each making use of half the stage-space; or they might be combined into a sort of arena; or the entire stage-space might be given up to one of the two auditoria, thus offering something in the nature of a proscenium-type theatre. Ralph Alswang and P. M. Rudolph, in a more fully conceived project design, use the "adapted theatre" concept to provide a playhouse wherein the use of films may "be combined with live stage action in one complete blending."

At first, it might well appear legitimate for the modern theatre to seize upon all that the past has to offer, to put the whole of that past to its immediate service, and, perhaps, to go further by offering facilities for the employment within a single production of both three-dimensional actors and two-dimensional films. Yet, when we examine these proposals more

246

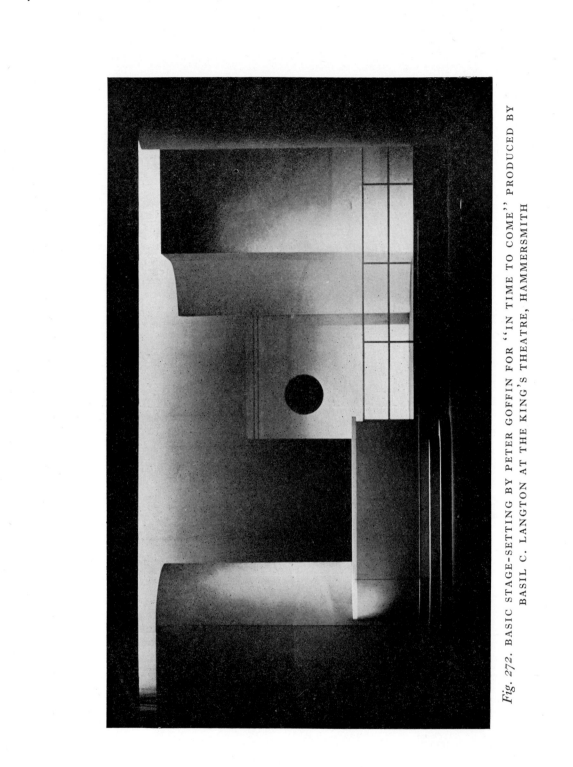

Fig. 272. BASIC STAGE-SETTING BY PETER GOFFIN FOR "IN TIME TO COME" PRODUCED BY BASIL C. LANGTON AT THE KING'S THEATRE, HAMMERSMITH

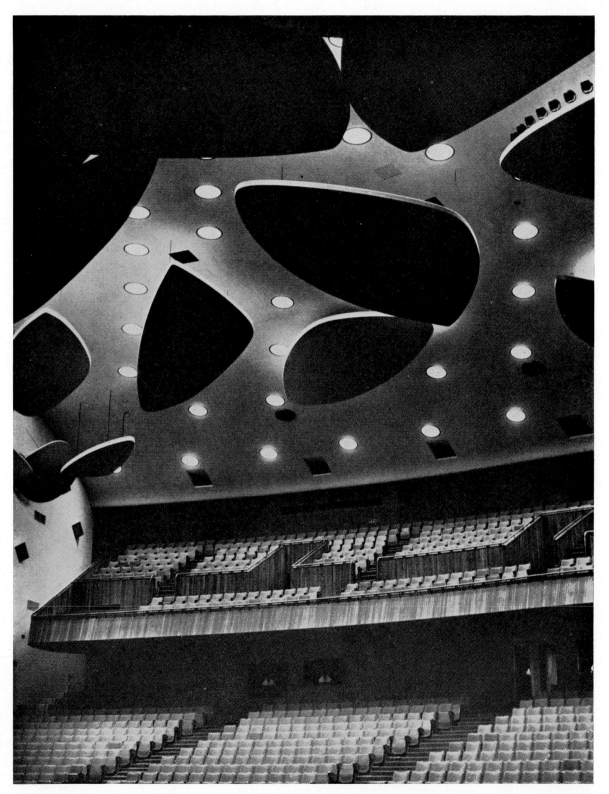

Fig. 273. THE AUDITORIUM OF THE "UNIVERSITY CITY" THEATRE, CARACAS, 1952–53,
DESIGNED BY CARLOS RAUL VILLANUEVA

248

Fig. 274. THEATRE PROJECT BY RALPH ALSWANG AND PAUL MARVIN RUDOLPH

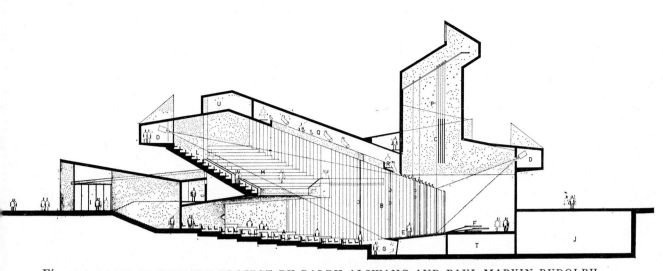

Fig. 275. PLAN OF THEATRE PROJECT BY RALPH ALSWANG AND PAUL MARVIN RUDOLPH
A. seats in groups separated by upholstered rails   B. translucent screens adjustable for stage, auditorium lighting, and movie projection   C. combination of three-dimensional elements flown from fly-tower used with lighting and movie projection   E. sliding doors on ramped stage   F. revolving cantilevered platforms   G. orchestra shell   I. foyer   J. workshops   Q. lighting gallery.

deeply, may not doubts arise in our minds? The film certainly engages the services of actors; but essentially it is an art-form entirely distinct from that of the stage. Here the basic intercommunication between those performing and those witnessing the performance is wholly absent; and the attempt to combine the two must ultimately lead to confusion. Quite apart from that, we may be led to believe that in eclecticism there is much more to be lost than

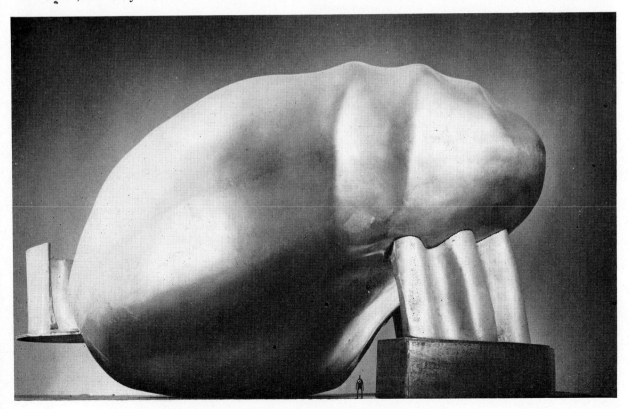

Fig. 276. THEATRE PROJECT BY FREDERICK JOHN KIESLER

gained. A really creative period in the theatre demands a playhouse structure intrinsically its own, not simply a building which incorporates within itself diverse elements taken from theatres of the past.

This, however, again brings us to still another dichotomy, the dichotomy between those who aim at fusing into a single structure all that is of significance in the past and those who clamour, often vaguely, that the theatre must be set free, seeking at all costs to project a playhouse which shall be utterly distinct from everything that has gone before. F. J. Kiesler, for example, thus envisages an architectural unit revolutionary and "modern" inside and out. In essence this takes shape as a sky-scraper erected on top of a main theatre; and in the sky-scraper, besides numerous offices and the like, there is "a variety of small theatres with capacities for seating 120 to 300 people." Not only, however, is the unit rebellious in the disposal of its space, it also boldly insists on its modernity in outward form; since concrete is

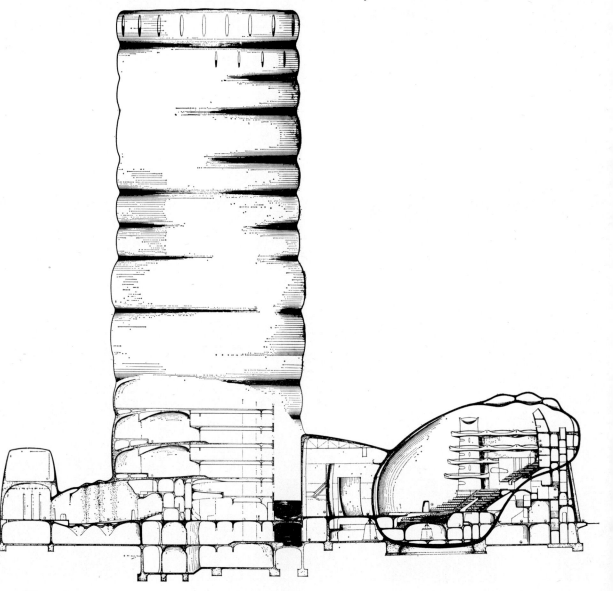

Fig. 277. LONGITUDINAL SECTION OF THEATRE PROJECT BY FREDERICK JOHN KIESLER

being employed, the architect argues that this building material should, as it were, be poured on rather than wrought into straight-line patterns.

These clashes and conflicts inevitably carry us back to Gaston Baty's words of 1949—"Le théâtre actuel est sous le signe de chaos." Everywhere there is a search for something new; but perhaps it may be suggested that, if this something new is to be truly effective, it will probably arise from a clear recognition that theatrical art cannot be confused with any other art such as the film, from the re-examination and re-exploration in a fresh light of the theatre's successes and failures in the past, from a rejection of modernism just for the sake of modernism, and from a hard and deliberate attempt to steer a passage through the whirlpool of this age's eclecticism.

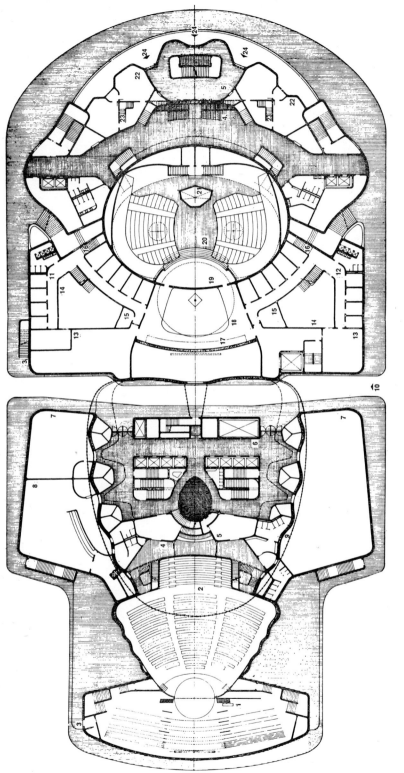

Fig. 278. PLAN OF THEATRE PROJECT BY FREDERICK JOHN KIESLER

1. stage house   2. small theatre   3. stage entrance   4–5. lobbies   6. entrance plaza   11–12. dressing rooms   20. arena stage.

Appendix

THE DIALOGUES OF LEONE DI SOMI

The *Dialogues on Stage Affairs*, by Leone di Somi, are here presented for the first time in their complete form. Although noted as early as 1789 by Risbaldo Orsini di Orbassano, they have never before (even in the original Italian) been printed as a whole; only small portions have hitherto been translated into English. Why they have not been put to greater use is a mystery, for they constitute an invaluable commentary on stage practice and on histrionic method at the period of their composition, probably about the year 1565, approximately when Shakespeare was born.

The author, Leone di Somi, belonged to a Jewish family of Mantua, that of the Portaleone, highly distinguished for its contributions to the art of science and medicine. Its real founder was Guglielmo Mizolo, who acted as body-physician to Ferdinando I of Naples, Galeazzo Sforza of Milan, and three Mantuan princes—Lodovico, Federigo, and Francesco Gonzaga. So richly were his talents regarded at Naples that he was accorded there the rare honour of knighthood—the only Jew of his age distinguished as a *cavaliere*. Guglielmo's two sons, Abraham and Lazzaro, were also doctors. The former acted for a period as court physician to Guidobaldo, Duke of Urbino, but towards the end of his life returned to his native Mantua under Federigo Gonzaga. His brother likewise left Mantua in his youth, attaching himself to Count Giovanni Sassatelli, general of the Venetian army, and he too found his way back under Lodovico Gonzaga. Lazzaro's two sons, Abraham and David, were during the early years of the sixteenth century duly licensed court physicians to Duke Federigo. David's son was still another Abraham, known to historians as the author of *Shilṭē hag-Gibbōrīm* (Mantua, 1612), and *De Auro, dialogi tres* (Mantua, 1584). David's line carries us, in a succession of notable doctors, well past the middle of the seventeenth century. His brother, Abraham, also had children, and from one of these was descended the author of the *Dialogues*. He was born at Mantua in 1527.

From 1567 to the time of his death we can trace this man's varied activities. Patronized by Mantuan nobility, he evidently became chief purveyor of theatrical entertainments to the court, and even projected the scheme for having a permanent public playhouse opened in his native city. From his activities he gained the distinction of becoming official *scrittore*, or author, to the famous Accademia degli Invaghiti, directed by Cesare Gonzaga. To commemorate the death of this prince he wrote and produced an "heroic pastoral," entitled *I doni*. Until his death in 1592 he seems to have proved an indispensable official in Mantuan service.

His activities embraced much more than the theatre. The social and religious work of his community occupied his attention. He founded a synagogue in Mantua; he was a noted writer of scrolls; and he came forward in his youth as a poet with a series of Hebrew and Italian verses "In Defence of Women." These are preserved now in a manuscript at the Bodleian Library, Oxford (Bodl. 2251). Another work, apparently even more interesting, is a Hebrew comedy, discovered and described by J. Schirmann. An Italian play, *L'Hirifile*, is all that remains of the large collection of his writings once preserved in the Biblioteca Nazionale in Turin.

Of the *Dialogues* there is extant only a copy, now in the Biblioteca Palatina of Parma. When these were written is a trifle difficult to determine. The address to the readers is dated 1556, but internal evidence demonstrates that, though they may have been begun in that year, they were certainly not completed until at least a decade later. The surest clues are the reference to Flaminia and to Leone Aretino. Flaminia made a great stir when she came to Mantua in 1567, and Leone Aretino's work for Duke Guglielmo's wedding was carried out in 1561. One might suggest that the composition of the original manuscript was undertaken about this time; it may be that the copyist's date 1556 was put in error for 1565.

Portions of the *Dialogues* are printed in Luigi Rasi, *I Comici italiani* (Florence, 1905), i, 106–112, and Alessandro D'Ancona, *Origini del teatro italiano* (Turin, 1891), ii, 411–422; short passages in English rendering appear in Winifred Smith, *The Commedia dell'Arte* (New York, 1912), and Kathleen M. Lea, *Italian Popular Comedy* (Oxford, 1934). The list of di Somi's works once preserved at Turin will be found in B. Peyron, *Codices Italici . . . qui in Biblioteca Taurinensis Athenaei . . . asservabantur* (Turin, 1904). The Portaleone family is dealt with in M. Mortara, *Un important document sur la famille des Portaleone* (*Revue des études juives*, 1886, xii, 113–116), David Kaufmann, *Leone de Sommi Portaleone* (*The Jewish Quarterly Review*, 1898, x, 445–461) and *Leone de Sommi Portaleone der Dramatiker* (*Gesammelte Schriften*, iii, 1915, 303–315), Vittore Colorni, *Note per la biografia di alcuni dotti ebrei vissuti a Mantova nel secolo xv* (*Annuario di studi ebraici*, 1934, i, 169–182), Luigi Carnevali, *Il ghetto di Mantova con appendice sui medici ebrei* (Mantua, 1884). Letters and documents relating to Leone's biography are presented in A. D'Ancona, *op cit.*, B. Peyron, *Note di storia letteraria del secolo xvi tratte dai manoscritti della Biblioteca Nazionale di Torino* (*Atti della R. Accademia delle Scienze di Torino*, 1884, xix, 743–759), Charles Dejob, *De la Condition des juifs de Mantoue au seizième siècle* (*Revue des études juives*, 1891, xxiii, 75–84), and A. Bertolotti, *Musica alla corte dei Gonzaga in Mantova del secolo xv al xviii* (Milan, 1890), 92. For the Accademia degli Invaghiti see Michele Maylender, *Storia delle accademie d'Italia* (Bologna, n.d.), iii, 363–366. The significance of Leone's Hebrew comedy is now widely recognized, largely thanks to the researches of J. Schirmann—in particular, *Eine hebräisch-italienische Komödie des xvi Jahrhunderts* (*Monatsschrift für Geschichte und Wissenschaft des Judentums*, 1931, lxxv, 97–118), *Hammahaze ha'ivri ha'rishon* ("The First Hebrew Drama," Jerusalem, 1946), and *Juda Sommo fondateur du Théâtre hébreu* (*Revue de la Pensée Juive*, No. 5, 1950, pp. 86–104), and *Theatre and Music in the Italian Ghetti between the 16th and 18th Centuries* (*Zion*, xxxix, 1964, 61–111). This drama is also dealt with by C. Roth in *The Jews in the Renaissance* (1959): the rôle played by its author forms a section of the second volume of S. Simonsohn's *The Jews in Mantua* (in Hebrew). The comedy itself, in an adapted form, was produced by the students of the Hebrew University of Jerusalem in 1963; and it is to be professionally presented by the Municipal Theatre of Haifa.

Lydia Pegna has an unpublished dissertation on *Leone de' Sommi* (Florence, 1930); she has presented *Alcune lettere inedite di Leone de' Sommi* in *La Rassegna mensile di Israel* (1933, vii, 549–57).

THE DIALOGUES OF LEONE DI SOMI

TO THE READERS

1556

I believe that these four Dialogues—which truly were composed more for my own personal convenience than from any desire of securing fame—may be of use to others and to myself as a set of rules, or at least as a record of what must be done in writing or in producing any dramatic poem; otherwise, I have no doubt, they would prove but useless and ill-pleasing. I earnestly beg whoever reads these dialogues for utility to accept whatever is to his purpose (for it is impossible that they can be entirely without service) and pardon me for the rest on account of the difficulty of my theme. I warn any persons who are not seeking for matter of information that they may expect neither usefulness nor pleasure in these writings, since my principal aim in this heavy task has been only to record, rather for myself than for others, in due order those more important rules and more necessary precepts of which I myself have often had to avail myself when obeying the commands of the authorities. Such rules and precepts have been taken from the writings of good authors whom I have not alluded to here lest I may seem to become by turns what one is accustomed to call familiarly a boorish pedant and a familiar Gratiano.

Sre. LEONE HEBo. DE SOMI

Assuredly with justice this terrestial existence has been styled by many philosophers both ancient and modern an earthly scene; for, while they stay on this earth, men must act even as the performers act on the stage. Just as the performers in tragedy, comedy, or similar pieces are costumed by the director—one set up as a prince and another as a citizen, one as a yeoman and another as a slave, others still in stranger guises—and then are turned forth on the stage each one to represent as well as he can the person he is told to interpret; and lastly, when the show is over, all are stripped of their borrowed clothes and returned to their former state, with praise or blame meted out in accordance with the manner, good or bad, in which they essayed their *rôles*; even so one sees men at birth tricked out in various guises by the Ruler of the universe, each one coming to play a part as best he can or as far as he wills till the drama of life arrives at its conclusion. Then, stripped and naked as he came, each one returns, bearing praise or blame—rather say, reward or punishment—according to the way he acted in the state and profession that was given him. But since not all men are accustomed to act at one time in the same play—some being introduced to-day in tragedies, others tomorrow in comedies, others only in farces or eclogues or in similar pastoral shows, others again in mimes, others in satires—so it happens that every man may frequently become, if he so desires, a spectator of many of his companions, and from the actions of others (if he be wise) can draw both use and pleasure; from their example he may profit, so that what he is called upon to do on this earthly stage will become such a show for the others as will leave no room for blame from those Arguses and Momuses who are ever lying in wait to blame us. This undoubtedly ought to be the aim of all dramatic performances; especially is it the scope of all the tragedies and comedies which are produced in well-regulated cities for honest entertainment—namely, to reveal those virtues which are to be imitated and those vices which are to be avoided and condemned. Thus, by such examples, is every one made aware of the manner in which he should govern his own actions. If, then, these dramatic performances (I refer, of course, to those which are worthy of esteem) have so much power to make us skilled in our own affairs—nay, if they are so prized that the whole world is none other than a scene or theatre where a continual spectacle is made of our actions—it seems to me that this dramatic method deserves to be dealt with much more carefully and in much greater detail than has been hitherto done by any writers ancient or modern. Hence—not in the belief that I can here entirely satisfy the need, but rather for the purpose of encouraging others to fill in what I leave blank—I have deemed it no vain task to set down these talks lately made by some of my friends on this subject. Since these conversations were entered into familiarly by men who make no pretensions to rhetoric or literary style, I have left them unaltered in their original purity, believing that often a meagre portion of natural beauty is more agreeable and valuable than a richly ornamented, but artificial, loveliness. With the same object, therefore, in which these four dialogues originated and with the same method and aim in which they were familiarly discussed by men who, as I said, made no professions toward poetry or oratory, I send them to your Illustrious Highness, so that by association with the glory of your name and the purity of your rare virtues the lowly state of that interlocutor who appears here under the name of Veridico may be granted a tinge of illustriousness. Veridico speaks without pomp of words and without intricacy of style; he would rather be held sincere and dutiful than witty and ambitious, learned and ingenious.

FIRST DIALOGUE

Interlocutors: MASSIMIANO, SANTINO, *and* VERIDICO

Massimiano. Let us call on Veridico, the embroiderer. I want to ask how he has got on with the cloak and circlet I ordered from him. I am very much afraid they won't be ready in time.

Santino. All right: let's go in. I should like to see the things.

Massimiano. And of course it's just possible we might be able to see a rehearsal of his play.

Santino. Oh? So the play we are to see at Tuesday's carnival is his doing, is it?

Massimiano. I believe so; and I should expect we'll see something rather fine. He has given good proof of his skill in these things on more than one occasion.

Santino. It is hard to credit that an ordinary workman can write a poem worthy of critical praise.

Massimiano. I tell you his talent is not to be laughed at. He is a most versatile man, and he excels particularly in playwriting. If I can persuade him I'd like you to see a rehearsal to-day. You would be surprised, I'm certain.

Santino. There's nothing I should enjoy more.

Massimiano. Here he is. Good day, my dear Veridico.

Veridico. Good day, sir, and good day to your friend. Pray be seated.

Massimiano. Well, how are my things getting on?

Veridico. Those two lads at the loom there are busy on them now; they say they'll be finished to-morrow morning. If you trust my word I'll stand surety for them.

Massimiano. That's all right, then.

Santino. What extraordinary costume is that you are holding? It is heavily ornamented with gold, and to me seems most effective and of a new cut.

Veridico. This is a costume designed for a Rainbow who is to conduct a noble lord to the lists at Sunday's tourney.

Massimiano. You don't tell us his name, eh?

Veridico. No, sir: just as I don't give up your secrets to others.

Santino. Just look, Massimiano, at that queer device on the shield over there.

Massimiano. I noticed it as we came in. I like it very much indeed. It shows a winged child throwing a stone into a river and watching the ripples circle outward in the water; childishly he seems to be trying to catch them. And the motto reads, "I catch naught." Besides being brief and from a well-known author, it is a most striking device.

Santino. Yes, but I rather suspect that those who refuse to admit the human figure into things of this kind will be inclined to condemn it.

Veridico. Pedants such as those do not worry me. The lord who is to bear this shield and I, its maker, might bring forward many arguments in its favour, but for us all that really matters is that this winged child harmonizes excellently with my lord's object and with his relations to his lady. She, I expect, will recognize the force of the motto and agree that the device is skilful and effective.

Massimiano. I think you are right.

Santino. And what new kind of headgear is that hanging there?

Massimiano. They are decidedly out of the common and pleasant to look at.

Santino. We won't ask whose they are, for you won't tell us; but I'd gladly know if they are to be used in our tourney or intended for some masquerade.

Veridico. Neither. To tell you the truth, confidentially, they are to be used in our play. The setting is supposed to be Constantina, and some of the women characters are dressed as Greeks with those ornaments in their hair.

Massimiano. I am simply dying to see your play. I'm sure I shall see and hear—in the poet's words— "things 'bove nature high and rare."

Veridico. May I remind you that in jesting at me you are jesting at one who is your most sincerely devoted servant?

Massimiano. Indeed, I protest, as I am your friend, as we came along here together we talked about you and agreed you have such talent (particularly in things of this kind) that we were certain to get from you not only the exquisitely beautiful but the novel and the fresh. But let that pass. Could we possibly be granted the favour of seeing a rehearsal of your play to-day?

Veridico. Not to-day, sir. I gave no instructions for the actors to meet to-day. To fetch them now would be a difficult task—nay, almost impossible.

Massimiano. I know what a job it is to collect people together even when they've had notice. At least, however, will you grant us the favour of entertaining us for half an hour—for we have nowhere special to go—saying something about this playwriting business?

Veridico. What do you want me to tell you?

Santino. What, in your opinion, is a play? Who first wrote plays? Of what use are they? Ought they to be in verse or in prose? Why are they divided into five acts? Things of that kind.

Veridico. These questions are difficult to answer: all the more so since those authors who have dealt with such subjects have treated them most confusedly. For my part, if I must, to please you, speak about this matter, I protest that I should not wish to repeat much of what others have written on this theme—not because I am so bold as to disagree with judgments made by men much wiser than myself, but because it were mere labour lost to repeat opinions of others regarding plot and plot-arrangement, decorum, and the various rules. In any case, since I am speaking to persons well skilled in these matters and well endowed with talent, I should like to leave all this aside.

Massimiano. Without any ceremonies, then, would you not say something on this subject for the brief period we are at leisure? We should esteem it and feel much obliged to you.

Veridico. Obliged to me? No, for it is my duty to do all in my power to serve you. Your request for me is a command. Here, then, I stand, prepared to give answers (though I know how inadequate they must be) to the questions you propose.

Massimiano. Without any further ceremony, then—save only that I must repeat how highly we esteem your skill in these matters—let us first put Santino's initial question: What is a play, and how did drama arise?

Veridico. Drama, according to the best authorities, is simply an imitation or mirror of human life, wherein vices are attacked and made odious and virtues praised in such a manner as to make people wish to follow them, by methods which will be more apparent when we have dealt with its origin and the manner by which it was introduced. Some think that the Athenian peasants were the first to provide an example of acting in that they, enraged at the authorities and having no other means of self-defence, used to march by night through the city streets traducing their oppressors; this, they say, developed to such an extent that crowds gathered to listen to their scandals, just as to-day love-lorn girls and lively youths gather on pleasant evenings for conversation. Since, however, opinions regarding this matter are diverse, and since I personally do not think it is of much importance to know who was the first actor, it being of far greater value to discover the first person who, in a dignified and judicious manner, composed a play suitable for and worthy of histrionic interpretation, I venture to put forward my own rather bold opinion on that subject. Very strongly do I object to our granting all credit to the lying Greeks. These Greeks have often laid claim to the glory of others, although in several ancient and sacred records we find ample proof of the existence of these arts and virtues long before their time. Tentatively, then, and rather as a theme for discussion than as an affirmation, I suggest that just as modern writers inherited the art of writing plays from Livius Andronicus, who is said to have been the first in time among the Latin dramatic authors, and later from Plautus and Terence, while these and other Romans inherited this art from Aristophanes, Menander, and possibly the still more ancient Eupolis, among the Greeks, so I believe that these Greeks might have learned the art of introducing diverse characters and of making them converse from the still more ancient sacred books of the Hebrews; this method may have been imitated later by Plato, and then came drama's first beginnings. If this be so, then Drama was not invented by some rude peasant, as others would have us imagine painting, kindred art to poetry, primarily arose. These critics say that a rustic shepherd standing with his flock in the sun saw the shadow of a goat cast on the ground and began idly to trace its outlines on the sand with his staff—hence the origin of that fine art which provides so gracious a mirror of nature. Not so, I say, do I believe drama to have been invented—neither by chance nor by rustic intellect. Drama is an imitation or mirror of human life, and I conceive it established by divine ordinance. The sublime genius of the holy legislator Moses, the famous leader of the Jews, after he had written his five books of divine law as delivered to him by oracle— nay, from the lips of Almighty God Himself—in 5550 verses, produced, as is demonstrated in the literature of the Jews, the magnificent and philosophic tragedy of Job, introducing therein just five human characters. No doubt this was not written to be represented on the stage (although it has been so represented many times since then), but it was cast in the form of a dialogue or discussion in which various characters took part—that is to say, in the form assumed by every poem suited for dramatic representation. One might perhaps believe that the first things recited publicly were (as the critics say) rustic colloquies, since some indication of this is given by the word "scene," which may be derived from *scigni*, the significance of which both in Greek and in popular Italian is "leafy," in allusion to the places where these primitive folk acted their rustic plays. Hence, they say, the origin of satyr plays and of pastoral eclogues. On the other hand, *scèhonà* is a Hebrew word meaning "way" or "street" where there is a group of houses, and it seems to me more likely that the first plays were presented by city folks in a habited spot with settings akin to those we have now. Of this I wish, at a more fitting time, to speak later. To add further proof, I may mention that

I have translated from the Chaldean a most ancient work, called *The Course of Life*, in which is introduced a youth inexperienced in the ways of the world and a guardian angel who briefly but skilfully and with mysterious power exhorts him to live a good life and counsels him to go dressed in a simple costume of pure white linen given to him by the angel. The youth seems well disposed to follow his advice, but when left alone he allows the Tempter, who appears before him with lovely aspect and conceals his monstrous horrid features, to flatter him with his lies and dress him up in rich, proud garments. On hearing this his better angel reproves him, and he, repentant, casts off the costly raiment. Then anew he is suborned by the Tempter, assuming once more the world's delights and all its transitory joys. In the end, after a long debate, through the admonitions of the good angel, who makes him look into a mirror, he recognizes his true self: in astonishment he looks—sees himself in the twinkling of an eye turned into an aged man—and in a fit of repentance strips off all those damnable worldly clothes of his. Then, with a devout and pious prayer, he submits to God's will. This piece is written so excellently and so well planned that one must assume it was composed for representation, and, indeed, that it was probably acted in public. From this, and for many other reasons, I argue that the origin of drama lies far back in the past—farther back than Greek authors would lead us to suppose. Thus—to continue with the main subject of our discussion—I declare that, in my opinion, I am right in affirming that from the afore-mentioned poem of Job (more ancient assuredly than any other of which we have record) these first poets must have derived the dramatic method; from this poem, too, I am prepared to believe they may have drawn the practice, much observed among the ancients, of making tragedies out of real events and historical episodes—for I assume, as many do, that the story of Job is literally true. Even if those are right who regard this holy poem as of divine but fictional invention for the purpose of introducing the concepts of the philosophers, and so of aiding the listeners (the genuine end of every theatrical work)—even following their opinion, we must agree that here there is the tragic weaving of some familiar tale with a moral aim and theological purpose. Although some moderns may believe that a poet be permitted to invent the whole subject of a tragedy (as, it seems, Aristotle does in the *Poetics*), they do not deny that it is better to search for a true tale, and that, unless there is any special reason against its adoption, this should be utilized; the reason being that a spectator, knowing that what he sees before him has a basis in truth, will be moved to greater terror and pity as he watches the tragic events and characters, and, being more deeply moved, will have his mind better purged of vices, will derive, too, more profit from the examples set on the stage, since these will be regarded as verities and not as fictions. Such tragedies, both in dialogue and in action, are to be expressed with an imagery the more vivid and the more elevated than that of comedy as the regal majesty of tragedy is elevated above the ordinary. Yet both tragedy and comedy are designed as things to give pleasure, even while they present warnings whereby may be learned, by means of eminent fictions and exemplars, the way to a good and temperate life; this is the end of every tragic poem and of every comic poem alike, whether put into representation or only described. The only essential difference between them is this, that tragedies introduce as their chief characters royal persons speaking serious dialogue in a majestic way and involved in terrible actions, all conceived in a style suitable to their grandeur, whereas in comedy (which is but a mirror of ordinary life) only honest citizens and their manners are depicted, in a style harmonious with their character, all for the purpose of taxing vice and lauding virtue. Here the terrors of tragedy are transformed into such pleasant delights as are suitable to comedy, the object of which is to instruct by example and rouse delight by means of quip and jest.

Santino. If it is only thus they differ—or, to be more correct, present variation—why are so many things allowed in the one which are regarded as faults in the other?

Veridico. What do you mean?

Santino. Is it not the peculiar property of tragedy to have a sad ending and of comedy to have a happy conclusion?

Veridico. No, sir, it is not the happy ending or the sad that gives to a poem the title of tragic or comic; the distinction lies in the quality of the persons introduced and of the situations in which they are involved. Indeed, we find tragedies which end on a note of consolation (as in the poem of Job I mentioned, although it starts with many horrors, disasters, and deaths). I share the view of the best critics that we cannot lay down any exact rule limiting tragedy to an unhappy ending. This, indeed, has led some to hazard the opinion that deaths and disasters are not prohibited to comedy, even although comedy does not deal with characters permitted, through their position of authority, to do with themselves or others what they please, as is true of the persons playing the principal *rôles* in tragedy.

Santino. Supposing—but not granting—that it is true, according to these critics' views, that so much is proper to tragedy as is allowed to a king or a great noble, and also that comedy may introduce only private citizens, may we not trace beyond that, in the matters that do not depend on this social difference in the characters, some measure of distinction between the two kinds?

Veridico. As for instance?

Santino. Well—say the introduction of an innocent virgin on the stage in a speaking part. This would be regarded as a great fault in comedy, and yet is readily allowed in tragedy.

Veridico. That, too, depends on the difference in position of the characters. It is easy to decide, when we wish to do so, what ought to be the actions of kings and what of citizens. I say what they ought to be, and not what they are, because the poet (as Aristotle says) must always represent things in the most perfect way possible. Here another thing occurs to me, and I trust you will permit a slight digression. It is important to observe that to this more than to anything else the poet ought to devote attention, for, if he does not give to all his characters the most perfect and natural existence, he will endeavour in vain to convince us that he is doing something worthy of esteem. He must apply to each one (as Horace indicates well in his *Poetics*) the qualities proper to their age, position, and profession, as well as to the situations in which they are placed— all in the manner most worthy of imitation. The ancients, therefore, did well in accepting the law that a virgin should not be permitted to appear in comedies lest by such an example citizens' daughters, who ought to be bashful and retiring, might be induced to gad abroad and engage in public gossip. On the other hand, a prince's daughter might be allowed to appear in public, for the reason that few would be so bold as to dare attack the honour of such a woman—where there is no hope love clearly can take no root. Love is universally recognized as arising from a certain equality between lover and object—equality in blood or constellation or position; speaking generally, where there is inequality there can be no love. Daughters of princes, therefore, may go out and speak to others in the streets, both because their position makes them freer and, more particularly, because it is presumed that no one will violate their honour, there being few persons (and those far distant) of an equality with them. Such procedure is not allowed to citizens' daughters because in the city there are thousands of their own class; going out of doors, therefore, brings to them much danger of evil hap. She who values her honour must avoid the chance of scandal, even if that be purely baseless. Comedy, therefore, which is designed to present good examples, ought not to permit anyone to say a word or to indulge in an action contrary to that person's position and quality. Although it does not seem wrong to bring in, say, a malicious and astute servant, a bold and shrewd waiting-maid, a flattering and mendacious parasite, a suspicious and avaricious old man, it would be an intolerable fault to apply these vices to a young gallant, a noble student, an honest girl, or an aged and wise father of a family. On the other hand, it is true that the poet is allowed—and often by this means gives great delight to his auditors—to tax vice by introducing a person marked by some single vice. Thus, in order to attack some contemporary social error (and particular attention ought to be given to this) there may be brought on the stage a doctor, or rather a prescription-monger, who thinks far more of his pennies than of curing his patients, endeavouring always to pocket some money, instead of honestly aiming at bringing health; or else a doctor of laws who cheats his client because he has been bribed by the other party in the case; or an old man whom love has turned into a fool and who is thus involved in ridiculous action. Such satirical touches not only are permitted, but give great delight when their object is to condemn vice or expose knaveries for the spectators' benefit. To conclude, I say that our first aim must be to treat everything in a natural manner, and that we must always think of giving instruction—otherwise we land ourselves in the booby's mathematics where naught from naught is naught.

Massimiano. I doubt not that, precisely because they aimed at this naturalness you speak of, the ancient writers of comedy refrained from introducing more than three speaking characters on the stage at one time, or, if they did introduce a fourth, from giving him more than a few lines of dialogue. For it is not natural that cultured men should indulge in confused conversation.

Veridico. Yes, indeed, and hence, too, comes the rule that no character should don disguise when he is actually on the stage, since it is unlikely that a person who changes his costume in order to go unrecognized, or for some other secret purpose of his own, should do so in public. For the same reason one of our play-wright friends has made a rule in a new comedy he has written that none of his characters should utter any lengthy soliloquies. All he has permitted is that some of them should make a few short jesting or angry asides. This gentleman declares it as his opinion that, just as it is esteemed a fault for an actor on the stage to address his remarks to the spectators, for these spectators never are in the place where the actor is supposed to be, so he deems it unfitting that a person who is supposed to be in a public street should raise his voice in long soliloquies beyond the custom of nature and, contrary to every practice of civilized life, talk like an idiot to himself—since, as has been pointed out, he has not the authority to address the spectators directly.

Massimiano. So far your answers, all concerned with our first question, have been most satisfying. In addition to having had a direct reply, we have learned about the origin of comedy, what comedy is, and how it has for its object the condemning of vices and the praising of virtues. Now I should like you to give us your opinion concerning the form to be employed in comedy—whether you think it should be in verse or in prose. I suppose we may put rimed verses out of account, since I imagine it is commonly agreed that such verse is unsuited for such dramatic compositions.

Veridico. This is a question on which opinions differ very considerably and each critic brings forward his own special arguments, authorities, and examples. The learned Bibiena, who was perhaps the first to produce a true vernacular comedy worthy of the name, wrote his *Calandria* in prose and had good reason for so doing. For if the value of a comedy (presupposing, of course, that it be substantial in content and well planned) is increased by its fidelity to nature, and so by its power of convincing the spectators into the belief that what they see before them are real events happening casually, and not merely things imagined by the poet, then its worth will be still further augmented if it be composed, not in verse, but in prose. It is obvious that in familiar speech we do not observe regularity of rhythm, and, however expert the actor may be, he cannot in speaking verse always conceal the presence of the verse form; indeed, many critics have attacked prose writings where some passages fall into verse rhythm through the carelessness of the authors. On the other hand, the judicious and truly unique Ariosto (whose comedies perhaps take first place among those written in Italian, even although they contain little of the purely laughable, which alone seems to please contemporary popular tastes), although he once held to this opinion, changed it later; all his prose comedies he rewrote in blank verse. So, too, the illustrious Ercole Bentivoglio, whose high genius and prime authority is universally recognized, has written all his comedies in verse, not so much, I believe, for the purpose of imitating the ancient Romans and Greeks and Hebrews as in the belief that so lovely and useful an art as comedy, to attain the rank of a perfect poem, demanded the dignity and the harmony of verse utterance. Truly, considering the matter generally, it would appear that this view is the just one; but, considering it particularly, it is obviously necessary to compare the nature of verse, especially dramatic verse, among the ancients with our vernacular verses. When this is done it will be immediately realized that, whereas theirs were excellently suited to comic composition, ours are but poorly adaptable for such a purpose. The chief reason is that our verses of eleven syllables, as opposed to those of the Romans, Greeks, and Hebrews, move so swiftly and end in such a regular note that we cannot escape in it a fettering and resonance which, in relation to the domestic subjects ordinarily introduced into comedy, become thoroughly artificial. The authors I have mentioned and other gifted modern writers have realized this, and (to avoid such a fault) have been consequently forced to make use of weak endings, so providing a lighter close to the line and a greater linking of verse to verse. Clearly this is nearer to the prose of common speech. So far as tragedy is concerned, we note that there has never been any author who made use of aught but verse for this kind of drama. Nor can I, for my part, counsel a change in such a method by the substitution of tragic dialogue in prose; for truly verse is more suited to the dignity out of which the tragic impression arises. The majesty inherent in the theme, the appearance of a king, of a queen, and of suchlike persons who are the normal characters in tragedy, seem to demand a speech more weighty and more rhythmical than that of common men. Of course, the poet must take care to avoid over-use of consonants in his verses and the repetition of sounds; he must, too, be careful to see that sentences do not always end at the close of verses, so escaping that severe rhetoric and that boring resonance, which, already condemned in comedy, would become un-utterably monotonous in tragedy. By frequent breaking of the lines, while keeping them pleasing and harmonious, the poet's verses will gain in dignity and nobility and at the same time they will have the ease of prose when they are recited; the combination of this ease with the majesty of verse produces an enjoyable and gracious effect. Furthermore, since tragedies and comedies are written to be presented on the stage as well as to be read, the author must take care, when introducing any subject, to relate it to the action and to the dialogue. The comic poet, indeed, can have no success unless he has qualified actors to interpret his work. Concerning these actors—a most important subject—I wish to speak to you later; so, too, I want to say something about the settings, for the stage, as the saying goes, is the trial of the play and many things delightful in the reading will be insipid when produced, and *vice versa*. Since I have touched on this matter—which is of much greater significance than most people realize—I may take an example to demonstrate what I mean. Among his prose tales Boccaccio introduces a charming one wherein Bruno and Buffalmacco persuade Calandrino that he has become invisible because of the Heliotropia he imagines he has discovered. With many jests they proceed to stone him—and the tale is most charming in the reading. I have, however, seen this plot reproduced on the stage in a blank-verse comedy, and the whole thing proved most boring—partly because of the regularity of the verse, which gave it a sing-song quality, but chiefly because of the abstract nature of the theme, which is ill-adapted for stage presentation. The spectators always had in front of their eyes this fool who thought he was invisible and consequently refused to believe that he could possibly be such a booby as to think no one saw him. Thus by these two things the naturalness of the story disappeared, and, deprived of that, it may be said to have been reft of its very spirit. Hence the great master of poetry well admonishes us that we ought rather to attempt a description of impossible or unnatural things than endeavour to introduce them physically on the stage. Thus, to conclude, it seems to me that both in words and in actions the author must employ those means which seem most natural and pleasing; hence, too, I deem, as I have said, that in comedies we ought to use prose, as being more fitting for familiar dialogue, while for tragedy verse, as possessing more of the majesty and loftiness suitable to the tragic mood, is to be preferred. Even here, however, it is desirable that the verse to be recited on the stage should approximate so far as possible to prose utterance.

Santino. You have expressed it as your belief that comedy and tragedy both spring from the same source and that both have the same aim, each in its particular manner pointing out virtues by good examples and discrediting vice. Yet, so far as medium of expression is concerned, you seem to allow a vast measure of difference between them by granting verse to the one and prose to the other.

Veridico. On the contrary, the difference is but a slight one. Ultimately each introduces simply a collection of words; the only distinction is that in verse the arrangement is more rhythmical and harmonious and consequently verse is, as I have said, more fitted for the majesty of a regal tale; while prose, because it is more colloquial and familiar, seems better suited for the easy tone of a less exalted theme. Please note, however, that I assume that this prose should ever have its own measure of perfection. Just as verse must have a measure of perfection of its own, we should recognize that prose too must possess its own fundamental standards and move on with a pleasing vigour, without lapsing into limping or insipid phrases. Prose has an art form of its own, together with rules that apply specifically to it and to it alone; and when it is judiciously written there is to be recognized in it a kind of rhythmic flow akin to that observable in formal verse.

Massimiano. There seems to me to be indeed great force in your arguments, and I believe there is no contradiction in your remarks. On just one matter I should like further explanation before you proceed to other things. What did you mean when you spoke of comedies having an entire theme? In other words what kind of themes do you accept as entire and which do you reject?

Veridico. By an entire theme I mean that which contains a double plot, since comedies with but a single development or of simple plot were little esteemed among the ancients and by us are regarded as of slight value. The reason is that double plots well harmonized together seize more powerfully on the imagination of an audience and avoid monotony by the variety of action introduced. Hence those comedies are worthy of greatest praise which cheat spectators into the belief that one action must end in a particular way and then conclude in another, for every one derives greater pleasure from witnessing a fresh and unexpected termination of events.

Massimiano. I think, Veridico, that so far you have answered our queries in a most able manner. Now will you please tell me about the division of comedies into five acts? Do you consider that this is done of conscious design or that the division is purely fortuitous? At the same time I should much like to know why these divisions are termed acts.

Veridico. It is my firmly held belief that, just as comedy was not of chance origin but, as I said, derived by imitation from a divine poem, so it was divided into five acts not fortuitously, but of set purpose. To reply briefly first of all to the second part of your question before proceeding to deal in greater detail with the original query—I should say that these parts of a comedy are called acts because of the actions occurring in them, since, as you are aware, comedy of movement is more worthy of esteem than static comedy, actions or deeds, together with the dialogues, being the principal means by which this kind of art is expressed. As I said before, the perfect comedy does not consist merely in fine descriptions, but demands also suitability for good stage representation.

Santino. Pray, before you proceed further, tell me—for I do not know it—the derivation of the word "comedy."

Veridico. The professors of Greek inform us that "comedy" is derived from *chomi*, meaning "song," and *odi*, meaning "discourse"; or else from *comos* and *ode*, which signify a rustic ditty. The latter derivation would be based on the assumption that, as we saw above, peasants were the first actors.

Santino. And how did the actors come to be called *histrioni*?

Veridico. They say that the ancient Tuscans, who are descended from the Lydians, employed the word *hister* for the entertainer who postured both in private houses and on the stage.

Massimiano. I am anxiously waiting now for you to tell us why comedies are divided precisely into five acts, and also—if this does not lie entirely outside the scope of the question—why the ancient comic dramatists did not permit their actors to come upon the stage more than five times.

Veridico. The latter is a rule which is but little observed even among the ancients, yet I trust I shall satisfy you that——

Santino. Wait a moment, please. Two, three, four, five. It is five o'clock, Massimiano—we are due at the castle.

Massimiano. Bother the necessity of service—I almost called it by a worse name! I am really grieved that it prevents me from hearing an answer to the question I was so eager to get answered.

Veridico. Every living person must serve some one; and he who serves so courteous a lord as yours is need not complain and style his service slavery. Go where your duties summon you, and I shall defer that last part of our discussion till to-morrow, when your costume will be finished. I shall then conclude our discourse, God willing, and seek as best I can to give you full satisfaction.

The *Second Dialogue* wherein there is a discussion concerning the division of comedy into five acts and concerning the arrangement and proportion to be desired in a dramatic poem.

SECOND DIALOGUE

Interlocutors: Santino, Massimiano, *and* Veridico

Santino. Every hour seems an age to me, so anxious am I to hear what the excellent man has to say about the division of comedies into acts.

Massimiano. There he is. Look—under the loggia, sitting and picking his teeth after dinner. Good day, Veridico. How are you?

Veridico. Good day, gentlemen. Since you have come so soon, I know now that no time had to be lost in getting your costume ready. Here it is all ready and carefully finished.

Massimiano. It was not for the costume we came so soon, although I am glad to see it finished. We have hurried back because we are so eager to hear what you have to say about the division of comedy into acts, and, too, about some other matters on which we want to ask you questions. First of all, will you give us your opinion concerning the rule proposed by certain of the ancients which would prohibit actors from entering the stage more than five times? I know, of course, that the moderns pay but scant attention to it.

Veridico. This rule of the grammarians seems to me to be utterly false whether we consider it generally or in its particular application. Terence—assuredly a most scrupulously exact playwright—broke it frequently. In the *Andria* he makes Davus come on the stage seven times, and in the *Heautontimoroumenos* I believe Chremes enters eight times. You will find the same licence, I think, elsewhere in plays I have not carefully examined from this point of view. Granted, however, that some persons think this rule should be kept, I am inclined to believe the reason that the early comic actors were not permitted to enter more than five times is the same that governs the division of comedy into five acts. In discussing this division perhaps we shall also indirectly resolve the other question. So far I have discovered no references of any kind to this subject. I do not propose at present to say much concerning the general significance of the number five, although that has a decided bearing on the point at issue; I shall limit myself to one explanation—a very pertinent one, methinks—of which I am rather proud. I shall indeed rejoice if it pleases you: should it not, then take it as propounded rather as part of a familiar discourse for the purpose of meeting your inquiries than as a formal argument intended to bring absolute conviction.

Santino. I know well we cannot but be satisfied; but please do not put aside this lengthy discourse which, you say, may be delivered on the number five. At least give us such part of it as is intimately related to our particular theme.

Veridico. The number five, as you are aware, includes within itself a two and a three—let us call them the even and the odd in one. The even is related to the feminine, and the odd, as being more perfect, to the masculine; whence the Pythagoreans called five the matrimonial number and the Gentile philosophers applied it to Mercury, god of sciences, particularly of mathematics, arithmetic, geometry, and music. In addition to this, we find that the number five is the mediator or mean of all numbers; these, as we all know, extend only to ten and are then repeated; hence the philosophers style it the number of justice. This is the first number which, multiplied by itself, returns to itself; just as the circle, a perfect figure, turns within itself. Doubled, it makes the entire number—as compasses, opened a further space, form a circle of double size. It is said, too, that this number five has great power over evil spirits, and one learns from occult philosophy that it is particularly potent against poisons. The swallow, which possesses such wonderful properties in matters supernatural, produces its young in fives.

Santino. May I interrupt to ask you one question? What are these properties?

Veridico. I shall not speak here of the virtue of certain stones which grow in its stomach or of some marvellous properties these birds have in relation to love and hate; sufficient be it that magicians lay great store on their plumage.

Santino. I myself have noted one extraordinary thing in connexion with swallows which I had certainly thought you would have mentioned.

Veridico. And that is—— ?

Santino. I have pierced the eyes of young swallows in the nest and left them there. Then the mother returned, found them blind, and by the aid of a herb restored their vision.

Veridico. Yes, I have often heard of that and of many other marvellous qualities they possess. However, lest we wander too far from the subject, let us get back to the question of the fivefold division of comedy. To begin at the beginning, I say that comedy—as, indeed, I indicated before—is nothing but an imitation or speculum of civil life, and, since its end is society, it is clear that the closer its relationship is to man the greater will be its perfection. Now, I need only show you that this form of art is an exemplum of human life to demonstrate that its structure is as mysterious and perfect as is the structure of man. That man is perfect, not only as being human but also as participating in the divine, is sufficiently manifest, since he includes within himself both the quality of this inferior world and that of the heavenly and divine. Because of this the Greeks termed man the microcosm, indicating thus that within himself he embraced something of the whole universe—the inferior world, the celestial world, and the spiritual—as, indeed, is affirmed by the authority of Holy Scripture, where (to select only one example from the beginning of Genesis) it is said, "God created man in his own image, in the image of God created he him." Man's structure, then, is sublime and perfect; and at once we recognize that he is made up in terms of five—five senses—seeing, hearing, tasting, smelling, and touching; five psychological qualities—vegetable, sensible, lustful, irascible, and rational; five extremities—head, two hands, and two feet (just as the world is divided into five zones). Not only has our body these five extremities, but each one of these extremities is divided into five: five fingers to each hand, five toes to each foot, five parts to the head—eyes with visual sense, ears with sense of hearing, nose with sense of smell, mouth with sense of taste, and finally, although the sense of touch is spread through all our members, we get the fifth, the sense of touch, specifically related to the supreme intellect, whose seat is in the brain. To sum up, there are five extremities to this microcosm, each with its own five extremities. Furthermore, we realize that the whole human body is made up of five chief parts—bones, nerves, veins, muscles, and flesh. The sacred law, therefore, which is divine and granted directly by God to mankind, was for this reason (among others more mysterious and arcane) divided into five books, which are to be read with but five principal vowels; on the front page of this law we see written the great name of God expressed in five letters, by means of which the cabalists declare the whole world was created. In five books and no more the Psalmist, Prophet, and King, David, composed his famous Song of Songs, and this truly cannot have been by chance, but must have come of set purpose for reasons partly revealed, partly shaded in solemn darkness. And so Moses, who was imitated by David and others, in instructing those early fathers in divine law and civil government, inspired by the Holy Spirit and with the consent of the All-Highest, chose this division by five—itself a symbol of the divine and intimately related to the essential nature of the microcosm, as we have already demonstrated. In writing his significant and philosophic poem of Job Moses, moreover, made use of but five characters. This being so, what better division could be sought for or discovered by the ancient Greek and Roman poets when they came to compose comedies—that most useful form of art, designed solely to instruct others delightfully how to pursue virtue and avoid vice?

Massimiano. We are to take it, then, from your discourse that comedy ought to be an image or mirror of a perfect human being?

Veridico. So I believe. Not only should there be five acts, corresponding to the five extremities of the human figure and to the five extremities of each of these taken separately, but every individual act must be associated with one of the extremities—the first with the head, the second with the left hand, the third with the right, the fourth and fifth with the left and right feet respectively—the whole taking shape as a well-planned organism, unified by a dominant spirit. Its soul will be the main theme which will give life to all the various parts, each of which must be proportioned to the shape of the entire body and not presented as though it was monstrously formed or maimed.

Santino. This I should like dealt with in greater detail.

Veridico. Well, just as a man sees and hears and understands through the senses located in his head, so the first act of a comedy with its exposition, which we might style the demonstration of the argument, must present to the understanding and sight the principal bases of the plot. Similarly, just as the left hand, being the weakest, does not aid man much in defending him against dangers, unless he is able to employ his stronger right hand to realize his aims, so the intrigues and mischances which ought to be introduced in a well-planned comedy throughout the course of the second act, would result in utter disaster were it not that, quite naturally, the third act carried these affairs to a happier conclusion. And just as we should, in traversing the ways of this weary world, stumble into many of the pitfalls and precipitous dangers placed around us were it not for the firmness of our right feet which God has given us as our stay and support, so the disasters and threats which occur at the climax of the intrigue—or, rather, the epitasis of the fourth act—might result in complete ruin for the characters and plunge our minds into hopeless gloom, if it were not that the fifth act, introducing catastrophe and peripeteia, brought everything to a fortunate conclusion. Summing up, we may say that, even as the heart distributes its spirit to all man's members, so the theme of a play should send its spirit into all the parts of the work, giving the impression that nothing has been brought in needlessly or without purpose any more than any member of our body has been created in vain.

Massimiano. We are to assume, then, that in your opinion the first act of a well-constructed comedy should contain the argument and exposition, in the second we should see various disturbances and hindrances, in the third some adjustment must be made, ruin and disaster must threaten in the fourth, while in the fifth a solution is to be reached, bearing all to a joyous and happy ending.

Veridico. Yes, that is my idea. At the end all the characters must reach a state of happy contentment.

Santino. According to your able demonstration, it is clear that comedy has been given five acts, neither more nor less, because of careful forethought. I am prepared to believe that the actors were forbidden to leave the stage empty except between these five acts in order that the audience should not imagine the play to be divided into more portions.

Veridico. I should think that was the reason.

Santino. A comedy, then, is divided into five acts. Now, every act is divided into scenes—have you by chance any opinion to express concerning the number of scenes each act should have?

Veridico. The number of scenes introduced in an act is left to the discretion of the author. I am inclined to accept the common view that an act should not include less than two scenes or more than nine. It is well, I think, to keep to these limits.

Massimiano. In accordance with what you have said, Veridico, I suppose you will not deny that those plays which have only three acts—called, I know not why, farces—are imperfect.

Veridico. Such plays cannot be termed imperfect simply for that reason. Granted that they are written cleverly and according to the rules, they deviate from the others only in having a simple theme. The comedies of double plot which, counting in the intermedii (of which we shall speak later), are designed to last in performance for four or five hours would certainly become boring without the provision of suitable intervals. The fivefold division, besides the reasons for its observance given above, has this virtue, that it provides the author with a period between each act which may stand for four, six, or eight hours, a lapse of time frequently necessary between one episode and another in a comedy which introduces various themes. But those pieces which in plot and scope did not come within the sphere of true comedy, and yet would be tedious in performance were they not provided with any intervals, were divided into three parts only. They could not bear the perfect fivefold division, the symbol of the human figure, but approached that human figure as nearly as they might. Please note that, although I have demonstrated the fivefold division to be that natural and proper to comedy, it by no means follows that poems unsuited to this division are consequently imperfect. Rather may we say that farces or eclogues with simple plots find their most fitting arrangement in three parts. This, too, harmonizes with the human figure, which may be considered as threefold also, a likeness of the three worlds. From the stomach, called the diaphragm, down to the legs man corresponds to the lower world; from the waist to the throat he corresponds to the celestial; while the head, the highest part of the body, is the genuine image of the spiritual world. All this I could easily demonstrate in detail if that had been the main subject of our talk. Moreover, we see that man is made up of soul, body, and spirit, the last uniting the first two. Thus it will be realized that farce adopts the same method of division as comedy—that is to say, it has the same number of acts as the parts of the body. Indeed, it may be argued in favour of this division that the five extremities of the human body are reducible to three—the head, the two hands taken together, and the two feet. And although it seems a little beyond our present subject, I should like to remark that verse is better than prose in satyr-plays and eclogues, since these are works wherein under the guise of shepherds, gods, and goddesses we see reflected that simplicity, purity, and joy of the early ages imaginatively described by our famous poets. I do not, of course, wish to affirm that no author may invent out of his own imagination tales and plots (provided they be full of marvels) in order to weave these into pastoral settings; on the contrary, I believe that such a licence is granted to them, as it is to writers of comedy. And, since the men of these times must be represented not only as happy in their sincerity but also virtuous and of high genius, it is fitting that they be brought on the stage embellished with certain resplendent and good qualities apt to arouse in the audience both commendation of the honesty existent in those times and admiration of the cultured genius and the integrity of the men of that period, alike in word and action. Just as verse, as being more choice and refined than common speech, is used in these works, so the presence of gods, denied to comedy, is permitted here. The tragic poet is, of course, allowed to introduce gods (perhaps following the example of Moses, who brought in the deity as a speaking character in his tragedy of Job); similar introduction of gods is permitted in pastoral plays even in our days. It cannot cause any hurt to religion, for there is no fear that such foolish idolatries should cheat men into error; we realize now throughout the whole world that there is only one God worthy of true adoration and reverence. I have touched on this subject to combat the views of some hypocrites, who in a pretence of devotion are used to condemn the appearance of pagan gods in plays of this kind, declaring that they present a bad example. These fools do not realize that such profane superstitions may be treated humorously in a way we could not permit with things sacred and divine.

Massimiano. In referring to these hypocrites you have brought to my mind an objection made by a certain zealous friend of ours who would not allow in any comedy the slightest word or phrase of a licentious kind. What do you think about this?

Veridico. There is no doubt that if comedies were to be witnessed always by wise and virtuous people they would be the more praised the farther removed they were from every lascivious and obscene thought. But since there will ever be among the audience more licentious persons stained by some vice than wholly virtuous ones, and since their humour must be met, I think that the introduction of a few licentious phrases in a comedy will not come amiss. Just as we praise a doctor who conceals a bitter medicine with a jam pleasing to the corrupt taste of his patient, so we should not blame the poet who, desiring to present in his plays salutary material, conceals this sometimes by appealing to the corrupt taste of an infirm age. The true beauty of comedy, after all, consists in its power to give entertainment to every one—and this particularly in our times. To do this adequately it must, as modestly as it may, appeal to men of every type, and endeavour to hold the attention even of those who will fall asleep during the philosophic scenes and moral discourses by which the poet interests others and will be aroused only by laughter at vulgar and immodest jests. These men are like the blacksmith's dog who sleeps through the sound of the hammer by means of which his master gains his livelihood, but wakens up at the sound of his master's teeth when he starts eating the bread he has won by his toil. Hence I should not condemn the introduction of some small obscenities in a comedy any more than I should condemn the human body, from which comedy takes its perfect form, because some of its limbs are shameful. Indeed, since comedy (as I have said) ought to follow otherwise the proportions of our bodies, so it undoubtedly ought to in this. Just so much and not more should it be allowed of licentiousness as is the proportion of shameful parts in respect of man's other members. This will not take from comedy the unity we have credited it with, but rather will make it more perfect and complete. Be this observed, however, that, as Nature places these shameful parts of the human body in a position easily concealed, so the poet ought, in his mirror of civil life, to hide every vicious element. And since all civilized men cover those parts either with clothes or animals' skins or at least leaves of the trees, it should be noted that every vulgar phrase ought to be concealed with virtuous words. This is easy to accomplish and is highly laudable. Here let us finish our talk for to-day.

Santino. In your speaking about these matters you have more than once said that you would tell us something about the stage business and the intermedii and the methods of acting. We don't want to tire you too much just at present, but we shall hold you to your promise and shall content ourselves now by hoping that you will fulfil it. Now we are going off. Good-bye.

In the *Third Dialogue* there are treated the rules of acting, the method of costuming, and everything that appertains to the stage, with many valuable comments.

THIRD DIALOGUE

Interlocutors: SANTINO, MASSIMIANO, *and* VERIDICO

Santino. We shall be in luck if this excellent fellow gives us as good material on the producing of plays as he has given in his other talks. I like his way of always presenting valid reasons for all his arguments.

Massimiano. For my part I should think his talk to-day will be even better than the others, because he has directed more plays than he has written. He is therefore likely to be more expert in matters of production than in those of play-construction. But here he is himself.

Santino. Dinner-time seemed an age to us, Veridico, we so longed to hurry over to you to get you to pay the debt which of your own volition you owe us.

Veridico. I am most glad to see you. Will you not sit down?

Massimiano. Perhaps we are disturbing you. I see you are engaged in some arithmetic.

Veridico. No, no. This is not an account of debit and credit. Indeed, it has to do precisely with the subject you wish to talk about.

Santino. In what way?

Veridico. This is a list I have made of the costumes and properties belonging to our actors. I drew it up so that we may be quite prepared when the time of performance comes.

Santino. Now we are here I propose to pounce directly on our prey. Let's start by inquiring how you would set about getting a play ready, supposing, say, the Prince ordered you to start producing one immediately.

Veridico. You are presuming, are you, that he has chosen the piece already?

Santino. No. I presume that you have the job of finding one.

Veridico. Well, first of all I should endeavour to obtain a play that satisfied me, one presenting those qualities which I said specially concern such works of art, above all written in a good prose style and not made tedious by many soliloquies or long-drawn-out episodes or useless dialogue; for I agree with those who declare that a play is perfect when the omitting of the smallest part renders it imperfect. If possible, I should try to get a new play, or at least one little known, avoiding as far as I could those already in print, however masterly they might be; partly because every novelty gives pleasure, and partly because it is certain that those comedies which the audience knows beforehand have little interest. There are many reasons for this, chief among which, I believe, is the fact that, since the actor has to try as hard as he can to cheat the spectator into the belief that what he sees on the stage is true, if the auditor knows already the dialogue and the action of the piece the cheat seems too open and absurd, the plot loses that impression of reality with which it must always be associated, and the spectator, as if he imagined that he had been laughed at, not only condemns the show but chides himself for having childishly gone, as the proverb says, on a wild-goose chase. This does not occur in the presentation of new plays, for, however much the spectator realizes from the beginning that he is going to listen to fictional things, yet as he remains intent upon the novelty of the events it seems that little by little he voluntarily permits himself to be cheated until he imagines—if the actors are as accomplished as they ought to be—that he is really looking upon an actual series of real events.

Santino. Certainly all you say is true, for I myself have attended good performances of really fine printed plays, and I, in common with others, have found myself dissatisfied. On the other hand, I have derived immense pleasure from seeing other plays which, while they were not nearly so good, were new to me.

Massimiano. Now you have told us about choosing a play would you say a few words about your method of production?

Veridico. First I have all the parts carefully copied out and then choose the actors who seem to me fittest for the various *rôles* (taking as much stock as possible of those particular qualities which I shall deal with later). I then gather them all together in one room and give each one that part for which he is most fitted. I get them, after that, to read the whole play in order that they, even the children who take a share in it, may learn the plot, or at least that portion which concerns them, impressing on all their minds the nature of the characters they have to interpret. Then I dismiss them and give them time to learn their parts.

Massimiano. This presents a clear start. Now we come to the question of choosing the actors and distributing the *rôles*—truly a most serious matter.

Veridico. You may be surprised to hear me say—indeed, I should set it forth boldly as a fundamental principle—that it is far more essential to get good actors than a good play. To prove the truth of this it is only necessary to call to your minds the number of times we have seen a poor drama succeed and give much pleasure to the audience because it was well acted; and how often a fine play has failed on the stage because of the poor performance. Now, supposing I have a good number of men skilled in acting and ready to follow my directions, first of all I endeavour to select those who speak with a good accent—for that is the primal consideration—then I consider their physical suitability for the part. Thus a lover must be handsome, a soldier stoutly built, a parasite fat, a servant nimble, and so on. I pay also great attention to their voices, for this I find of major importance. I should not give the part of an old man, unless I were positively forced to do so, to an actor with a childlike voice, or a woman's part (particularly the part of a girl) to a deep-voiced actor. So, too, suppose I had to choose some one for a ghost in a tragedy, I should endeavour, in order to produce the impression demanded, to secure an actor with naturally shrill tones or at least one who could counterfeit a trembling falsetto. I should not pay so much attention to the actual facial features, since so much can be done by the aid of make-up in the way of altering the colour of a beard, simulating a scar, turning the cheeks pale or yellow, or rendering an appearance of vigor, ruddiness, weakness, or darkness as occasion demands. Masks and false beards I should never employ, since they impede the voice too much. If I were forced to give an old man's part to a beardless actor I should simply paint his chin to make him appear shaven, with a fringe of hair showing under his cap; I should give him a few touches with the make-up brush on his cheeks and forehead, and by so doing I should make him seem aged, decrepit, and wrinkled. Now, since I can't think of anything else concerning the selection of play or actors, I shall let you ask any questions that occur to you.

Santino. I should like to inquire first of all what precepts and methods have to be followed by these actors.

Veridico. You set me a very hard task. To give you a general idea of the way I set about this matter, I shall say that in the first place I tell them all to speak firmly without raising their voices to shouting pitch; I instruct them to speak in such a manner as to make their words clearly audible to all the spectators, thus avoiding those uproars which often occur among those in the back seats who cannot hear and which completely disturb the action of a play. The only remedy is having an actor with a naturally fine voice, which, as I said, is the next necessity after a good pronunciation.

Massimiano. That is very true.

Veridico. I prohibit entirely as a very serious fault any tendency to haste in utterance: nay, I am always counselling them to go as slowly as possible. For this purpose I make them pronounce their words very deliberately, without letting their voices drop on the last syllables. Through this fault the spectators often lose the ends of sentences.

Santino. If, as I think, the actors have to imitate ordinary speech I should have imagined that this slow and deliberate utterance would have seemed unnatural.

Veridico. No, it does not in the least, for, apart from the fact that this slow enunciation is no bad thing in itself and is the special feature of dignified persons—those, indeed, who should be imitated by us—the actor must watch to give time to the auditors for appreciating the poet's words and relishing his sentences, which are by no means ordinary and commonplace. I should like you to observe that, while an actor may think he is talking slowly, the spectator does not get that impression, provided that the words are not separated but given continuous delivery without being so mannerized as to raise annoyance. Regarding other rules or methods of acting I do not believe I can say anything precise. In general let us state that, granted the performer has a good accent, good voice, and suitable presence, whether natural or achieved by art, it will be his object to vary his gestures according to the variety of moods and to imitate not only the character he represents but also the state in which that character is supposed to be at the moment.

Massimiano. Could you make that a trifle clearer, Veridico?

Veridico. Well, to take an example. It will not be enough for a person taking, say, the part of a miser to keep his hand always on his purse as if he were constantly in terror lest the key of his desk should be lost; he must learn as occasion demands to imitate the frenzy (for instance) he will experience when he learns that his son has stolen some of his money. If the part is that of a servant, then the actor must learn how, on an occasion of sudden joy, to break into a lively dance; in a moment of grief to tear his handkerchief with his teeth; in a moment of despair to pull his cap to the back of his head, and so on with suitable effects which give life to the performance. And if he has the part of a fool, besides speaking ill to the point as indicated by the author in his dialogue, he must learn on occasion to play the ninny, catching flies, searching for fleas, and suchlike. If he is taking the part of a waiting-maid he must learn to make an exit by tossing up his skirts in a vulgar manner or biting his thumb and so on—actions which the author has not been able explicitly to indicate in his script.

Massimiano. I remember hearing of some actors who were able to make their cheeks go pale on hearing bad news as though in reality they had experienced a great misfortune.

Veridico. This is referred to by the immortal Plato in his dialogue on poetic fury. He makes Ion say, "Every time I recite a mournful poem my eyes fill with tears; every time I come on some terrible passages my hair rises on my head," and so on. But in fact these things cannot be displayed very well on the stage, and certainly cannot be learned if they do not come by nature. Although there are references among the ancients to many skilled players, and although one recognizes that theirs was a peculiar art, yet we cannot frame any rules for this profession; truly it must be born in the individual. Among the many gentlemen who take delight in acting to-day (such as the wonderful Montefalco, the excessively witty Verrato of Ferrara, the piquant Olivo, sharp Zoppino of Mantua, and that other Zoppino of Gazzolo, besides many others we have witnessed) I have always thought and still think that the acting of a young Roman girl called Flaminia is the most extraordinary. Besides being gifted with many beauteous qualities, she is judged so unique in her profession that I do not believe the ancients ever saw or the moderns are likely to see a more brilliant actress. When she is on the stage the audience gets the impression not of a play composed and finished by an author, but rather of a series of real events taking shape before them. She so varies her gestures, tones, and moods in accordance with the diverse nature of her scenes that every one who sees her is moved to wonder and delighted admiration.

Santino. I remember hearing her, and I know that many wits, inspired by her rare playing, have written sonnets and epigrams and other poems in her praise.

Massimiano. I should like to hear one of these.

Veridico. I remember only two—one is "Mentre gli occhi fatali hor lieti, hor mesti, etc.," and the other "Donna leggiadra a cui la più gradita, etc." Now, to get back once more to acting in general, let me say again that the performer must have a natural disposition for his work, otherwise he can never succeed. On the other hand, the man who learns his part well and has the requisite skill finds movements and gestures of an appropriate kind to make his part seem real. For this, as for other things, it is useful to have the author of the play as a director; he generally has the ability to demonstrate some ideas not expressed in the text which improve the play and consequently make the actors seem more lively. I say lively, for above all other things the actor must be vivacious and bright in his diction, except, of course, when he has to express grief, and even on such an occasion he must express it in a vital manner so as not to bore the audience. In fine, just as the poet has to hold the attention of the spectators by a seeming naturalness and a well-planned vivacious dialogue, so the actor has the business of keeping the variety of his actions appropriate to the situations, of maintaining a constant alertness, and of avoiding a tedious dullness; this last simply bores an audience in the theatre and comes from cold interpretation, lacking the necessary fire and fighting power. To remedy this defect the actors (and particularly those who are not very expert in their art) must introduce this vivacity I have spoken of even in their rehearsals; otherwise when they appear before the public they show up but ill.

Santino. Assuredly the actor takes a greater place in a play than I imagined. I suppose few realize this.

Veridico. I have spoken already to you about actions and words and have indicated that a comedy is built up from them, as our bodies are composed of flesh and spirit; the poet corresponds to one of these parts, the actor to the other. The actor's movements, styled by the father of the Latin tongue the body's eloquence, are of so great importance that perhaps the power of words is not more than the power of gesture. Proof of this is to be found in those silent comedies familiar in certain parts of Europe, wherein the story is so clearly and pleasantly presented by means of action alone that only those who have witnessed this kind of play would credit its force. To this corporal eloquence, although it is of tremendous importance, called by some the soul of rhetoric, and consisting in dignity of movement in head, countenance, eyes, hands, and body, we can apply no laws. I can say only that the actor ought in general to have a lithe body with free-moving limbs, not stiff and awkward. He must place his feet on the ground naturally when he speaks, move them easily when occasion demands, turn his head without artificiality—not as though it were fastened to his neck by rivets. His arms and hands, too, when there is no need to make gestures with them, ought to hang naturally at his sides. The actor should avoid the manner of those many persons who introduce inappropriate gestures and seem to know not what they are doing. To take an example, if a woman playfully puts her hand on her hip or a young man puts his on his sword, neither should remain standing in this position for long; whenever the situation that called for this action is over a change should be made and another gesture should be adopted suitable to the speech that follows. When an appropriate gesture cannot be found or when no movement is called for, then the actor should, as I said, leave his arms and hands in a natural position, loose and easy, without raising or folding them as though they were attached to the body with sticks. He should always employ in his actions just such demeanour as is demanded from the character he represents; and likewise in the tone of his voice, now arrogant, now calm, now timorous, now fervent, with due emphasis on the essential points. In all he has to observe and imitate the natural manner of those persons whom he represents, above all avoiding as a capital crime what I shall call, for want of a better word, a pedantic manner of interpretation, after the style of school-children repeating their lessons before their master. That method of acting, I say, which makes the words seem like a passage learned by rote, must be avoided; and endeavour must be made above all other things to render whatever is spoken thoroughly effective, with suitable alteration of tones and appropriate gestures. The whole dialogue must seem like a familiar talk, wholly improvised. Beyond this I can give you no rules; and since I suppose this subject in general is sufficiently understood, let us dwell on it no longer, but pass on to the question of costume. In speaking about costume—and leaving aside the methods of the ancients whereby old men were all dressed in white and youths in coloured robes, parasites in folded cloaks thrown over their shoulders, and courtesans in yellow garments, because such symbolic indications, owing to variety in usage, would now be useless or but little appreciated—I may say that I always aim, first of all, at dressing the actors as richly as possible, yet with proportionate variations, since sumptuous costumes (particularly in these times when show is at its highest, and above all things we must consider time and place) seem to me to add much to the beauty of comedies and more so to that of tragedies. I should not hesitate to dress a servant in velvet or coloured satin, provided that his master's costume had sufficient embroidery and gold ornament to make a proper distinction between them; nor should I endeavour to clothe a waiting-maid in a torn skirt or a valet in a shabby doublet; on the contrary, I should give to the former a fine petticoat and to the latter a magnificent jacket—increasing at the same time the richness of their master's clothes to match the brightness of the servants' dresses.

Massimiano. Unquestionably the sight of those rags which are sometimes worn by a miser or a servant detracts from the impression created by a play.

Veridico. A miser or a servant may be clad in garments which have something rich about them and yet are true to nature.

Santino. That is true, particularly when one takes into account what you said about the usages of our own times.

Veridico. I try so far as possible to give the actors widely differing costumes. This is of double service in that the variety adds to the beauty of the show and at the same time aids in making the plot clear. For the latter reason, I believe, rather than for any other, the ancients employed characteristic dresses with particular colours allocated to the social position of the persons. To take an example, supposing I had to provide costumes for three or four servants, I should clothe one in white with a hat, another in red with a small cap, another in mixed livery, while to the fourth I might give a velvet hat and a pair of knitted sleeves should his position permit this. (I am speaking, of course, of a comedy introducing Italian fashions.) Similarly, if I had to dress two lovers I should try both in the colours and the cut of their suits to make them as different as possible. One would wear a cape, the other a short cassock; one would sport some feathers in his cap, the other a gold ornament without any feathers. All would be contrived in such a way that as soon as either came on the stage he would be immediately recognizable, not merely by his countenance, but by the form of his clothes, so that the audience would know who he was without having to wait for him to announce his identity. I may observe that the method of wearing a hat is the most distinguishing characteristic in both men and women; for that reason these should be as different as possible, in both colour and shape.

Santino. How often have I been in doubt for a time about the identity of a particular character on the stage, precisely because he is not dressed differently from another actor or servant!

Veridico. The diversity of colours gives great pleasure in the theatre. In general the costumes ought to be worked out in clear and bright shades. Black should be used as little as possible, and also any sombre tones. Not only do I aim at contrasting one actor with another, but I try to transform each one so that he shall not be immediately recognized by those spectators who have daily business with him. Of course, I endeavour not to fall into the error of the ancients who, to conceal the real identity of their players, painted their faces with wine-lees or mud. I am content to transform, not to transfigure them, trying as much as I can to make them seem persons unknown to the audience. When a spectator recognizes an actor he loses some of that pleasant pretence which it is our object to maintain; for we must always try to make him believe that our play is a real series of events. But, since novelty is always sure to please, an audience takes delight in seeing foreign and strange costumes on the stage; it is for that reason that comedies in the Greek style are usually so successful. For this more than for any other reason I have contrived that the setting of the comedy you are to see on Tuesday should be Constantinople, so that I can introduce men's and women's dresses of a kind we do not wear. I hope by this means to add not a little to the beauty of the show, and, apart from that, there is the fact that theatrical situations affecting strange persons we do not know invariably seem more probable than the situations introduced into most of our comedies where the characters are citizens with whom we have daily business. And if this plan is good for comedy, as experience amply shows us, it is still better for tragedy. In costuming tragedies a careful producer must not be satisfied with modern clothes, but must dress his actors after the fashion of antique sculptures or paintings, with those mantles and attires in which these persons of past centuries were so beautifully depicted. Since, too, the finest stage spectacles have introduced a troop of armed men I recommend that where possible there be brought in as a bodyguard to a king or a general some soldiers and gladiators, costumed in antique style after the manner of old paintings.

Santino. Certainly it is true that such spectacles are poor unless they are presented by princes who have sufficient grandeur of spirit to spend lavishly on the settings and accoutrements.

Veridico. I don't want to speak about the settings to-day; to-morrow, I promise, I shall come back to that subject. But, lest you fall into the error of supposing that one needs a whole treasury to furnish out a tragedy, let me just say that no prince's wardrobe is so poorly equipped as to lack materials for the dressing of a great tragedy so long as the producer is a clever man who can make use of what is given him and who has the skill to convert pieces of stuff, draperies, and the like into mantles, cloaks, and vestments, with girdles and knots after the antique fashion, without cutting or destroying them at all.

Massimiano. Assuredly a whole treasury (as Santino said) would have to be expended if one wanted to make all these dresses especially for the occasion.

Veridico. Yes, a whole treasury, or little less, would have to be expended on even a comedy or a pastoral play if all the dresses had to be specially made. Because of this we generally contrive to use up existing material.

Massimiano. Now you have brought it to my mind I should be glad if you would tell us something about these costumes and scenes suitable for pastoral plays. I personally do not think I have ever seen one on the stage.

Veridico. I shall deal with pastoral settings to-morrow when I turn to the subject of scenery in general. Concerning the manner of costuming, I should say that if the poet has introduced a god or a similar imaginative character we must try to follow his intentions; but for pastoral costumes generally the same rule holds good as appertains to comedy—namely, that the characters must be dressed as differently from one another as possible. In general the method of costuming such persons is as follows: the legs and arms are covered with flesh-coloured cloth, or if the actor is young and handsome they are left naked. No actor, however, must go barefoot; a well-fashioned cothurnus or the sock has to be worn. He should have a small, sleeveless shirt of taffeta or of some similar material pleasantly coloured; and over this two leopard or other skins such as were described by Homer in his account of the Trojan shepherd, one worn on his breast, the other on his back. The legs of the animals' skins should come over his shoulders and under his thighs; but variety may be introduced by making a few characters wear them over one shoulder only. Some of the actors should have at their girdles a small flask or a wooden bowl; others a pouch slung over the shoulder and hanging down on the opposite side. Each one ought to have a stick, some of these sticks being cut and polished, others left untrimmed—the more extraordinary they are in shape the better. Their hair may be either natural or false, some curly and others combed out straight. Thus are the shepherds suitably dressed according to their positions and distinguished from one another by their colours, different kinds of skins, varying complexions, and variously arranged headdresses, as well as by other devices determinable only through actual experimentation. For the nymphs, after a careful examination of their qualities as outlined by the poets, there will be found necessary sleeved slips variously embroidered. I personally am in the habit of soaking the materials in starch so that when the dresses are bound with jewellery or else with coloured or golden girdles they spread out and present a pleasing picture to the eyes. In addition skirts of good coloured material are worn, girdled up so as to show the instep. The feet are clad either in elegant golden shoes of an antique pattern or else in boots of coloured leather. Finally a sumptuous mantle is demanded, passing from one of the hips and gathered together at the opposite shoulder. These nymphs ought to have thick, fair hair so as to seem natural, some flowing freely over their shoulders with a small garland; others, for variety's sake, may have a frontlet of gold, and still others may bind their locks with silk ribbons and cover them with such thin veils floating down on their shoulders as in ordinary dress add so much beauty to a woman's costume. This, I say, is permissible even in pastoral shows since generally the floating veil is the principal head ornament worn by women and yet has a sufficient appearance of innocence and simplicity to accord with the dress of a wood-nymph. Some of these nymphs should carry bows with a quiver at their hips, others should merely carry a hunting spear, while still others may be equipped with both. He who attempts one of these pastoral shows must be a real expert, for it is much more difficult to win success in them than in comedies, although when success is secured the spectacle assumes much more gracefulness and beauty.

Santino. You do not, I suppose, include under the name of nymphs all kinds of women appearing in these plays—any more than you would include under the name of shepherds all the men?

Veridico. Assuredly no; for if, for example, the poet were to introduce in such a play the person of a witch we should have to dress her in fitting robes; or if a peasant we should have to put him in coarse rustic garments. Should shepherdesses be introduced, then the nymphs' dresses will serve, with the exception that no cloak will be worn and nothing held in the hands save a crook. The costumes may vary from the plain to the elaborately rich. It adds to the spectacle if the shepherds bring in one or two dogs, and I like to see some of the nymphs bringing them in too. The latter, however, should be more graceful dogs, with pretty collars and light coverings. To conclude what I have to say about these plays, I shall affirm that, just as verse is required for their dialogue, so an harmonious accompaniment is needed in the costuming and direction as well as in the stature and movements of the players.

Massimiano. I should not imagine that it would be possible to assign more particular rules than those you have already given to these pastoral plays. Let us therefore get back to our former theme—the arrangements to be made for the prologues to comedies.

Veridico. Before one comes to the prologue, however, one must run over the characters to see if all are provided with such things as they may require; these things must be noted down in a property list (such as that which I was but now engaged in preparing), for to forget even some small article may put the players very much out. Besides this, I personally am in the habit of doing another thing which is very useful and necessary; I note down all the scenes in order, with the names of the characters appearing in them, together with an indication of the house or street by which they are to enter, their cues, and the first words they have to utter on the stage; by the aid of this plan the director can arrange always to get all the actors ready in time at their places of entrance, to put them on stage at their cues, and prompt them with the first words they have to speak.

Santino. With this device there is no danger of the stage remaining empty between one scene and another. Now let us go to the question of the dropping of the curtain, or *sipario*, as the ancients called it.

Veridico. Before the curtain falls I recommend the sounding, after the fashion of the early actors, of trumpets or flutes or of similar loud instruments. This has the effect of awakening interest, which may be flagging owing to the long wait which commonly the great majority of the spectators have before the beginning of the play. It serves also to give warning to the groups of actors.

Massimiano. My experience is that this does make a strong impression. Now let us come to the question of prologues and their forms.

Veridico. So far as kinds of prologues are concerned, I believe that those have greatest dignity and are most fitting which were used by the ancients. In these an actor clad in a toga and crowned with laurel, dressed in a sumptuous yet dignified costume, entered in the guise of the poet. It adds much to place under the wreath a false wig, both to conceal the actor's individuality and to make him seem an antique character. He must come on stage, immediately the curtain falls, walk very slowly and with dignified demeanour from the extreme edge of the stage, and, when he has at last arrived in the very middle, remain motionless for a time until he recognizes that the chatter common in such places is quite stilled. Then with smooth diction he may commence. I do not counsel him to move; it is much better for him to stay in one spot as he majestically delivers his words; should he be forced to move from one position to another he may take a single step, or two, but slowly, without turning his back on the audience. Since I have referred to this, it may be appropriate to mention that neither the speaker of the prologue nor any of the actors should ever turn their shoulders to the audience; this is a universal rule. Also it is always well for them to act as much in the middle of the stage and on the proscenium line as possible, and to face the spectators. The actor should also try to avoid going too close to the scenic perspectives, since if he gets near them they lose their verisimilitude, while the distance he actually is from them seems but slight to the audience. This is well proved in practice. In general, too, I may say that while an actor is speaking he ought never to walk about unless he is forced thereto by great necessity.

Massimiano. That is assuredly true. Now please tell us this: if the scene is supposed to be, let us say, Rome, and the play is being acted, say, in Florence, whom is the actor speaking the prologue to address and where is he supposed to be?

Veridico. Leaving aside just now those fantastic prologues where gods and other extraordinary characters are introduced (of these we shall deal when speaking of visible intermedii), I may say that the person who, speaking in the name of the poet, delivers the prologue must always directly address his speech to the spectators (contrary to what the actor has to do) and make himself seem their fellow-citizen, giving them information regarding the city represented in the setting, the nature of the play, and its title, besides begging their silence, and other similar things.

Santino. You don't want to say anything to-day about the intermedii?

Veridico. I want to leave over till to-morrow this question of stage intermedii. I shall then give you my opinion concerning the way in which they may add to or detract from the plays with which they are associated. Just now, however, I shall say that plays need musical intermissions at least, both to refresh the spectator's minds and to grant the dramatic poet (as I started to tell you yesterday) an interval to give proportion to his play, since every one of these intermedii, however brief, may serve to indicate a space of four, six, or eight hours. Obviously the play, however long it may be, cannot last more than four hours, yet the action often spreads over a whole day and sometimes half of another; the fact that during the interval no actors are on stage makes the fictional passage of time more efficacious.

Massimiano. What kind of intermedii seem to you best adapted to the needs of tragedy and pastoral?

Veridico. Tragedies, as I believe I have indicated before, do not need to be divided into acts (although the moderns so divide them on their own authority), and the choruses which are introduced in them by the poets ought to serve for that part which marks the passage of time from one action to another. But as it is the custom in our times to distinguish separate acts (owing to the fact that the moderns introduce lengthier themes) I shall tell you to-morrow what kind of intermedii may be judged most fitting. At the same time we shall talk about the intermissions suitable for pastoral plays. To-day our discussion has been long enough, and, indeed, it is time that I tried out the lighting for our comedy, to see that nothing is amiss. Therefore with your leave I shall make an end of my discourse, unless perchance you too wish to come and see the rehearsal.

Santino. We certainly do wish to accept this gracious invitation—do we not, Signor Massimiano?

Massimiano. Undoubtedly.

Veridico. Let us go, then, to the theatre.

Santino. Yes, let us go.

FOURTH DIALOGUE

Interlocutors: VERIDICO, SANTINO, *and* MASSIMIANO

Veridico. Quick, Marcletto, and you, you booby, get one of these ladders each and start lighting the lamps. We shall sit here, gentlemen.

Santino. I should like to sit a trifle farther back, so as to see better the excellent effect of that perspective.

Veridico. All right: I too will come over there. Ready? Light all these reliefs.

Massimiano. Assuredly this art of painting is a wonderful thing when it is in capable hands. Standing here, I am completely cheated by the illusion. Though I know, of course, that there is only a flat cloth in front of me, I seem to see a real street running back a good half-mile.

Veridico. Precisely the same power is at the command of the accomplished actor. Though you are perfectly well aware that he *is* only play-acting, if he does his part well a series of real events will seem to unfold themselves before you.

Massimiano. That is quite true.

Santino. Apart from the painting, the architecture of this set appears to my eyes to be excellent. I do not recall having seen so beautiful buildings at Naples or Rome or Florence or Milan.

Veridico. I do not wish to speak at large about the special qualities of the scenery, partly because my business is not that of architect or painter, partly because it would be impossible to provide you with adequate examples. The manners and styles of the painters vary considerably, and the material they work in is infinite; equally varied are the settings which they may devise—house fronts, squares, porticoes, streets embellished with arches, columns, statues of diverse kinds—the models being taken from this city or that, ancient or modern, according to the demands of the script. However, just as I said that the actors' costumes should be rich in appearance, so I say that the sets ought always to be based on the finest possible models. The details of such matters I leave to those who practise such arts, but I may remark—with all due deference to the moderns—that the sets of which we have so full descriptions among the ancients must have possessed an almost absolute beauty. On this subject Ercole Bentivoglio touches pleasantly and briefly in one of his prologues, when he declares that:

> Marcus Scaurus, citizen of Rome,
> So beauteous a theatre made, and scene,
> Of glass and marble joined in harmony,
> With rich carved columns all embellishèd,
> And statues hewn by sculptors famed.
> 'Tis said another theatre was made,
> By Caius Antonius, a glittering dream
> Of silver; and of gold a third Petreius
> Fashionèd; of ivory white was that
> Of Quintus Catulus. Most marvellous
> Were those two theatres of Curio,
> Which wondrously did turn and, facing each
> To each, an amphitheatre made—

and so on. From these accounts we may deem that our modern sets, lovely as they may seem, are but shadows to those of that more glorious time. During that period plays were held in greatest esteem, their end being, as I have said, the civil institution. Because of this, theatres were erected among the more important civic buildings; as Virgil, in the first book of the *Aeneid* observes, concerning the founding of Carthage:

> And then the firm and ample base was laid
> For the great stages.

Massimiano. In my opinion that was a magnificent setting which his Highness the Duke of Mantua caused to be erected in the courtyard of his castle for his wedding celebrations. Though it was not used for anything but the tourney held that evening, it would have served excellently for the presentation both of comedies and of tragedies.

Veridico. Cavalier Leone, accomplished architect as he is, could not have created anything but what was perfect; and that set, I agree, was perfect—enriched with so many reliefs, embellished by such admirable architecture, with such variety of lovely inventions.

Santino. Had it been constructed of firm and durable substance, maybe one might have compared it—perhaps even put it above—those settings you have just been speaking of. Unfortunately, it was made entirely of lath and plaster.

18

Veridico. But all the greater was Duke Guglielmo's magnanimity in spending so many thousands of ducats on that marvellous set and then destroying it when it had served its immediate purpose.

Santino. Perhaps so, but let us dwell on this subject a trifle longer. I want you to tell me one thing, Veridico. Here on your stage are many lighted lamps, giving ample illumination and making a most lovely show; what, then, is the use of and how originated those many lamps burning on the roofs of the stage-house? They do not seem to me to aid the perspective, and for ordinary purposes of illumination there are torches enough.

Veridico. I think I have said more than once that plays are produced for the purpose of providing pleasant instruction and of alleviating noyance of mind. Whence I declared, and again I repeat it, the actor should above all other things endeavour to enunciate his lines in a bright and joyous manner. Such, granted that the author provides us with a pleasant, charming plot and that the actor gives to this a vivid interpretation, surely it is equally essential that the architect should represent gladness and joy on the stage. Now it has been a custom, both in ancient and modern times, to light bonfires and torches in the streets, on the house-tops, and on towers, as a sign of joy; and hence arises this theatrical convention—the imitating of such festive occasions. The lights are put there for no other purpose but to imitate, in the very first scene, this mood of gaiety.

Santino. I suppose, then, that these lights would not appear in a tragedy.

Veridico. Perhaps they would not be so wholly out of place even in such a play. Quite apart from the fact that there are tragedies with happy endings, we note that nearly all tragedies open in a happy strain; and consequently it will not be unfitting to arouse the mind, so far as we may, to this happiness, although disasters and deaths are to ensue later. I remember once I had to produce a tragedy of this kind. During all the time when the episodes were happy in mood I had the stage brightly illuminated, but so soon as the first unhappy incident occurred—the unexpected death of a queen—while the chorus was engaged in lamenting that the sun could bear to look down on such evil, I contrived (by prearrangement, of course) that at that very instant most of the stage lights not used for the perspective were darkened or extinguished. This created a profound impression of horror among the spectators and won universal praise.

Santino. It could not have called forth anything but praise.

Massimiano. Will you now please tell us why most of your lights have in front of them transparent or coloured glasses?

Veridico. This was invented by some men who realized a little-appreciated fact—that a brilliant light striking directly upon the eye for any length of time becomes exceedingly irritating. Since, then, the spectator must keep his eyes fixed on the stage, watching the actions proceeding now on this side, now on that, the shading of the lights was devised to minimize the annoyance.

Massimiano. I should be willing to bet that not ten persons out of a hundred who make use of these shades appreciate their object.

Veridico. They would at any rate say that the shades were used to produce a more beautiful effect, and in so doing they would be enunciating part of the whole. Not by my own theorizing, certainly, but from long practice and experience I have made observation of these things and have tried to get at their origins. I have found that it was the ancients who, as the saying goes, snatched them from obscurity. While we are dealing with this subject I should like to point out also that the small mirrors which some managers set at appropriate places in the perspective settings and the far sides of the wings are very effective. They reflect those concealed lights which the architects cleverly place behind columns and in the openings between the wings, thus serving to make the set more gay and bright. Not only can these reflections give no annoyance to the eyes; they have the further advantage that here we obtain light without smoke—a great consideration. I may take this occasion to remark that the producer who does not take care to have a number of holes made behind the scenes so that the smoke from the lamps may have a means of escape will land himself in serious difficulties, for otherwise this smoke, gradually increasing and becoming thicker, will produce so effective a screen that before the second act be done the actors will seem to be not men but shadows, while the spectators, as if blinded, will, without realizing the cause, get the impression that they are losing their sight. Great care ought to be taken of this, though it is a matter to which few pay sufficient attention. So far as my experience goes, there is no real difficulty provided adequate pains are taken beforehand.

Massimiano. Now that you bring these things to my attention I do recall that at the close of plays we have often found our eyes smarting uncomfortably and that we have not been able to see nearly so much as we did at the beginning. I realize that this must have been due to the cause you have referred to.

Veridico. To avoid the smoke screen I have found that the best remedy is to open as many windows as possible under the proscenium, so that the air, entering from below, drives all the smoke through the holes bored in the roof behind the scenery.

Massimiano. That, I believe, would be an excellent device.

Veridico. It is, I assure you.

Santino. I see, Veridico, that on your stage there are many lamps both behind the scenes and in front of them; yet in the auditorium here you have made arrangements for but twelve standing candelabra. The reason I can't imagine; for I have often counted as many as 250 torches in this large hall.

Veridico. It is a natural fact—as no doubt you are aware—that a man who stands in the shade sees much more distinctly an object illuminated from afar; the reason being that the sight proceeds more directly and without any distraction towards this object, or, according to the peripatetic theory, the object impinges itself more directly upon the eye. Wherefore I place only a few lamps in the auditorium, while at the same time I render the stage as bright as I possibly can. Still further, these few auditorium lights I place at the rear of the spectators, because the interposition of such lights would but be dazzling to the eyes. Over them, as you see, I have made small openings so that their smoke can cause no damage.

Santino. By thus introducing only a few lights in the auditorium, then, you obviate the trouble of smoke-fumes and to a certain extent you render the seeing clearer.

Massimiano. There is yet another advantage: he saves the Duke fifty ducats in respect of the torches usually set in the hall.

Veridico. That, I confess, had not come into my mind, nor does his Excellency need to think of such economies, but, as the proverb says, in the end every good proves good.

Santino. Concerning the illumination of the scene you have said, in my opinion, all that can be said; concerning the details of the set you yourself declared you were unwilling to say more since you are not an architect by profession. But would you not now care to tell us something about the pastoral settings, since for those at least a knowledge of architecture is not demanded?

Veridico. At your request, then, I shall say this: If the pastoral play which is to be produced demands the usual setting of an open country in summer-time, then the scene will have to be rich and full of foliage. On being discovered to the spectators it ought to give an impression of great loveliness. This is best done by using leaves and flowers and fruit-trees to represent a summer season, with, among the branches, diverse birds whose songs may arouse a feeling of joy. At times, too, one may cause various animals, such as rabbits and hares and so on, to wander over the stage. Thus the likeness of pleasing landscapes and solitary woods may be drawn to the life. Similarly, prospects may be shown of mountains, valleys, cottages, springs, caves, and suchlike, according to your desire—the distant views, of course, being rendered in conformity with the laws of perspective. At the front so much space, adorned to represent a flower field, may be left clear for the ordinary purposes of the play as the stage permits. If, however, a night scene is demanded, then painting must be employed, and special care must be taken to see that the lamps are concealed as much as possible. No more can I say about such settings in matter of detail; one must depend on the judgment of the writer of the play and the skill of the director, just as is the case in scenes of a maritime sort.

Santino. What do you mean by maritime scenes?

Veridico. Such as I saw not many years ago in Portugal. The set called for a great ship in the harbour at Rhodes. This indeed made a brave show, both because of the great colossus which, according to the ancients, once stood above this harbour, its legs straddling over the ships that sailed in or out, and because of the number of characters who in the various scenes performed now on shore, now on board ship.

Santino. That, I doubt not, was a novel and beauteous show. Now would you not be so good as to say a few words concerning the method of presenting perspective or open scenes which, it is said, is frequently used—indeed, generally used—in Spanish theatres?

Veridico. By open scenes I presume you mean those where we look into a room and see some one acting there?

18*

Santino. Yes, these are the kind I refer to. What do you think of them?

Veridico. Although there is a certain beauty in seeing presented on the stage an open, well-appointed room in which, for example, a lover has an interview with a bawd, and although this gives a strong impression of verisimilitude, yet it goes so contrary to reality—in that the room is lacking (as it must) a fourth wall—that it appears to me rather awkward; besides which, I am by no means sure that the actor in such a scene can be said to be on a stage at all. One might, of course, avoid these inconveniences by opening the scene on a loggia or a terrace where some persons come to converse, but, for myself, I should not take the licence to leave the front stage otherwise empty and accordingly should contrive that such conversations appeared at the end or the beginning of an act—so that they might almost be called intermedii. Since I have thus made reference to visible intermedii, I may give you a few thoughts on this subject. First of all, in regard to extraordinary prologues, I should say that those of a fantastic kind do not harmonize very well with plays, for plays, after all, ought to deal with things which may seem natural. However, when these prologues have some connexion with the plot or with the occasion of the performance, then they will become more tolerable.

Santino. Would you be so good as to give us an example?

Veridico. Well, this will do. Suppose in a comedy designed to celebrate the establishment of a new prince we introduce, say, a god who, drawing lots with his brothers, gains the rule of the heavens, and suppose this god is made to say something concerning the good governing of a state. Similarly if the performance were to take place on the occasion of the birth of a prince, then we might, for example, introduce a Lucina to prognosticate immortal glory arising from his birth. Or else at a nuptial festival one might introduce a Hymen. Indeed, it is easy to invent suitable topics for all sorts of occasions.

Santino. And if it were not for any special performance, but merely, as is more usual, for a carnival show, how would the poet harmonize his matter to the occasion?

Veridico. Easily, for there is no lack of subject-matter having some bearing on the plot.

Santino. What do you mean?

Veridico. I shall give you some examples from those which a few years ago we saw in this city; these will make it all clear to you. Don't you remember the success of the prologue to that tragi-comedy presented last carnival, when the poet introduced an argument between Comedy and Tragedy? Do you not recall also the prologue to *Fortunata*, a comedy acted four years ago, in which appeared a new show of Fortune and Fame?

Santino. Of course I do; but surely one could not find similarly appropriate prologues for all plays?

Veridico. I grant that: but when this is the case it is always possible to bring in matter relating to the city or to the places in which the plays are given—one might introduce the rivers that irrigate the surrounding country, the men who first built the town, those born there who had become famous for their heroic virtues. A friend of ours did this when in a Mantuan play he introduced Virgil; another time he brought in a Mincio, and still another the Theban Manto—thus varying his fancies in the prologues to diverse plays. However, I do not want to spend too long a time on this matter, since I want to speak of visible intermedii. Such, I say, are little suitable for comedies, since by their novelty they so distract the mind of the spectator that when he turns again to the plot of the drama it seems to him less interesting, for truly we shall be more powerfully attracted by the spectacle (say) of a Cadmus sowing the teeth of the slain dragon and raising his crop of armed men, or of a Perseus ascending on his Pegasus to defend an Andromeda, than when we watch a slave astutely disentangling himself from the dangers encompassing him or a lover planning a *tête-à-tête* with his adored one. Hence I say that when a play has such extraordinary fancies in the intermedii these will be more looked to, and the play as a consequence fail in its success. Sometimes, however, we see certain bizarreries which, without drawing away the attention, give a good deal of pleasure. Thus, for example, between two acts of a play eight or ten artisans might come on the stage from different streets; these might sing in concert, and on entering each might indicate his profession, some of them playing on instruments concealed in the tools of their trade. Thus a small lyre would be in the locksmith's pan, a violin in a boot belonging to the mender of old shoes, a flute in the handle of the broom borne by the chimney-sweep, a harpsichord in the basket of the pastry-cook, with similar other devices which, being things commonly seen in cities, do not draw away the mind and detract in no wise from the interest we take in the plot of the play.

Santino. Of this sort were the intermedii brought forward by our own Cardo; he introduced four pilgrims who went about singing and with a number of engaging quips, begging alms from the ladies. In another intermedio he called for four porters, who, after a brief argument in rustic terms concerning the division of some money, came to blows and kicks, all in morris time.

Veridico. We may conclude, then, that those intermedii which are concerned with such ordinary things as one may see in comedies may be tolerated. Those of an extravagant kind, introducing matters of an unnatural sort, seem to me to be entirely inappropriate. In tragedies divided into acts and also in pastoral poems undoubtedly may be permitted things more out of the ordinary, since in the body of the play itself appear ghosts, furies, gods, and strange characters; but unquestionably these intermedii will be the better the more definite relationship they bear to the plot. Thus, for example, in a play which is to bring ruin or death on the stage the Fates may be introduced; these may sing as they spin and wind on their distaffs the thread of a king or a queen until it is violently cut by Clotho. Or else one may bring on the Furies of Hell, with burning torches in their hands; these, moving about in morris time, would set alight Rage and Ruin around some royal palace. Things of this kind would make pleasing shows without entirely distracting attention from the subject-matter of the play.

Massimiano. Verily I believe that any man of good judgment could easily discover diverse extravagant fancies of this sort, for most legends and many historical anecdotes could readily be dramatized in this way. For instance, at Bologna I saw some years ago an intermedio which brought on an Amphion; at the sound of his music the rocks began to pile up one on top of the other, and thus were reared the walls of Thebes. In the second intermedio an eagle appeared to seize a Ganymede. During the interval of the third act Deucalion and Pyrrha came on and threw stones over their shoulders, whence arose little by little tiny nude children. The fourth intermedio introduced a giant, who brought on an enormous globe and placed it in the middle of the stage; after he had given it some blows with a club the ball opened, and out stepped four satyrs, who executed a delightful morris dance. In a tragi-comedy recently presented here in our city I saw a battle between the three Horatii and the three Curiatii, produced so effectively to the time of a morris dance, with real weapons, that it made a magnificent show. In conclusion I say that I believe that any man might easily invent things of this kind, although the harmonizing of them to the theme of the play seems to me rather difficult. Wherefore I should like to have some specific example.

Veridico. I wish to give you to read a pastoral in five acts. You will find that the intermedii introduced in it are so thoroughly appropriate that they seem almost part of its structure. I am sure you will not regret looking at it. While I am searching for it among my books I shall take the opportunity of telling you about a pastoral feast which followed this play. It proceeded thus. Our illustrious Lord had got built in a great hall two orders of square rustic columns, evenly spaced and bearing vaulted arches. Although it was winter-time, these were all covered with green boughs. Thus were formed two lovely, long, and leafy loggias with diverse festoons of fruits and flowers, some artificial (since it was out of their season), some real. Within the columns (which were hollow) there had been concealed many lamps, which, shining forth from shades made of coloured glass and skilfully placed, illuminated the whole room in a delightful way; still greater splendour was provided by several great globes filled with water, cleverly set in the middle of each archway. Above these, lamps had been placed in such number that each arch seemed lit up by a blazing sun. Indeed, it seemed brighter than at high noon. Between the two loggias was a space of about ten cubits; it was considerably higher than the two loggias and was entirely roofed with a blue sky set with stars and having a magnificent great moon in the middle. The rays from this moon fell on a deliciously set table which stretched the whole length of the open space, and on which was spread a rich supper of diverse fruits—mostly artificial sugar fruits or else real fruits preserved in sugar. As soon as the play was over—this was given in another hall and had marvellous success—an Orpheus appeared, followed by many shepherds and nymphs. In a few lines of verse, to the harmonious accompaniment of a lyre, he invited the assembled audience to a pastoral and rustic feast; and accordingly the accompanying shepherds—following their instructions—went off to welcome the guests. Each shepherd acted as escort to one of the gentlemen, masked or unmasked as the case might be; similarly every nymph took one of the ladies under her guidance; and so, couple by couple, all the guests were led into the room set apart for this purpose—the sudden sight of which caused great wonderment among them all. The lord of the feast, who was masked as a shepherd, together with many of his men, took the mask from his face, and they all followed him. Then, after some pleasant jesting, they washed their hands and sat down in festive spirit at the table, where they were richly served by the shepherds and the nymphs, without the least confusion or disorder.

Massimiano. You have filled me with delight by the mere retelling of this device. Just imagine how transported I should have been had I actually been present.

Veridico. And what would you have done had you seen all the dishes borne with various devices to the table?

Massimiano. Then some art was employed in bringing the food to the table?

Veridico. Yes, indeed; that was the best part of the feast. Nothing was brought in already cooked; but the contents of each dish were first displayed either alive or uncooked, with a series of delightful fancies.

Massimiano. Please give us an example so that we may imagine the rest.

Veridico. Willingly. First there appeared four youths clad as monks; these, bearing baskets of various rich salads, greeted a sister of the Lord who sat at the head of the table, and on behalf of the Mother Prior gave them to her as an offering of affection. Then, seeing all the company were seated at the table, they sang a lovely benediction in unison, and meanwhile the dressed salads were brought in. And since the banquet was a sumptuous one, when the fish arrived there appeared first a number of fishermen, each dressed in the fashion of a different locality, and as they made their bows at those moments the produce of their various regions were brought in. Similarly when the time came for kids or other like domestic meat a shepherd or a peasant arrived to lead them in alive; he would then present them to the lord and to the guests with many witty remarks, and immediately the table would be served with these courses. In the same way, before the bird course came, hawkers brought them in alive, accompanying them now with music, now with verses, now with doggerel rimes. Similarly before the meat was served a number of hunters appeared with sound of horn and hounds, and presented to one guest a boar's head, to another a hare, to this man a deer and to that a roe, and so with all. What, however, aroused the greatest amount of pleasant laughter was that certain vile, lecherous, or vicious things were presented by two facetious persons (not to call them buffoons)—a old man and a youth who had been called in specially for this purpose. When they brought in their various objects they aroused great laughter by the variety of their witty remarks.

Bibliography

The following list of books attempts to do no more than offer a guide which may introduce the student to the area of theatre history as a whole and to some of its particular parts. Most of the volumes referred to are of recent publication: it would obviously have been impossible to have included even a small proportion of earlier studies, and the vast extension of investigation into this subject which has been a marked feature of the past thirty or forty years seemed to make it advisable to give preference to modern historical and critical works. The student should also observe that the list itself, following the scope of the text, deals almost exclusively with works concerning theatre-building, staging methods, and scenic practice, and that, accordingly, it leaves out of account numerous fields of investigation which must be included in any complete survey of the history of the theatre. Efforts to describe and analyse varying acting styles are thus omitted here; not only are studies devoted to drama left out of account, but no references even are made to works which seek to provide chronological records of play-performances; only a few selected writings on theatrical audiences are mentioned. References to such works may readily be obtained from the bibliographies in the *Enciclopedia dello spettacolo* and elsewhere.

1. General

Perhaps the most important and useful tool for the student of theatrical history is the great Italian *Enciclopedia dello spettacolo*, of which nine volumes have been issued since 1954, and which will be completed by a tenth volume shortly to be published: this encyclopedia not only provides authoritative information, together with a rich array of illustrative material, relating to all aspects of theatrical activity, but also provides up-to-date bibliographical references; consequently it is of great service even to those who cannot read Italian. The single-volume *Oxford Companion to the Theatre* (2nd edition, 1957) is also serviceable, although clearly far less extensive in scope. Among the various general surveys published during recent years the most significant are the *Histoire générale illustrée du théâtre* (5 vols, 1931–34), prepared by Lucien Dubech, and Heinz Kindermann's *Theatergeschichte Europas* (1957–65, in progress). These largely supersede such historical surveys as Giulio Ferrari's *La Scenografia* (1902), Karl Mantzius' *A*

History of Theatrical Art (6 vols, English translation, 1903–21), Christian Gaehde's *Das Theater vom Altertum bis zur Gegenwart* (1921), Lee Simonson's *The Stage is Set* (1932), and Joseph Gregor's *Weltgeschichte des Theaters* (1933). In *Sources of Theatrical History* (1952) A. M. Nagler has collected an interesting anthology of comments on stage affairs; Carl Niessen's *Das Bühnenbild* (1924–27) provides another useful anthology of illustrations and Richard Southern's *The Seven Ages of the Theatre* (1962) presents a thoughtful schematic survey of theatrical forms.

During the past few years many journals devoted to the history of the theatre have been established, and their articles have markedly increased the available body of evidence relating both to the stages of individual countries and to particular aspects of the playhouse. The following may be especially noted: *Theatergeschichtliche Forschungen* (1891–), *Archiv für Theatergeschichte* (1904–5), *Bulletin de la Société des Historiens du Théâtre* (1933, continued as *Revue d'histoire du théâtre* from 1949), *Theatre Notebook* (1946–), the publications of the Schweizerische Gesellschaft für Theaterkultur (1948–), together with the *Schweizer Theater-Jahrbuch* (1928–), *Pamiętnik teatralny* (1952–), *Maske und Kothurn* (1955–), *Theatre Survey* (1960–), *Theatre Annual* (1942–), *OSU Theatre Collection Bulletin* (1953–), and *Theatre Research* (1958–).

2. Oriental

A fairly extensive literature exists on the two chief forms of the Japanese stage. "*Noh*" *or Accomplishment* (1917), by E. F. Fenellosa and E. L. Pound, is a serviceable early study and Arthur Waley's *Nō Plays of Japan* (1921) is important; P. G. O'Neill has a scholarly investigation of *Early Nō Drama* (1959); in *La Tradition secrète du Nō* (1960) René Sieffert gives valuable information on this subject and also presents in translation an original treatise by Zeami; an authoritative brief record of the form appears in the anonymous *Japanese Noh Drama* published in Tokyo in 1955. On the more "popular" stage Zoe Kincaid's *Kabuki* (1925), A. C. Scott's *The Kabuki Theatre of Japan* (1955), and Earle Ernst's *The Kabuki Theatre* (1957) may be consulted. A very important study of the Japanese stage as a whole, together with an anthology of plays in Italian translation, is Marcello Muccioli's *Il Teatro giapponese* (1962). The conventions of the Chinese stage have been described by A. E. Zucker (1925), L. C. Arlington (1930), and C. S. L. Zung (1937). A. K. Yajnik's *The Indian Theatre* (1933) examines both the ancient Sanskrit stage and modern theatrical activities.

3. *Greece and Rome*

Owing to the fact that for long centuries classical studies formed the core of humanist education, the Greek stage has attracted an attention greater and more exact than that devoted to playhouses of other periods. Vitruvius' *De architectura* was first printed in 1486, and during the sixteenth and seventeenth centuries there were several reprintings of this work accompanied by commentaries; among these, that by Daniele Barbaro (1556) is of particular significance. In 1521 appeared an Italian version, in 1547 both a German and a French, in 1602 a Spanish, while in 1692 was issued an English abridgment of a later French translation (1673) by Claude Perrault. M. H. Martin's *The Ten Books of Architecture* (1914) is a carefully prepared modern rendering, and E. Capps' *Vitruvius and the Greek Stage* (1893) provides an excellent commentary. The *Onomastikon* of Pollux was first printed in 1502 and several times reprinted and re-edited.

Das griechische Theater (1896) by W. Dörpfeld and E. Reisch is a very important study, based on the results of archaeological investigation of extant remains of the classical Athenian stage, and from it has stemmed a considerable library of later exploratory volumes devoted to the examination of a variety of theatres from early times to the Hellenistic period. A. E. Haigh's *The Attic Theatre* (3rd edition, revised by A. W. Pickard-Cambridge, 1907) is a useful short general study of the classical stage; Margarete Bieber's *History of the Greek and Roman Theater* (2nd edition, 1961) offers a much wider canvas, in which full account is taken of recent contributions to the subject, and which carries the survey on to the last days of the Roman Empire; and there are several significant works which aim at interpreting the known facts and at presenting a picture of Greek productional method, such as R. C. Flickinger's *The Greek Theatre and its Drama* (1918), J. T. Allen's *Stage Antiquities of the Greeks and Romans* (1927), T. B. L. Webster's *Greek Theatre Production* (1956), and P. D. Arnott's *An Introduction to the Greek Theatre* (1959). Among other important volumes may be specially noted A. W. Pickard-Cambridge's *The Theatre of Dionysus in Athens* (1946) and *Dramatic Festivals of Athens* (1953), A. Neppi Modona's *Gli Edifici teatrali greci e romani* (1961), P. D. Arnott's *Greek Scenic Conventions of the Fifth Century B.C.* (1962), and C. Anti's *Teatri greci arcaici da Minosse a Pericle* (1947). A recent study by N. C. Hourmouziades, *Production and Imagination in Euripides* (1965), excellently surveys the evidence for the use of "scenic space" in the classical theatre.

The Roman Stage (1955) is specifically surveyed by W. Beare; J. A. Hanson discusses *Roman Theatre-Temples* (1959); much information concerning Roman theatrical remains in France is conveniently summarized in the second volume of A. Grenier's *Manuel d'archéologie gallo-romaine* (1931–60).

4. *The Middle Ages*

During the last decades of the nineteenth century the subject of the staging of medieval plays (as distinct from their literary style and content) began to attract considerable attention. In France these studies led towards Gustave Cohen's *Histoire de la mise-en-scène dans le théâtre religieux français du moyen âge* (1906), followed by his edition of the extensive Mons prompt-book (1925), his *Le Théâtre en France au moyen âge* (1929–31), and *Etudes d'histoire du théâtre en France au moyen âge et à la Renaissance* (1956). An English study of the *Medieval French Drama* (1954) has been published by Grace Frank. The staging of the Lucerne mystery play was first examined by Franz Leibing (1869); and several other more general investigations, such as G. Milchsack's *Die Oster- und Passion-spiele* (1880) and R. Froning's *Das Drama des Mittelalters* (1891), discuss both productional methods and dramatic content of medieval German plays. Medieval staging as well as early Renaissance efforts are expertly analysed in Max Herrmann's *Forschungen zur deutschen Theatergeschichte des Mittelalters und der Renaissance* (1914). A similarly wide sweep is taken by Glynne Wickham in his *Early English Stages, 1300 to 1600* (1959–63). E. K. Chambers' *The Medieval Stage* (2 vols, 1903) is a mine of information concerning all kinds of entertainments during the medieval period; F. M. Salter discusses in detail the *Medieval Drama in Chester* (1955); R. Southern essays to reconstruct the original performance of *The Castle of Perseverance* in his *Medieval Theatre in the Round* (1957). After having been sadly neglected, the early Tudor interludes are beginning to receive adequate attention: T. W. Craik (1958), in particular, examines their staging. For a long time the standard work on the Italian medieval stage was the *Origini del teatro italiano* (1891) by Alessandro D'Ancona, and this still remains a basic study; much new material, however, has been gathered since its publication, and various volumes supplement its contents; C. Molinari's *Spettacoli fiorentini del quattrocento* (1961) is of special importance. The fortunes of the Spanish stage are traced in E. Cotarelo y Mori's *Estudios sobre la historia del arte escénico en España* (1896–97) and in H. A. Rennert's *The Spanish Stage in the Time of Lope de Vega* (1909). A more recent study is the *Historia del teatro español* (1956) by A. Valbuena Prati: valuable new documentary material relating to the presentation of later religious plays is presented by N. D. Shergold and J. E. Varey in *Los Autos Sacramentales en Madrid, hasta 1636* (1959).

B. Hunningher, in *The Origin of the Theatre* (1955), argues strongly for the theory that the early European religious stage was influenced by relics of Roman theatrical entertainments.

5. *The Renaissance*

The theatres of the Renaissance and Baroque periods have recently attracted perhaps more detailed study than any others. Particularly significant is G. R. Kernodle's *From Art to Theatre* (1944), a stimulating discussion of conventions in painting and architectural form. The work of the humanists is examined by M. Herrmann in *Die Entstehung der berufsmässingen Schauspielkunst* (1962), a posthumous work unfortunately left incomplete because its author was among the millions destroyed in German concentration camps. Lily B. Campbell's earlier *Scenes and Machines* (1923) deals with the general background; Hélène Leclerc adroitly traces *Les Origines italiennes de l'architecture théâtrale* (1946), as does T. E. Lawrenson in *The French Stage in the Seventeenth Century* (1957). L. Magagnato's *Teatri italiani del Cinquecento* (1954) is an excellent survey; the Teatro Olimpico and its origins have been well examined by L. Puppi (1963), and there is a detailed study by Leo Schrade of *La Représentation d'Edipo Tiranno au Teatro Olimpico* (1960). Alfredo Puerari's *Sabbioneta* (1956) provides excellent illustrations of that theatre. Among earlier studies, Angelo Solerti's *Musica, ballo e drammatica alla corte medicea dal 1600 al 1637* (1905) may be particularly noted; A. M. Nagler devotes detailed attention to the *Theatre Festivals of the Medici, 1539–1637* (1964). B. Hewitt, in *The Renaissance Stage* (1958), has edited translations of the theatrical essays by Serlio, Sabbatini, and Furttenbach; commentary on Sabbatini accompanies Willi Fleming's German translation (1926), Maria and Renée Canavaggia's French version (1942), and the facsimile reprint of the original, edited by Elena Povoledo (1955); an analysis of Sabbatini's methods by Orville K. Larson has been separately reprinted from his articles contributed to the *Players Magazine* (Oct.–Nov. 1962).

On early "street theatres" and associated activities a wealth of material is presented in two volumes edited by Jean Jacquot, *Fêtes de la Renaissance* (1956) and *Fêtes et cérémonies au temps de Charles Quint* (1960). Many significant comments by the same author appear in the catalogue of a 1963 exhibition, *La Vie théâtrale au temps de la Renaissance*, and another volume edited by him, *Le Lieu théâtrale à la Renaissance* (1964), ranges widely over early stage plans.

Much research has been concentrated on the Elizabethan theatre. E. K. Chambers' *The Elizabethan Stage* (4 vols, 1923) provides a comprehensive array of documentary and other evidence, and it has been followed by G. E. Bentley's equally thorough *Jacobean and Caroline Stage* (5 vols, 1941–56). A conspectus of more recent investigations appears in *Shakespeare Survey 1* (1959) and the twelfth volume of that periodical (1959) is also largely devoted to this subject. W. W. Greg's *Dramatic Documents from the Elizabethan Playhouses* (1931) is an invaluable collection of original documents; Greg also has a very important edition of *Henslowe's Diary* (2 vols, 1904–8) which, however, has for long been out of print; a carefully prepared new transcript of the original document, with a short introduction, has been prepared by R. A. Foakes and R. T. Rickert (1961). A. Feuillerat has edited the relevant documents belonging to the Office of the Revels (1908, 1914). All W. J. Lawrence's numerous volumes are inspired by keen, acute observations; the general surveys of Elizabethan playhouses by A. H. Thorndike (1916) and J. Q. Adams (1917), although of earlier date, still remain of service; Muriel C. Bradbrook's *Elizabethan Stage Conditions* (1932) has many suggestive comments, and A. M. Nagler's *Shakespeare's Stage* (1958) provides a useful survey; M. Channing Linthicum examines stage costume (1936); B. L. Joseph deals with Elizabethan acting (1951); and Alfred Harbage closely analyses such evidence as remains concerning the audience of the time (1941). In 1940 G. F. Reynolds broke fresh ground by devoting attention to a single selected playhouse, the Red Bull, and slightly later J. C. Adams essayed to do the same for the Globe (1942): more recent studies of a similar kind are I. Smith's *Shakespeare's Globe Playhouse* (1956), J. L. Hotson's *Shakespeare's Wooden O* (1959), and C. W. Hodges' *The Globe Restored* (1953). C. T. Prouty's *Studies in the Elizabethan Theatre* (1961) deals with several currently debated aspects of this subject, and numerous significant contributions to the study of particular parts of the stage (notably those made by Richard Hosley) have appeared in article form. On the court masques, the studies by R. Brotanek (1902), Paul Reyher (1909), and Enid Welsford (1927) should be consulted: the present writer has a volume on *Stuart Masques and the Renaissance Stage* (1937, reissued 1964); the Chatsworth designs are expertly catalogued by P. Simpson and C. F. Bell (1924).

J. L. Hotson presents much interesting material relating to the theatre from 1640 to 1700 in his *Commonwealth and Restoration Stage* (1928); *The Restoration Court Stage* (1932) is minutely examined by Eleanore Boswell; the public theatres are discussed in the first volume of the present writer's *History of English Drama 1660–1900* (1952), and in Montague Summers' *The Playhouse of Pepys* (1935).

Three important studies of the French stage during these periods are the *Histoire de la mise en scène dans le théâtre français de 1600 à 1657* (1933), by Wilma Holsboer, *The Early Public Theatre in France* (1960), by W. L. Wiley, and T. E. Lawrenson's already cited volume. H. C. Lancaster's *French Dramatic Literature in the Seventeenth Century* (1929–42) incidentally discusses various questions concerning the staging of the plays, and the same author's edition of the *Mémoire de Mahelot* (1920) is an invaluable record of production methods at the Hôtel de Bourgogne. Numerous other earlier studies, such as H. Prunières' *Le Ballet de cour en France avant Benserade et Lully* (1914) and E. Rigal's *Le Théâtre français avant la période classique* (1901), remain of considerable value. J. Lough seeks to analyse the composition of *Paris Theatre Audiences in the Seventeenth and Eighteenth Centuries* (1957).

The structure of the Dutch *Amsterdamse Schouwburg* is carefully examined by B. Hunningher (1959).

6. The Baroque Period

Obviously, several among the books listed above deal partly or wholly with the theatres of the baroque style, and to this subject there have been numerous contributions during recent years. P. Bjurström has a detailed critical volume on *Giacomo Torelli and Baroque Stage Design* (1962); M. Viale Ferrero in *La Scenografia del '700 e i fratelli Galliari* (1963), L. Rovere, V. Viale, and A. E. Brinckmann in *Filippo Juvarra* (1937), G. Fiocco in *Giovambattista Crosato* (2nd edition, 1945), and H. J. Scholtz and A. H. Mayor in *Baroque and Romantic Stage Design* (2nd edition, 1962) reproduce numerous hitherto unknown or neglected drawings. B. Bożyk has a Polish study of the *Historia architektury budynku teatralnego i techniki sceny w teatrze europejskim* (1956); R. Southern's *Changeable Scenery* (1952) treats the same subject with special reference to the English stage; and W. H. Bruford surveys *Theatre, Drama and Audiences in Goethe's Germany* (1950). S. Towneley-Worsthorne's *Venetian Opera in the Seventeenth Century* (1954) reproduces many interesting designs, and rich collections of iconographic material appear in J. Gregor's *Monumenta scenica* (1925–30), Corrado Ricci's *La Scenografia italiana* (1930), and the same author's *I Bibiena* (1915); other related material is presented in P. Zucker's *Theaterdekoration des Barock* (1925) and *Theaterdekoration des Klassizismus* (1925), and in J. Gregor's *Wiener szenische Kunst* (1924). A very important recent work is Franz Hadamowsky's *Die Familie Galli-Bibiena in Wien* (1962), and further information on the work of these scenographers appears in A. H. Mayor's *The Bibiena Family* (1945). F. Mancini has a general study of *La Scanografia napoletana dell' età barocca* (1965). The relationship between stage and pictorial art during the period is examined by H. Tintelnot in *Barock Theater und barocke Kunst* (1939).

During the last years of the eighteenth century and on through the nineteenth many volumes on theatre building were published, extending from P. Patté's *Essai sur l'architecture théâtrale* (1782), through G. Ferrario's *Storia e descrizione de' principali teatri antichi e moderni* (1830) and A. Donnet's *Architectonographie des théâtres* (1837), on to A. Gosset's *Traité de la construction des théâtres* (1886) and the *Parallèle des principaux théâtres modernes* (1860) by A. C. Contant and J. de Filippi; other works published during these years present plans of the playhouses of particular cities; on French architectural experiments *Les Salles de spectacle construites par Victor Louis*, by H. Prudent and P. Guadet (1903), and *Victor Louis*, by C. C. Marionneau (1881), may be consulted. An important study of Swedish, and other court theatres is Agne Beijer's *Slottsteatrarna på Drottningholm och Gripsholm* (1937); Barbara Król-Kaczorowska (1961) describes the Warsaw court theatre in the Łazienki park. R. Southern's *The Georgian Playhouse* (1948) discusses remaining examples of English eighteenth-century houses; chapters on English theatrical conditions during this period are included in the present writer's *History of English Drama*, vols 2 and 3, and in the various volumes of *The London Stage* (1961, in progress).

7. Nineteenth Century and After

Much information concerning playhouse structure during the latter part of the nineteenth century is presented in Edwin O. Sachs' *Modern Opera Houses and Theatres* (3 vols, 1896–98) and in M. Hammitzsch's *Der moderne Theaterbau* (1906). Descriptions of earlier English houses will be found in *The Covent-Garden Journal* (1810) and in T. Gilliland's *Dramatic Mirror* (2 vols, 1808); Errol Sherson's *London's Lost Theatres* (1925) and Bradlee Watson's *Sheridan to Robertson* (1926) are excellent guides, and G. C. D. Odell's *Shakespeare from Betterton to Irving* (2 vols, 1924), although specifically concerned with Shakespearian production, contains much useful material on changing stage methods. The nineteenth century teems with actors' memoirs, and theatrical conditions are discussed in various volumes concerned mainly with the drama of the period, such as the present writer's *History of English Drama*, vols 4 and 5, and G. Rowell's *The Victorian Theatre* (1956). An account of Charles Kean's work is given in J. W. Cole's record of his career (2 vols, 1859); A. N. Vardac, in *Stage to Screen* (1949), traces the wide development of nineteenth-century realism and spectacularism; L. A. Hudson has a survey of the theatre from 1850 to 1950 (1951). Numerous volumes of a similar kind provide documentation for the playhouses of many countries: obviously it would be impossible here to cite the individual titles, and such procedure would be of little service since the relevant literature is adequately listed in the *Enciclopedia dello spettacolo*. Attention, however, may be drawn to a few special studies: stage decoration in France from about 1800 to 1850 is well surveyed in *La Mise en scène en France dans la première moitié du dix-neuvième siècle* (1938) by Marie-Antoinette Allevy; the work of Francesco

Bagnara and of Giuseppe and Pietro Bertoja, as illustrated by Gino Damerini in *Scenografi veneziani dell'Ottocento* (1962), shows the developing scope of Italian design; theatrical practice in nineteenth-century Moscow and St Petersburg is examined by S. S. Danilov (1957; in Russian), while F. Syrkina (1956; also in Russian) gives attention to scenic design in those playhouses; contemporary activities in Poland are dealt with by E. Szwankowski in *Teatr polski drugiej polowy XIX wieku* (1957); among volumes devoted to theatrical development in other countries particular note may be made of M. Valsa's *Le Théâtre grec moderne de 1453 à 1900* (1960). Recently D. Bablet has published a critical account of *Le Décor de théâtre de 1870 à 1914* (1965). The development of fresh machine and lighting devices is described in E. M. Laumann's *La Machinerie au théâtre depuis les Grecs jusqu'à nos jours* (1897), G. Moynet's *L'Envers du théâtre* (1874), and *La Machinerie théâtrale; trucs et décors* (1893), A. de Vaulabelle's *La Science au théâtre* (1908), and J. Lefèvre's *L'Électricité au théâtre* (1894).

The new movement in the twentieth-century theatre, of course, owed much to the inspiration of Gordon Craig and Adolphe Appia. Enid Rose has an account of the former's career, but the best study is that in Italian by Ferruccio Marotti (1961); Craig's own writings, in particular *On the Art of the Theatre* (1911), *Towards a New Theatre* (1912), and *The Theatre Advancing* (1921), are all of great significance. Appia's *La Mise-en-scène du drame wagnérien* (1895) and *Die Musik und die Inscenierung* (1899) outline the concepts of that great innovator: two of his essays have recently been published in English translation by B. Hewitt (1960).

No attempt can be made here to record all the dozens of volumes which were published from about 1914 onward on the "modern" theatre, but the following may be specially mentioned: H. K. Moderwell's *The Theatre of Today* (1914), K. MacGowan's *Continental Stagecraft* (1922) and *The Theatre of Tomorrow* (1923), J. Mason Brown's *The Modern Theatre in Revolt* (1929), Hallie Flanagan's *Shifting Scenes of the Modern European Theatre* (1928), Sheldon Cheney's *The Art Theatre* (1925), *Twentieth-century Stage Decoration* (1928) by W. R. Fuerst and S. J. Hume, Léon Moussinac's *Tendances nouvelles du théâtre* (1930), and Raymond Cogniat's *Décor au théâtre* (1930). Joseph Urban's *Theatres* (1930), R. E. Jones' *Drawings for the Theatre* (1925), and Norman Bel Geddes' *Project for a Presentation of the Divine Comedy* (1924) well illustrate the questing experimentation of those years. Several later volumes, such as G. Frette's *Stage Design, 1909–1954* (1955) and the collections of representative settings issued under the sponsorship of UNESCO, *Stage Design throughout the World* (1956 and 1964), reproduce numerous examples of more recent scenographic work. General surveys of playhouse structure and practice are given by H. Gussmann and W. Eberhard in *Theatergebäude* (2 vols, 1955) and by O. Schubert in *Das Bühnenbild* (1955). R. Aloi's *Architetture per lo spettacolo* (1958), besides offering a collection of illustrations showing the historical development of theatrical forms, provides interesting information on a series of experimental playhouses built from about 1940 onward, and this subject is critically examined in *Le Lieu théâtrale dans la société moderne*, edited by J. Jacquot (1963). A useful short survey of recently built German theatres is Victor Glasstone's *Auditoria Galore* (1963), reprinted from *Achitectural Design*. Much consideration has been given to the question of planning theatres which might alter the relationships between spectators and actors, and this topic was actively discussed at the third congress of the Association internationale des techniciens de théâtre; these discussions are presented in full or summarized in *Adaptable Theatres* (1962). The striving for novel theatrical forms as well as the current interest in "adaptability" is reflected in *The Ideal Theatre: Eight Concepts* (1963), a volume sponsored by the American Federation of Arts.

The technical resources of the modern theatre are dealt with in *Bühnentechnik der Gegenwart* (1929–33) by F. Kranich, and in *Trattato di scenotecnica* (1962) by Bruno Mello: *Orientamenti della scenografia* (1961) discusses the function of scenery in present-day playhouses. E. F. Kook has an interesting and detailed *Images in Light for the Living Theatre* (1963, duplicated volume); W. O. Parker and H. K. Smith's *Scene Design and Stage Lighting* (1963) is an excellent practical handbook.

Apart from more general works of the kind listed above, the number of books devoted to twentieth-century theatrical activities in various individual countries is legion, and here again no attempt can be made to indicate their scope. Attention may, however, be drawn to the useful series of illustrations given in *Das amerikanische Theater und Kino* (1931) and *The Russian Theatre* (1930) by René Fülop-Miller and Joseph Gregor. In view of the fact that the Moscow Art Theatre was the first and the most influential playhouse of its kind in the twentieth century, reference may also be made to the fully illustrated record, in Russian, prepared by Nicolai Efros on this theatre's activities from 1898 to 1923 (1924); another similar record provides a survey of the activities of the Bolshoi Theatre from 1825 to 1925 (1925).

There is now a fairly large library of writings on the work of prominent actor-managers and directors from the time of Sir Henry Irving onward, and these are supplemented by scores of actors' biographies and autobiographies. Since Max Reinhardt's reputation and influence spread far beyond Germany and Austria, particular mention may here be made of two critical studies of his career, those by O. M. Sayler (1924) and Hans Rothe (1930).

Index